Oxford Revise

T0347356

AQA GCSE

GEOGRAPHY

COMPLETE REVISION AND PRACTICE

Series Editor: Tim Bayliss

Tim Bayliss

Andrew Crampton

OXFORD
UNIVERSITY PRESS

Contents

 Shade in each level of the circle as you feel more confident and ready for your exam.

How to use this book

This book uses a three-step approach to revision: **Knowledge**, **Retrieval**, and **Practice**.
It is important that you do all three; they work together to make your revision effective.

Knowledge

Knowledge comes first. Each chapter starts with a **Knowledge Organiser**. These are clear easy-to-understand, concise summaries of the content that you need to know for your exam. The information is organised to show how one idea flows into the next so you can learn how everything is tied together, rather than lots of disconnected facts.

Case study

The **Case study** box highlights a popular case study that you may have studied in class.

SPECIFICATION TIP

Specification tips offer useful guidance and reminders about the specification.

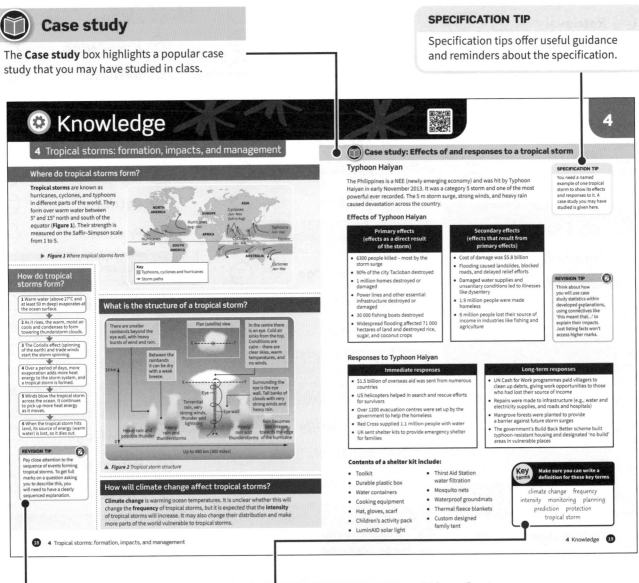

Other features:

REVISION TIP

Revision tips offer you helpful advice and guidance to aid your revision and help you to understand key concepts and remember them.

Key terms — Make sure you can write a definition for these key terms

The **Key terms** box highlights the key words and phrases you need to know, remember and be able to use confidently.

WATCH OUT

Watch out boxes highlight common mistakes and how to remember not to make them.

LINK

The **Link** box highlights a reference to a related topic you may want to refer to.

Retrieval

The **Retrieval questions** help you learn and quickly recall the information you've acquired. These are short questions and answers about the content in the Knowledge Organiser you have just reviewed. Cover up the answers with some paper and write down as many answers as you can from memory. Check back to the Knowledge Organiser for any you got wrong, then cover the answers and attempt all the questions again until you can answer *all* the questions correctly.

Make sure you revisit the retrieval questions on different days to help them stick in your memory. You need to write down the answers each time, or say them out loud, otherwise it won't work.

Previous Questions

Each chapter also has some **Retrieval questions** from **previous chapters**. Answer these to see if you can remember the content from the earlier chapters. If you get the answers wrong, go back and do the Retrieval questions for the earlier chapters again.

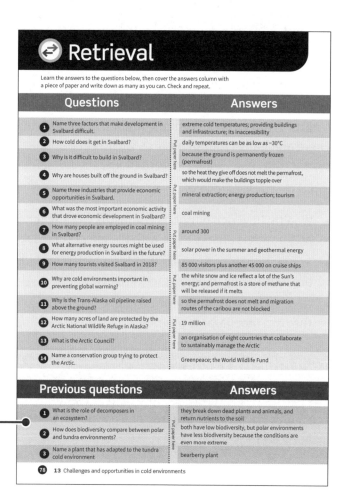

Practice

Once you think you know the Knowledge Organiser and Retrieval answers really well, you can move on to the final stage: **Practice**.

Each chapter has **exam-style questions**, including some questions from previous chapters, to help you apply all the knowledge you have learnt and can retrieve.

Answers and Glossary

You can scan the QR code at any time to access the sample answers and mark schemes for all the exam-style questions, glossary containing definitions of the key terms, as well as further revision support go.oup.com/OR/GCSE/A/Geog

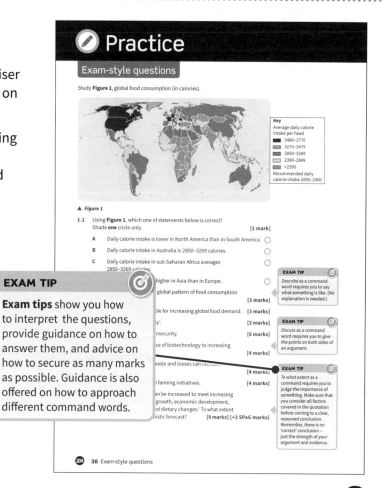

⚙ Knowledge

1 Natural hazards and tectonic hazards

Natural hazards

A **natural hazard** is an extreme natural event that threatens property and human life. There are many types of hazards such as earthquakes, volcanoes, tsunamis, tropical storms, droughts, wildfires, tornadoes, and floods.

Different factors affect the risks that hazards pose:

- Wealth: how rich or poor a country is will affect how well it prepares for a hazard, and how it is able to cope with the effects of a hazard.
- Population density: areas that have high population densities (e.g., urban areas) are more likely to be severely impacted.
- Geographical location: the location of a place (e.g., close to a volcano) influences the risks that hazards pose.

Tectonic hazards

The Earth's surface is divided into different sections called tectonic plates. Earthquakes and volcanoes are **tectonic hazards** and happen at **plate margins** (where two plates meet) (**Figure 1**).

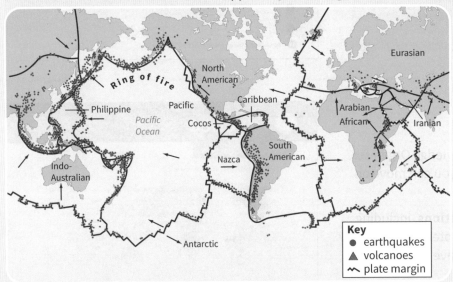

- Not everywhere in the world is at risk of tectonic hazards.
- Places near plate margins are more at risk than others.
- There is a pattern of earthquakes and volcanoes occurring in lines where tectonic plates meet.
- Tectonic plates can move apart, move towards each other, or move side by side.

▲ **Figure 1** The relationship between plate margins and the **distribution** of tectonic hazards

Why do tectonic plates move?

The Earth has four different layers (**Figure 2**).

There are two theories for why the Earth's plates move:

- Convection currents in the mantle move the plates.
- Ridge push/slab pull – heavier oceanic crust sinks into the mantle, pulling the plate downwards.

▶ **Figure 2** The structure of the Earth

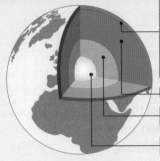

Crust: this is the surface of the planet and is divided into tectonic plates. There are two types of crust. Oceanic crust is denser and heavier than continental crust.

Mantle: this is molten rock.

Outer core: this is liquid iron and nickel.

Inner core: this is solid iron and nickel.

What happens at plate margins?

There are three types of plate margins.

1. Destructive margin

Process:

- An oceanic plate moves towards a continental plate.
- The denser oceanic plate is subducted beneath the continental plate.
- Friction between the plates as they move causes earthquakes.
- The oceanic plate melts in the mantle and mixes with sea water. This liquid rises up through cracks in the mantle as a volcanic eruption.

Hazards: powerful earthquakes and violent composite volcanoes.

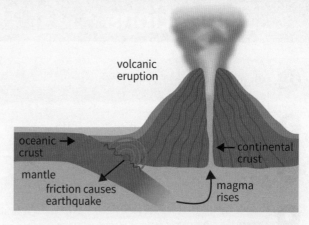

2. Conservative margin

Process:

- Two plates slide past each other.
- As they move, they get caught on each other.
- Pressure builds up and is released as an earthquake when the plates suddenly jolt free.

Hazards: earthquakes.

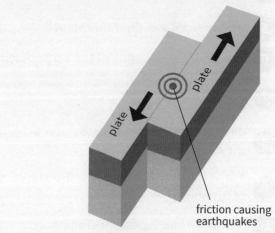

3. Constructive margin

Process:

- Two plates move apart from each other.
- This creates a gap in the Earth's crust.
- Magma from the mantle rises to fill this gap and a volcanic eruption occurs.
- Small earthquakes also happen due to the movement of the magma.

Hazards: gentle earthquakes and gently sloping shield volcanoes.

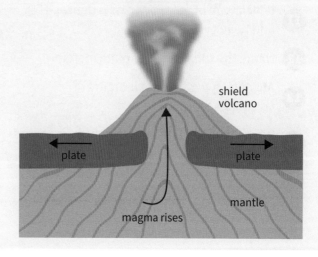

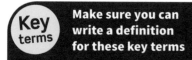

Key terms

Make sure you can write a definition for these key terms

conservative margin   constructive margin   destructive margin
distribution   natural hazard   plate margin   tectonic hazard

Learn the answers to the questions below, then cover the answers column with a piece of paper and write down as many as you can. Check and repeat.

	Questions		Answers
1	What is a natural hazard?		an extreme natural event that threatens property and human life
2	Give an example of a natural hazard.		tropical storm, tornado, earthquake, volcano, flood, etc.
3	Name a factor that affects the risk that hazards pose.	Put paper here	the wealth of a country; population density; geographical location
4	Is everywhere on Earth at risk from tectonic hazards?	Put paper here	no
5	Where do tectonic hazards occur?		at plate margins
6	What is the very centre of the Earth called?		the inner core
7	What is the layer of the Earth on which oceans and continents sit?	Put paper here	the crust
8	What is the layer of the Earth on which the crust sits?		the mantle
9	Name the two theories for why tectonic plates move.	Put paper here	convection currents in the mantle; ridge push/slab pull
10	Name the two types of tectonic crust.		oceanic and continental
11	Which type of tectonic crust is denser and heavier?		oceanic
12	Name the three types of plate margin.		destructive, constructive, conservative
13	At which types of plate margin are volcanoes found?	Put paper here	destructive and constructive
14	Which type of plate margin only experiences earthquakes?		conservative

Practice

Exam-style questions

Study **Figure 1**, a pie chart showing the deaths by natural hazard type in the USA between 1970 and 2004.

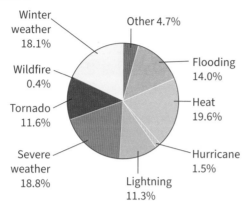

▲ *Figure 1*

1.1 Using **Figure 1**, identify which hazard type was responsible for the most deaths. **[1 mark]**

1.2 Give a reason why a pie chart is an appropriate type of graph to display this data. **[1 mark]**

1.3 Name a natural hazard that might form part of the 'other' category. **[1 mark]**

> **LINK**
>
> To understand the skill of reading pie charts, see the Geographical Skills section, page 229.

Study **Figure 2**, a map showing the global distribution of earthquakes and volcanoes. **[1 mark]**

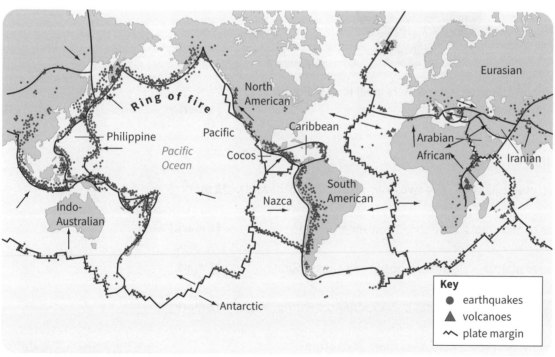

▲ *Figure 2*

Exam-style questions

2.1 Using **Figure 2**, which one of the following statements is true?
Shade **one** circle only. [1 mark]

A   South America only experiences earthquakes. ○

B   Africa is the continent with the highest number of earthquakes. ○

C   The Pacific Plate is moving towards the Nazca Plate. ○

D   There are earthquakes and volcanoes on the west coast
     of North America. ○

2.2 Using **Figure 2**, name the type of plate margin between the
North American and Eurasian Plate. [1 mark]

2.3 Using **Figure 2**, describe the global distribution of tectonic hazards. [2 marks]

2.4 Using **Figure 2** and your own knowledge, explain why countries on
the west coast of South America are at risk from tectonic hazards. [6 marks]

> **EXAM TIP**
>
> *Describe* as a command word requires you to say what something is like. (No explanation is needed.)

> **EXAM TIP**
>
> *Explain* as a command word requires you to give reasons why something is the case. Identify which tectonic hazards (plural) the west coast of South America is at risk from and use your knowledge of plate margins to explain why this is.

Study **Figure 3**, a cross-section of the Earth

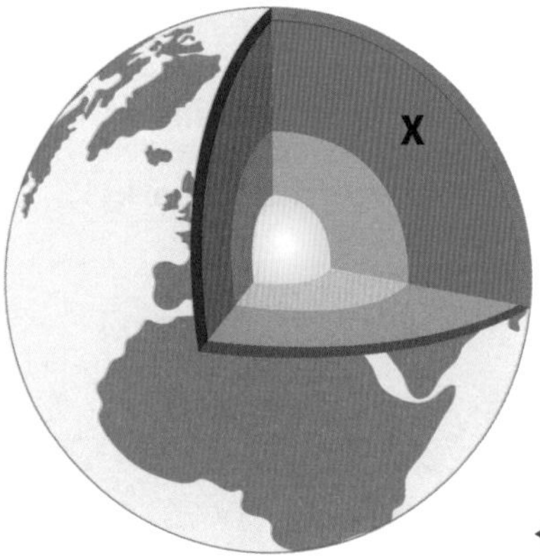

◀ *Figure 3*

3.1 Which one of the following is the correct label for **X** in **Figure 3**?
Shade **one** circle only. [1 mark]

A   Core   ○   C   Crust   ○

B   Mantle   ○   D   Outer Core   ○

3.2 Other than tectonic hazards, give **two** examples of natural hazards. [2 marks]

3.3 At what type of plate margin are shield volcanoes found? [1 mark]

3.4 At what type of plate margin are composite volcanoes found? [1 mark]

3.5 Name the type of plate margin that only experiences earthquakes. [1 mark]

3.6 Suggest reasons why some places are more at risk from
natural hazards than others. [4 marks]

> **EXAM TIP**
>
> *Suggest* as a command word requires you to give a well-reasoned guess to explain something.

3.7 Explain why earthquakes take place at conservative
plate margins. [4 marks]

3.8 Give **one** reason why the Earth's tectonic plates are moving. [1 mark]

3.9 Explain why volcanoes take place at constructive plate margins. [2 marks]

3.10 Explain why volcanoes take place at destructive plate margins. [4 marks]

▼ *Figure 4*

	Country	Magnitude	Deaths
14 August 2021	Haiti	7.2	2248
28 January 2020	Jamaica	7.7	0
7 January 2020	Puerto Rico	6.4	4
7 October 2018	Haiti	5.9	18
21 August 2018	Venezuela	7.3	5
12 January 2010	Haiti	7.0	220 000
29 November 2007	Martinique	7.4	6
21 November 2007	Dominican Republic	6.3	1
22 September 2003	Dominican Republic	6.4	3
22 April 1997	Trinidad and Tobago	6.7	2
13 January 1993	Jamaica	5.5	1

Study **Figure 4**, a table showing the magnitude and number of deaths of the most significant earthquakes in the Caribbean between 1990 and 2021.

4.1 Using **Figure 4**, calculate the mean number of deaths. [1 mark]

> **LINK**
> For help understanding means and ranges, see the Geographical Skills section, page 232.

4.2 Using **Figure 4**, calculate the range of deaths. [1 mark]

4.3 Using **Figure 4**, calculate the median number of deaths. [1 mark]

4.4 Using **Figure 4**, what is the modal number of deaths? [1 mark]

4.5 Using **Figure 4**, calculate the inter-quartile range for the number of deaths. Show your workings. [2 marks]

4.6 Using **Figure 4**, suggest why the mean number of deaths might not be a useful figure when assessing earthquake risk. [2 marks]

4.7 Name the type of graph that could be used to investigate whether there is a correlation between the magnitude and the number of deaths. [1 mark]

Knowledge

2 The impacts and management of tectonic hazards

 Case study: Tectonic events in two contrasting countries

Background to countries and cities affected by the earthquakes

	New Zealand	**Nepal**
Type of country	**HIC** (high income country)	**LIC** (low income country)
GNI per capita	$31 220 (ranked 46 out of 195)	$2500 (ranked 162 out of 195)
City impacted	Christchurch	Kathmandu (and surrounding villages)
Population of city	375 000	1 200 000
Population density of city	1300 per km²	20 200 per km²

SPECIFICATION TIP

You need named examples of two tectonic hazards to show how the effects and responses vary between two areas of contrasting levels of wealth. A case study you may have studied is given here.

Earthquake details

	New Zealand earthquake	**Nepal earthquake**
Date	22 February 2011	25 April 2015
Margin	Conservative – Pacific Plate sliding past the Australian Plate	Destructive (collision) – the Indian Plate colliding with the Eurasian Plate
Focus depth	Very **shallow focus** – 5 km	Shallow focus – 15 km
Richter scale strength	6.3	7.8

◀ *Figure 1 Many poorly built buildings collapsed in Kathmandu*

Effects of the earthquakes

Primary effects (effects that are a direct result of the earthquake)

New Zealand	**Nepal**
• 185 deaths	• 9000 deaths
• 7000 injured	• 22 000 injured
• 100 000 buildings damaged	• 600 000 buildings damaged
• Water and sewage pipes damaged	• Water tanks and pipes destroyed

 REVISION TIP

Learning key facts and statistics about these earthquakes will help you discuss and compare them in detail in an exam.

Secondary effects (effects that result from primary effects)

New Zealand
• US$40 billion worth of damage
• 10 000 homeless
• Many businesses closed for weeks
• 10 000 people left Christchurch
• 163 schools closed for two weeks
• Five Rugby World Cup matches were cancelled

Nepal
• US$5 billion worth of damage
• 3 million homeless
• Tourist economy impacted
• 300 000 people left Kathmandu
• 1 million children could not return to school for at least a month
• Landslides blocked rivers, creating dangerous lakes
• 50% of people living in temporary shelter two years later

Responses to the earthquakes

Immediate responses

New Zealand
• US$7 million received in aid
• Search and rescue teams from many countries like the UK, Australia, and the USA
• Aid workers from the Red Cross
• Zoning of areas to assess damage and safety
• 30 000 chemical toilets installed
• Temporary field hospital established

Nepal
• US$1 billion received in aid
• Search and rescue teams from countries like the UK, India, and China
• Aid workers from the Red Cross
• Half a million tents from UNICEF and a tent city established in Kathmandu
• Temporary field hospitals established

Long-term responses

New Zealand
• Water and gas reconnected
• Earthquake building codes tightened even further
• 10 000 affordable homes built
• Buildings demolished or repaired and rebuilt

Nepal
• Earthquake drills education was introduced
• US$200 million in aid from the Asian Development Bank
• Millions of homes rebuilt with stricter building codes
• Lakes formed behind dammed rivers were drained

Evaluation of differences

Effects

New Zealand is an HIC. It had strict earthquake building codes and well-trained and well-resourced emergency services. This reduced the number of deaths, but the cost of damage was higher in New Zealand because replacing expensive **infrastructure** costs more. Population size and density was higher in Nepal, meaning more people were likely to be affected.

Responses

The immediate responses were similar, but because Nepal is an LIC it relied more on outside help and had fewer resources readily available. It also had more damage to contend with. It took longer to tackle homelessness and get children back into school.

REVISION TIP

Try to think about which earthquake was worse and the reasons for this. Which facts should you remember to demonstrate this?

Knowledge

2 The impacts and management of tectonic hazards

Living with and managing risk in hazard-prone areas

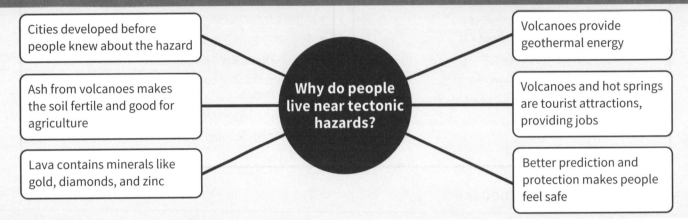

Cities developed before people knew about the hazard

Ash from volcanoes makes the soil fertile and good for agriculture

Lava contains minerals like gold, diamonds, and zinc

Why do people live near tectonic hazards?

Volcanoes provide geothermal energy

Volcanoes and hot springs are tourist attractions, providing jobs

Better prediction and protection makes people feel safe

How management reduces the risk from tectonic hazards

	Earthquakes	**Volcanoes**
Monitoring and prediction	• Patterns of activity monitored with seismometers • Cannot be predicted until moments before	• GPS and satellites monitor changes in volcano shape • Gases escape prior to eruption • Eruptions can be predicted
Protection	• Earthquake-proof buildings with shock absorbers	• Lava can be diverted away from settlements
Planning	• Earthquake drills and education of population • Residential homes made earthquake-safe (e.g., furniture fixed to walls)	• Exclusion zones around volcanoes • Evacuation to safe areas • Emergency supplies stockpiled

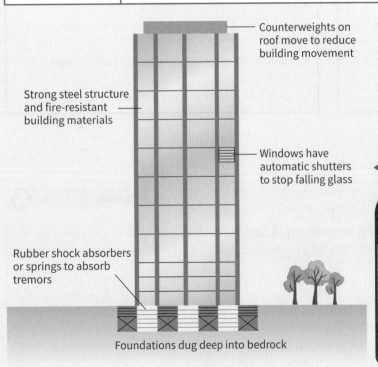

Counterweights on roof move to reduce building movement

Strong steel structure and fire-resistant building materials

Windows have automatic shutters to stop falling glass

Rubber shock absorbers or springs to absorb tremors

Foundations dug deep into bedrock

◀ **Figure 2** *A building with earthquake adaptations*

Key terms — **Make sure you can write a definition for these key terms**

HIC   immediate response
infrastructure   LIC
long-term response   population density
primary effect   secondary effect
shallow focus

Learn the answers to the questions below, then cover the answers column with
a piece of paper and write down as many as you can. Check and repeat.

Questions | Answers

#	Question	Answer
1	What is a primary effect of an earthquake?	an effect that is the direct result of the earthquake
2	What is a long-term response to an earthquake?	a response to the earthquake that is concerned with long-term recovery
3	What was the population density in Christchurch in 2011 compared to Kathmandu in 2015?	Christchurch: 1300 per km²; Kathmandu: 20 200 per km²
4	How many people died in the 2011 Christchurch earthquake?	185
5	How many people died in the 2015 Nepal earthquake?	9000
6	How many buildings were damaged in Christchurch and Nepal due to the earthquakes?	Christchurch: 100 000; Kathmandu: 600 000
7	163 schools were closed in Christchurch after the earthquake. Is this a primary or secondary effect?	secondary
8	Did New Zealand or Nepal have the highest cost of damage resulting from their earthquake?	New Zealand
9	Name two reasons why people continue to live near volcanic hazards.	jobs in tourism; precious minerals; they feel safe; fertile soils; geothermal energy
10	How can volcanic eruptions be predicted?	detecting changes in the volcano's shape; detecting small earthquakes; gases escaping from the volcano
11	How can people be protected from earthquakes?	earthquake-proof buildings
12	Name one feature of an earthquake-proof building.	shock absorbers in the foundations; rolling weights; reinforced walls; shutters on the windows
13	Name a low-cost measure that can reduce the impact of earthquakes.	education of the population; earthquake drills

Put paper here

Previous questions

Now go back and use these questions to check your knowledge of previous topics.

Previous questions | Answers

#	Question	Answer
1	Name the two types of tectonic crust.	oceanic and continental
2	Which type of plate margin only experiences earthquakes?	conservative
3	At which types of plate margin are volcanoes found?	destructive and constructive

Put paper here

Practice

Study **Figure 1**, showing earthquake damage in Chile and the effects of a volcano in Java.

▲ *Figure 1*

1.1 Using **Figure 1**, state **one** primary effect of tectonic hazards. **[1 mark]**

1.2 Using **Figure 1**, suggest **one** secondary effect caused by tectonic hazards. **[1 mark]**

> **EXAM TIP**
> *Suggest* as a command word requires you to present a possible case, to propose an idea, solution or answer.

1.3 Using **Figure 1** and your own knowledge, explain why primary effects of tectonic hazards often result in secondary effects. **[4 marks]**

1.4 Using **Figure 1** and your own knowledge, explain how tectonic hazards have primary and secondary effects. **[6 marks]**

> **EXAM TIP**
> Remember to use connectives like 'this means that…' and 'because of this…' to help you develop your explanations.

1.5 Using **Figure 1** and your own knowledge, assess whether a tectonic hazard's primary effects are worse than its secondary effects. **[6 marks]**

> **EXAM TIP**
> *Assess* as a command word requires you to present evidence and make an informed judgement.

1.6 For **two** tectonic hazards you have studied, compare the primary effects of these hazards. **[4 marks]**

2.1 Using **Figure 1**, suggest an immediate response to **either** the earthquake or the volcano. **[1 mark]**

2.2 Using **Figure 1**, suggest a long-term response to **either** the earthquake or the volcano. **[1 mark]**

2.3 Using **Figure 1** and your own knowledge, explain why immediate and long-term responses are both needed when responding to tectonic hazards. **[4 marks]**

2.4 For a tectonic hazard you have studied, assess how effective the responses to this hazard were. **[6 marks]**

3.1 For a tectonic hazard you have studied, evaluate the factors that contributed to the effects of this hazard. **[6 marks]**

> **EXAM TIP**
> *Evaluate* as a command word requires you to make judgements about what is most important or significant. Factors like wealth, population density, and the strength of the earthquake all might be significant.

3.2 For **two** tectonic hazards you have studied, to what extent can differences in wealth explain the different impacts of these hazards? **[9 marks]**
[+3 SPaG marks]

Study **Figure 2**, a photograph showing an earthquake drill in Japan.

▲ *Figure 2*

4.1 Using **Figure 2**, explain why earthquake drills might reduce the risks from tectonic hazards. **[4 marks]**

4.2 Using **Figure 2** and your own knowledge, suggest why planning can reduce the risks from tectonic hazards. **[6 marks]**

4.3 Using **Figure 2** and your own knowledge, suggest why people continue to live in areas prone to earthquakes. **[6 marks]**

4.4 Explain how volcanoes can be monitored to predict dangerous eruptions. **[4 marks]**

4.5 Suggest why people continue to live near volcanic hazards. **[4 marks]**

4.6 Evaluate the effectiveness of methods to reduce the risks from earthquake hazards. **[9 marks]**
[+3 SPaG marks]

Questions referring to previous content

5.1 Explain why earthquakes take place at destructive plate margins. **[4 marks]**

5.2 Identify at which types of plate margin volcanoes are found. **[2 marks]**

# Knowledge

3 Global atmospheric circulation

How does air circulate in the atmosphere?

The circulation of air in the atmosphere in cells moves heat around the planet, creating different climate zones. The way that air moves is called global **atmospheric circulation (Figure 1)**.

1 The Sun's energy is concentrated at the equator, making the temperature hot. Hot air rises, creating a low-**pressure belt**. When the air reaches high altitudes it moves north and south.

2 As the air moves away from the equator it cools and begins to sink. Sinking air creates a high-pressure belt at 30° north.

3 Wind is the movement of air from **high pressure** to **low pressure**. When the sinking air reaches the surface, some moves back to the equator as **trade winds**. This completes the Hadley cell. Some air moves north as **westerlies** to start the Ferrel cell.

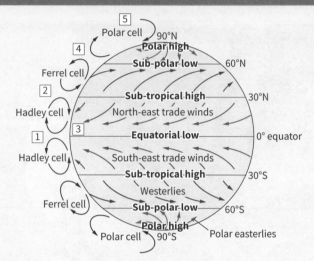

▲ **Figure 1** *Global atmospheric circulation*

4 Winds moving north meet cold winds from the Polar cell. The warmer Ferrel cell winds are forced to rise, creating another low-pressure belt at 60° north.

5 Air moving north in the Polar cell cools and sinks at 90° north. This creates high pressure. Winds move from high pressure at 90° north to low pressure at 60° north, completing the Polar cell.

Climate zones are created by the circulation of air

Pressure belt/ Climate zone	Equator	Sub-tropical high-pressure belt	Sub-polar low-pressure belt	Poles
Weather	Hot and wet	Hot and dry	Mild and wet	Cold and dry
Why?	Concentrated **solar insolation** creates a hot climate. Hot air rises, creating low pressure. It cools and condenses to give predictable convectional rainfall.	Sinking air loses moisture, giving clear blue skies, and little precipitation. It is hot because it is still quite close to the equator.	Air moving north in the Ferrel cell is forced up when it meets cold air from the Polar cell. It cools and condenses, giving frontal rainfall.	The Sun's insolation is spread out over a large area, making it cold. Sinking air in the Polar cell gives high pressure and dry weather.

Key terms — Make sure you can write a definition for these key terms: atmospheric circulation   high pressure   low pressure   pressure belt   solar insolation   trade winds   westerlies

Learn the answers to the questions below, then cover the answers column with a piece of paper and write down as many as you can. Check and repeat.

Questions | Answers

Put paper here

1. Why is it hot at the equator? — the Sun's energy is more concentrated
2. Is there rising air or sinking air at the equator? — rising air
3. Why does air rise at the equator? — because it is hot, and hot air is less dense and rises
4. Is rising air linked to wet or dry conditions? — wet
5. Does rising air create high or low pressure? — low
6. Why is rising air associated with rainfall? — because as the air rises, it cools and condenses, forming clouds that lead to rainfall
7. What type of weather is associated with low pressure at the equator? — warm and wet
8. Is there a high-pressure or low-pressure belt 30° north and south of the equator? — high pressure
9. Do high-pressure belts have rising air or sinking air? — sinking air
10. What type of weather is associated with high atmospheric pressure? — dry
11. Is there high or low pressure 60° north and south of the equator? — low
12. What type of climate is found where the Ferrel cell meets the Polar cell? — mild and wet
13. What are the winds called that blow from 30° north towards the equator? — trade winds
14. Why is it cold at the poles? — the sun's energy is spread out over a large area
15. Why is it dry at the poles? — there is sinking air with high atmospheric pressure

Previous questions

Now go back and use these questions to check your knowledge of previous topics.

Previous questions | Answers

1. Name a factor that affects the risk that hazards pose. — the wealth of a country; population density; geographical location
2. Name the three types of tectonic plate margins. — destructive, constructive, conservative
3. How can volcanic eruptions be predicted? — detecting changes in the volcano's shape; detecting small earthquakes; gases escaping from the volcano

Practice

Exam-style questions

Study **Figure 1**, the global atmospheric circulation system.

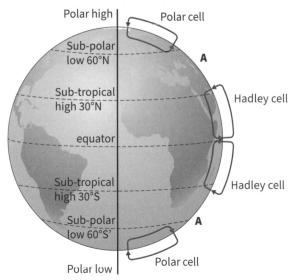

▲ *Figure 1*

1.1 Using **Figure 1**, what is the name of the cells at point **A**? [1 mark]

1.2 Describe the typical climatic conditions found in the sub-tropical high-pressure belt 30° north of the equator. [2 marks]

> **EXAM TIP**
>
> *Describe* as a command word requires you to say what something is like. (No explanation is needed.)

Study **Figure 2**, a photo of wet and humid conditions at the equator.

▲ *Figure 2*

1.3 Explain why the weather conditions shown in **Figure 2** are found at the equator. [4 marks]

1.4 Name the winds that blow from 30° north towards the equator. [1 mark]

> **EXAM TIP**
>
> *Explain* as a command word requires you to give reasons why something is the case.

1.5 Name the winds that blow from 30° north towards the sub-polar low at 60° north. [1 mark]

1.6 Suggest a reason why winds blow from 30° south towards the equator. [2 marks]

Study **Figure 3**, a wet day in the UK.

▲ *Figure 3*

1.7 Suggest why the UK often experiences rainfall. [4 marks]

1.8 Explain why Antarctica is a desert. [2 marks]

> **EXAM TIP**
>
> *Suggest* as a command word requires you to present a possible case, to propose an idea, solution or answer.

Questions referring to previous content

2.1 For **one** tectonic hazard you have studied, describe the physical processes leading to the hazard. [4 marks]

2.2 Which of these is a secondary effect of an earthquake? Shade **one** circle only. [1 mark]

A	People are left homeless.	◯
B	People are injured.	◯
C	Buildings collapse.	◯
D	Infrastructure is damaged.	◯

⚙ Knowledge

4 Tropical storms: formation, impacts, and management

Where do tropical storms form?

Tropical storms are known as hurricanes, cyclones, and typhoons in different parts of the world. They form over warm water between 5° and 15° north and south of the equator (**Figure 1**). Their strength is measured on the Saffir–Simpson scale from 1 to 5.

▶ **Figure 1** Where tropical storms form

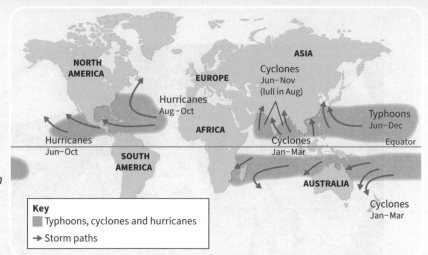

NORTH AMERICA
EUROPE
ASIA
Cyclones Jun–Nov (lull in Aug)
Hurricanes Aug–Oct
AFRICA
Typhoons Jun–Dec
Hurricanes Jun–Oct
SOUTH AMERICA
Cyclones Jan–Mar
Equator
AUSTRALIA
Cyclones Jan–Mar

Key
■ Typhoons, cyclones and hurricanes
→ Storm paths

How do tropical storms form?

1 Warm water (above 27°C and at least 50 m deep) evaporates at the ocean surface.

2 As it rises, the warm, moist air cools and condenses to form towering thunderstorm clouds.

3 The Coriolis effect (spinning of the earth) and trade winds start the storm spinning.

4 Over a period of days, more evaporation adds more heat energy to the storm system, and a tropical storm is formed.

5 Winds blow the tropical storm across the ocean. It continues to pick up more heat energy as it moves.

6 When the tropical storm hits land, its source of energy (warm water) is lost, so it dies out.

> **REVISION TIP** ☑
>
> Pay close attention to the sequence of events forming tropical storms. To get full marks on a question asking you to describe this, you will need to have a clearly sequenced explanation.

What is the structure of a tropical storm?

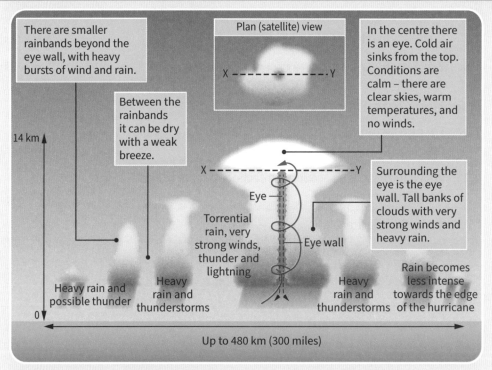

There are smaller rainbands beyond the eye wall, with heavy bursts of wind and rain.

Between the rainbands it can be dry with a weak breeze.

Plan (satellite) view
X - - - - - - - - - Y

In the centre there is an eye. Cold air sinks from the top. Conditions are calm – there are clear skies, warm temperatures, and no winds.

14 km

X - - - - - - - - - Y

Eye

Torrential rain, very strong winds, thunder and lightning

Eye wall

Surrounding the eye is the eye wall. Tall banks of clouds with very strong winds and heavy rain.

Heavy rain and possible thunder

Heavy rain and thunderstorms

Heavy rain and thunderstorms

Rain becomes less intense towards the edge of the hurricane

0

Up to 480 km (300 miles)

▲ **Figure 2** Tropical storm structure

How will climate change affect tropical storms?

Climate change is warming ocean temperatures. It is unclear whether this will change the **frequency** of tropical storms, but it is expected that the **intensity** of tropical storms will increase. It may also change their distribution and make more parts of the world vulnerable to tropical storms.

📖 Case study: Effects of and responses to a tropical storm

Typhoon Haiyan

The Philippines is a NEE (newly emerging economy) and was hit by Typhoon Haiyan in early November 2013. It was a category 5 storm and one of the most powerful ever recorded. The 5 m storm surge, strong winds, and heavy rain caused devastation across the country.

Effects of Typhoon Haiyan

Primary effects (effects as a direct result of the storm)	Secondary effects (effects that result from primary effects)
• 6300 people killed – most by the storm surge • 90% of the city Tacloban destroyed • 1 million homes destroyed or damaged • Power lines and other essential infrastructure destroyed or damaged • 30 000 fishing boats destroyed • Widespread flooding affected 71 000 hectares of land and destroyed rice, sugar, and coconut crops	• Cost of damage was $5.8 billion • Flooding caused landslides, blocked roads, and delayed relief efforts • Damaged water supplies and unsanitary conditions led to illnesses like dysentery • 1.9 million people were made homeless • 6 million people lost their source of income in industries like fishing and agriculture

Responses to Typhoon Haiyan

Immediate responses	Long-term responses
• $1.5 billion of overseas aid was sent from numerous countries • US helicopters helped in search and rescue efforts for survivors • Over 1200 evacuation centres were set up by the government to help the homeless • Red Cross supplied 1.1 million people with water • UK sent shelter kits to provide emergency shelter for families	• UN Cash for Work programmes paid villagers to clean up debris, giving work opportunities to those who had lost their source of income • Repairs were made to infrastructure (e.g., water and electricity supplies, and roads and hospitals) • Mangrove forests were planted to provide a barrier against future storm surges • The government's Build Back Better scheme built typhoon-resistant housing and designated 'no build' areas in vulnerable places

Contents of a shelter kit include:

- Toolkit
- Durable plastic box
- Water containers
- Cooking equipment
- Hat, gloves, scarf
- Children's activity pack
- LuminAID solar light

- Thirst Aid Station water filtration
- Mosquito nets
- Waterproof groundmats
- Thermal fleece blankets
- Custom designed family tent

Knowledge

4 Tropical storms: formation, impacts, and management

Reducing the effects of tropical storms

Monitoring and prediction

The development of tropical storms can be monitored with satellites. Satellite photos can be used to predict where tropical storms will hit land.

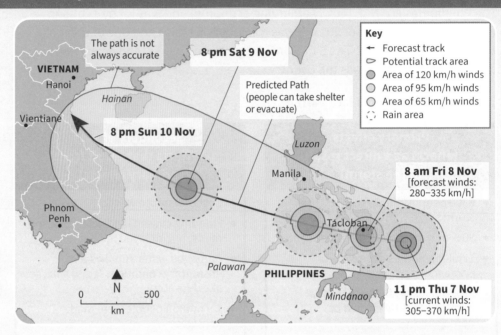

Figure 3 *Satellites helped to predict the path of Typhoon Haiyan*

The path is not always accurate

8 pm Sat 9 Nov

Predicted Path (people can take shelter or evacuate)

VIETNAM
Hanoi
Hainan
Vientiane
8 pm Sun 10 Nov
Phnom Penh
Luzon
Manila
Tácloban
Palawan
PHILIPPINES
Mindanao

Key
← Forecast track
◠ Potential track area
⬤ Area of 120 km/h winds
◯ Area of 95 km/h winds
◯ Area of 65 km/h winds
⬡ Rain area

8 am Fri 8 Nov [forecast winds: 280–335 km/h]

11 pm Thu 7 Nov [current winds: 305–370 km/h]

0   N   500
km

Protection

Protection measures are actions taken before a hazard strikes to reduce its impact. This includes:

- building specially designed storm shelters
- boarding up windows
- building sea walls to protect against storm surges
- planting mangrove forests to provide a natural barrier against storm surges.

Planning

Planning is one of the most cost-effective ways of reducing the impacts of tropical storms. Countries can:

- teach disaster preparation in schools
- run regular hurricane drills
- train emergency services
- train volunteers to deliver cyclone warnings to exposed populations
- signpost evacuation routes
- ensure citizens keep an emergency supply kit.

High-income countries (HICs) are better able to reduce the impacts of tropical storms. They can invest more in **monitoring** and **prediction**, and build storm defences. Their populations are also easier to reach through television, radio, and social media. LICs rely instead on lower-cost measures such as storm shelters and education campaigns.

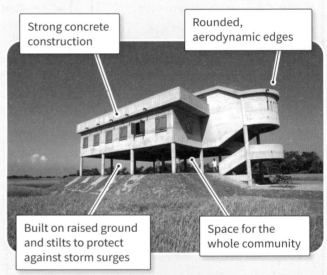
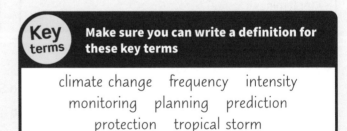

Strong concrete construction

Rounded, aerodynamic edges

Built on raised ground and stilts to protect against storm surges

Space for the whole community

▲ **Figure 4** *Cyclone shelter in Bangladesh*

Key terms — Make sure you can write a definition for these key terms

climate change   frequency   intensity
monitoring   planning   prediction
protection   tropical storm

Learn the answers to the questions below, then cover the answers column with a piece of paper and write down as many as you can. Check and repeat.

Questions | Answers

#	Question	Answer
1	What must the sea temperature be for a tropical storm to form?	27°C and above
2	How deep must the ocean be for a tropical storm to form?	50 m
3	Why do tropical storms spin?	because of the trade winds and the Coriolis effect
4	What happens when a tropical storm hits land?	it loses energy because it no longer has warm water from which to draw energy
5	Name two weather conditions associated with tropical storms.	strong winds and heavy rain
6	How many people died in Typhoon Haiyan?	6300
7	What is a storm surge?	a wall of water that hits land as the tropical storm hits
8	What was the total cost of damage caused by Typhoon Haiyan?	$5.8 billion
9	Name an illness caused by damaged and polluted water supplies from Typhoon Haiyan.	dysentery
10	Why were mangrove forests planted after Typhoon Haiyan?	to provide a barrier against future storm surges
11	How can people protect their properties from a tropical storm?	board up the windows
12	How can societies protect themselves from storm surges?	build sea walls; plant mangrove forests
13	State one protective feature of a tropical storm shelter.	it is built on stilts; it has shutters on the windows; it has rounded corners

Put paper here

Previous questions

Now go back and use these questions to check your knowledge of previous topics.

Previous questions | Answers

#	Question	Answer
1	Which type of tectonic crust is denser and heavier?	oceanic
2	Name two theories for why tectonic plates move.	convection currents in the mantle; ridge push/slab pull
3	What type of weather is associated with low pressure at the equator?	warm and wet

Put paper here

Practice

Exam-style questions

Study **Figure 1**, a map showing the distribution of tropical storms.

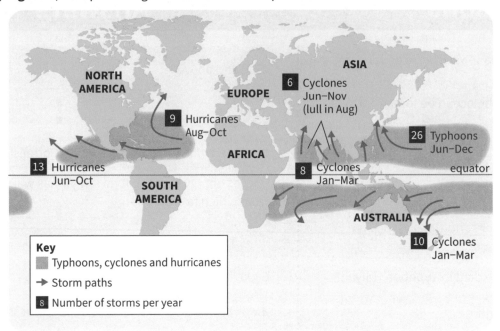

Key
▨	Typhoons, cyclones and hurricanes
➜	Storm paths
8	Number of storms per year

▲ *Figure 1*

1.1 Using **Figure 1**, which of the following statements is true?
Shade **one** circle only. **[1 mark]**

A   South America experiences a high number of tropical storms.   ◯

B   The west coast of Africa experiences tropical storms.   ◯

C   Europe experiences tropical storms.   ◯

D   The east coast of North America experiences tropical storms.   ◯

1.2 Calculate the total number of tropical storms per year
shown on the map. **[1 mark]**

1.3 Which of the following statements about tropical storms is **not** true?
Shade **one** circle only. **[1 mark]**

A   Tropical storms form on the equator.   ◯

B   Tropical storms require ocean temperatures of 27°C.   ◯

C   Tropical storms form between 5° and 30° north and south of
the equator.   ◯

D   The number of tropical storms varies from year to year.   ◯

1.4 State **one** condition needed for a tropical storm to form. **[1 mark]**

1.5 Explain how a trapical storm is formed. **[4 marks]**

> **EXAM TIP** ◎
>
> When explaining physical
> processes, make the
> sequence of events clear
> but do not use bullet
> points. Examiners like to
> see written paragraphs.

1.6 Describe the different weather conditions you might experience if you travelled through a tropical storm from its outer edge to the eye in the centre. **[4 marks]**

EXAM TIP

Describe as a command word requires you to say what something is like. (No explanation is needed.)

Study **Figure 2**, a table showing the number of tropical storms worldwide from 2011 to 2021.

▼ *Figure 2*

Year	2011	2012	2013	2014	2015	2016	2017	2018	2019	2020	2021
Number of tropical storms	75	88	90	77	95	83	84	103	98	104	94

2.1 Calculate the mean number of tropical storms per year. **[1 mark]**

2.2 Calculate the range of tropical storms per year. **[1 mark]**

2.3 Calculate the median number of tropical storms. **[1 mark]**

2.4 Calculate the inter-quartile range for the number of tropical storms between 2011 and 2021. Show your working. **[2 marks]**

LINK

For help understanding means, medians, and ranges, see the Geographical Skills section, page 232.

Study **Figure 3**, a bar chart showing the number of tropical storms worldwide from 2011 to 2021.

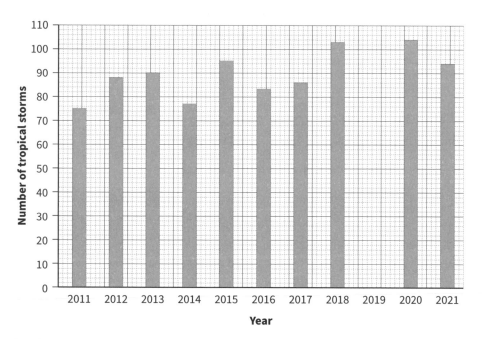

▲ *Figure 3*

2.5 Using the data in **Figure 2**, draw a bar for 2019 on **Figure 3**. **[1 mark]**

LINK

To understand the skill of constructing and reading bar graphs, see the Geographical Skills section, page 227.

Exam-style questions

3.1 State what is meant by the primary effects of tropical storms. **[1 mark]**

3.2 Identify **one** primary effect of tropical storms. Shade **one** circle only. **[1 mark]**

A	Loss of employment	◯	**C**	Flooding	◯
B	Spread of disease	◯	**D**	Homelessness	◯

3.3 Which **one** of the following countries is likely to be vulnerable to tropical storms? Shade **one** circle only. **[1 mark]**

A	Bangladesh	◯	**C**	South Africa	◯
B	France	◯	**D**	Canada	◯

Storm death toll rises

Hundreds of thousands of people were displaced from their homes after the storm surge created by the devastating category 5 storm flattened vast areas of the country. There were scenes of total devastation as well as no electricity, no clean water, and no food. Authorities fear that diseases will spread in infected water and that the cost of the damage will be hugely significant in this country. Livelihoods face being lost as it is estimated that 33 million coconut trees have been washed away.

▲ *Figure 4*

Study **Figure 4**, a newspaper report about a tropical storm.

3.4 Using **Figure 4**, identify **one** primary effect of the tropical storm. **[1 mark]**

3.5 Using **Figure 4**, explain **two** secondary effects of the tropical storm. **[4 marks]**

3.6 Using **Figure 4**, suggest **two** possible effects that the tropical storm will have on people. **[2 marks]**

EXAM TIP ◎

Suggest as a command word requires you to present a possible case, to propose an idea, solution, or answer. What can you infer from the text?

3.7 Using **Figure 4**, suggest **two** reasons why many deaths occurred during and after the tropical storm. **[4 marks]**

3.8 With reference to **Figure 4**, suggest **two** ways that the tropical storm affected the environment. **[4 marks]**

3.9 'The primary effects of tropical storms are more significant than the secondary effects.' To what extent do you agree with this statement?

Use **Figure 4** and your own knowledge to explain your answer. **[6 marks]**

EXAM TIP ◎

Make it clear whether you agree or not, but remember you can qualify your answer using phrases like 'mostly agree' or 'partially disagree'. Your examples can act as evidence to support your opinion.

3.10 'Long-term responses to tropical storms are more important than immediate responses.' Do you agree? Use an example to explain your answer. **[9 marks]**

[+3 SPaG marks]

3.11 Using an example you have studied, evaluate the immediate and long-term responses to a tropical storm. **[9 marks]**
[+3 SPaG marks]

3.12 'The impact of tropical storms is more significant for people than the environment.' Do you agree? Use an example to explain your answer. **[6 marks]**

▲ *Figure 5*

4.1 Using **Figure 5**, suggest **two** ways that this would be an effective tropical storm shelter. **[2 marks]**

4.2 Using **Figure 5** and your own knowledge, explain how the effects of tropical storms can be reduced. **[6 marks]**

4.3 Outline **two** ways that prediction might help reduce the effects of a tropical storm. **[4 marks]**

4.4 Explain how planning and protection might help reduce the effects of a tropical storm. **[6 marks]**

4.5 Describe how satellite images can be used to respond to tropical storms. **[4 marks]**

Questions referring to previous content

5.1 Explain why hot deserts are often found 30° north and south of the equator. **[2 marks]**

5.2 Outline **two** ways that planning and protection can reduce the impacts of earthquakes. **[4 marks]**

Knowledge

5 Weather hazards in the UK

Where does the UK's weather come from?

The UK sits at a meeting point for several different air masses bringing different weather systems (**Figure 1**). This can lead to different types of extreme weather.

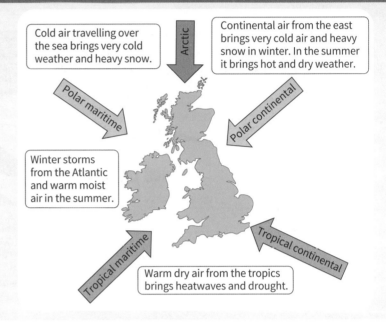

Cold air travelling over the sea brings very cold weather and heavy snow.

Continental air from the east brings very cold air and heavy snow in winter. In the summer it brings hot and dry weather.

Arctic

Polar maritime

Polar continental

Winter storms from the Atlantic and warm moist air in the summer.

Tropical maritime

Tropical continental

Warm dry air from the tropics brings heatwaves and drought.

▶ *Figure 1 The UK is affected by different weather systems*

Types of extreme weather in the UK

Type of extreme weather	Description	Impacts
Thunderstorms	Heavy rainfall in a short period of time	Flash flooding
Prolonged rainfall	Higher than average rainfall over a long period of time	Severe river flooding
Drought	An extended period of time with below average rainfall	Water shortages and reduced crop production; the UK had recent severe droughts in 2003, 2014, and 2018
Heatwaves	Extreme temperatures for a short period of time	Increased mortality, especially for the elderly; in 2022 temperatures reached a record 40.3°C
Heavy snow and extreme cold	Very cold temperatures and lots of snow; more likely to affect Scotland and the north of England	Travel disruption and school closures; the 'Beast from the East' in 2018 brought up to 50 cm of snow and temperatures of −12°C
Strong winds and gales	Exceptionally strong winds	Damaged power lines, trees, and property; storm Arwen in Scotland in November 2021 damaged 16 million trees

Is the UK's weather becoming more extreme?

With global warming it is likely the UK will experience more extreme weather.

- There will be more rain, and more days of extreme rainfall, meaning more flash flooding.
- Temperatures will be warmer, with more heatwaves. All of the 10 hottest years in the UK have occurred since 2002, and 2022 has brought the record high temperature.
- There is no evidence for increased wind or increased drought.

📖 Case study: A recent extreme weather event in the UK

The Somerset Levels

The Somerset Levels are low-lying land in south-west England that experienced extreme flooding between December 2013 and February 2014.

SPECIFICATION TIP

You need a named example of a recent extreme weather event in the UK. A case study you may have studied is given here.

▲ *Figure 2 The Somerset Levels*

Causes of the flooding

Physical causes
• Prolonged heavy rainfall. January 2014 was the wettest on record
• Saturated soils meant water ran off quickly into rivers
• High tides prevented river water escaping out to sea

Human causes
• The rivers (e.g., River Tone) had not been dredged for 20 years, reducing channel capacity
• Urbanisation on the flood plain increased impermeable surfaces

Impacts of the flooding

Social impacts
• 600 homes were flooded
• Residents were evacuated and living in temporary shelters
• Villages like Muchelney were cut off
• Some people could not get insurance after the floods

Economic impacts
• The cost of the flood damage was over £100 million
• 80% of businesses were affected by the flood
• £200 million was lost in the tourism industry
• The Bristol to Taunton railway was damaged and main roads were closed

Environmental impacts
• Floodwater was contaminated with sewage, chemicals, and oil
• Ecosystems were destroyed
• Soil was damaged by stagnant water, leading to agricultural losses
• Debris needed to be cleared from land

Management strategies to reduce flood risk

Immediate strategies
• The Met Office issued flood warnings
• Residents used sandbags to protect their property
• Temporary pumps pumped water back into rivers
• Facebook and Twitter were used to communicate news by FLAG (Flooding on the Levels Action Group)
• Boats were used to get help and food to stranded people

Long-term strategies
• A 20-year Somerset and Moors Flood Action Plan was launched, costing £100 million
• Rivers Tone and Parrett were dredged, costing £6 million
• Some road levels were raised
• Pumping stations were made permanent
• A tidal barrage will be built at Bridgwater

Key terms Make sure you can write a definition for these key terms

economic environmental
human cause management strategy
physical cause social

Retrieval

Learn the answers to the questions below, then cover the answers column with a piece of paper and write down as many as you can. Check and repeat.

Questions

Answers

#	Question	Answer
1	What is extreme weather?	weather that is much hotter, colder, wetter, drier, or windier than normal
2	Name a type of extreme weather brought by air from the north and east.	extreme cold or heavy snow
3	What evidence is there that the UK is getting hotter?	10 of the hottest years have occurred since 2002
4	Name an example of an extreme cold event in the UK.	the 'Beast from the East' in 2018
5	When did the Somerset Levels experience extreme flooding?	between December 2013 and February 2014
6	Name a physical cause of the Somerset Level floods.	prolonged heavy rainfall; saturated soils; high tides
7	Why would saturated soils lead to flooding?	water cannot infiltrate the soil, so it runs off into rivers
8	Name a human cause of the Somerset Level floods.	the rivers had not been dredged; urbanisation on the flood plain
9	What were the social impacts of the Somerset Level floods?	600 homes flooded; residents evacuated; villages cut off; people could not get insurance
10	What were the economic impacts of the Somerset Level floods?	flood damage cost £100 million; 80% of businesses affected; the tourism industry lost £200 million; railway and main roads closed
11	What were the environmental impacts of the Somerset Level floods?	contaminated floodwater; ecosystem damage; debris on the land
12	Name two immediate responses that took place before the floodwater reached very high levels.	the Met Office issued flood warnings; sandbags were put out to protect properties
13	What community group used social media to communicate news during the flood?	FLAG (Flooding on the Levels Action Group)

Put paper here

Previous questions

Now go back and use these questions to check your knowledge of previous topics.

Previous questions

Answers

#	Question	Answer
1	Name one feature of an earthquake-proof building.	shock absorbers in the foundations; rolling weights; reinforced walls; shutters on the windows
2	What must the sea temperature be for a tropical storm to form?	27°C and above
3	What type of climate is found where the Ferrel cell meets the Polar cell?	mild and wet

Put paper here

Exam-style questions

1.1 Define the term 'extreme weather'. **[1 mark]**

1.2 Name **one** type of extreme weather experienced in the UK. **[1 mark]**

1.3 Outline the evidence for extreme weather becoming more common in the UK. **[4 marks]**

Study **Figure 1**, a table showing monthly precipitation in the north-east of England in 2021.

▼ *Figure 1*

Month	Jan	Feb	Mar	Apr	May	Jun	Jul	Aug	Sep	Oct	Nov	Dec
Rainfall (mm)	139	87	41	19	106	24	74	59	47	121	73	98

Source: *Alexander, L.V. and Jones, P.D. (2001) Updated precipitation series for the UK and discussion of recent extremes. Atmospheric Science Letters doi:10.1006/asle.2001.0025*

1.4 Which type of graph would be most appropriate to display the precipitation data shown in **Figure 1**? Shade **one** circle only. **[1 mark]**

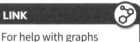

A Pie chart ◯   **C** Climate graph ◯

B Bar graph ◯   **D** Line graph ◯

> **LINK**
> For help with graphs and maths, see the Geographical Skills section, pages 227-229, and 232.

1.5 Using **Figure 1**, which month had the highest amount of precipitation in 2021? **[1 mark]**

1.6 Using **Figure 1**, calculate the total precipitation in 2021. **[1 mark]**

1.7 Using **Figure 1**, calculate the range of precipitation. **[1 mark]**

1.8 Using **Figure 1**, calculate the median precipitation. **[1 mark]**

1.9 Using **Figure 1**, calculate the inter-quartile range for precipitation. Show your workings. **[2 marks]**

Study **Figure 2**, a graph showing mean temperatures in the UK compared to the 1961–1990 average.

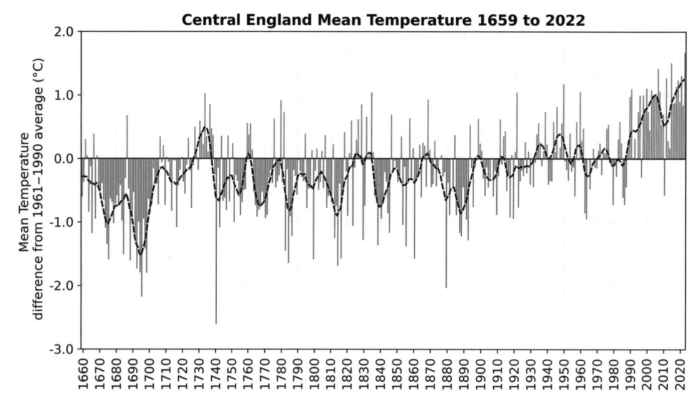

Source: *HadCET* © Crown copyright

▲ *Figure 2*

2.1 Using **Figure 2**, which of the following statements is **not** true? Shade **one** circle only.

[1 mark]

A	1740 was the coldest year.	◯
B	2022 was the warmest year.	◯
C	1660 to 1700 had many years warmer than average.	◯
D	Since 1990 most years have been warmer than average.	◯

> **EXAM TIP**
>
> For questions like this, take each statement one at a time. Check all the statements before deciding on your answer.

Study **Figure 3**, a news report from February 2014.

Gales bring chaos to the UK

The UK was hit by strong winds and gales yesterday, bringing chaos to road and rail networks and leaving 21 000 people without power.

Electricity networks went down in South Wales and the West Midlands, with a top wind speed of 105 mph recorded in Aberdaron in South Wales. Many trees were brought down by the strong winds, and transport networks were disrupted when the Clifton Suspension Bridge near Bristol was closed for the first time in its history.

Flooding, trees falling, and strong winds also led to parts of the West Coast rail line being closed. Coastal areas were battered with high waves and heavy rain, resulting in 14 severe flood warnings being issued.

▲ *Figure 3*

2.2 Using **Figure 3**, which of these is an environmental impact of the strong wind? Shade **one** circle only.   [1 mark]

A   21 000 people were without electricity.   ◯

B   Many trees were brought down.   ◯

C   Rail networks were damaged.   ◯

D   Clifton Suspension Bridge was closed.   ◯

2.3 Using **Figure 3** and your own knowledge, assess whether the economic effects of extreme weather events are worse than the environmental effects.   [6 marks]

EXAM TIP

When asked to use a Figure, ensure that something in the Figure appears in your answer. Read the article carefully and pick out an economic impact and an environmental impact to refer to. Then combine this with your own knowledge (e.g., your own example) to make a judgement.

2.4 For a recent extreme weather event in the UK you have studied, name **one** physical cause of this event.   [1 mark]

2.5 For a recent extreme weather event in the UK you have studied, describe the causes of this event.   [4 marks]

2.6 For a recent extreme weather event in the UK you have studied, explain the economic impacts of this event.   [4 marks]

2.7 For a recent extreme weather event in the UK you have studied, describe **one** immediate response.   [2 marks]

2.8 For a recent extreme weather event in the UK you have studied, explain why **one** management strategy was needed.   [4 marks]

2.9 For a recent extreme weather event in the UK you have studied, assess the effectiveness of the management strategies in reducing risk.   [9 marks]
[+3 SPaG marks]

Questions referring to previous content

3.1 Identify **one** way that the risks posed from volcanic hazards can be reduced.   [1 mark]

3.2 Outline **one** way that monitoring might help reduce the effects of a tropical storm.   [2 marks]

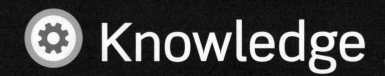
6 The evidence and reasons for climate change

Earth's temperature in the Quaternary period

Climate change is the long-term change in Earth's temperature. The **Quaternary period** is the last 2.6 million years. For most of the Quaternary period, the Earth's temperature has been colder than it is today (**Figure 1**).

The Earth's temperature has not been constant. It has fluctuated through cold glacial periods and warmer interglacial periods. The Earth's temperature has increased rapidly since the 1850s as many countries have developed more industry (**Figure 2**).

> **WATCH OUT**
>
> Figure 1 uses a 'temperature difference from average' on the y-axis. So a temperature of 1°C does not mean the actual temperature was 1°C, it means the temperature was 1°C *warmer than the average temperature.*

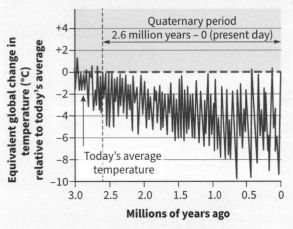

▲ **Figure 1** Earth's temperature fluctuated in the Quaternary period

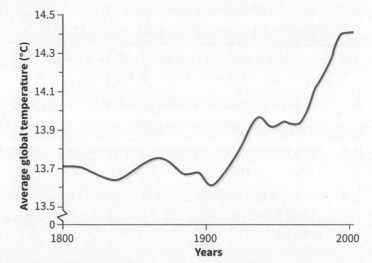

▲ **Figure 2** Earth's temperature has increased rapidly since 1850

Evidence for climate change

Ice cores: these are tubes of ice drilled out of the Arctic and Antarctic ice caps. Each layer in an ice core is a frozen record of the snow that fell that year. By studying gases trapped in the ice, scientists can tell whether the Earth was warmer or colder. Lots of carbon dioxide (CO_2) means the Earth was warmer. Ice cores give a pristine and reliable record of the climate stretching back 800 000 years.

Tree rings: the number of rings in a tree's trunk tell scientists the age of the tree, because each ring is one year of growth. Wider rings suggest a warmer and wetter climate because the tree grew faster. Tree rings are reliable records of the Earth's climate going back 13 000 years.

Global temperature data: global temperature data has been collected since 1850. All of the ten hottest years on record have taken place since 2010. Temperature records are reliable but older data was not collected on equipment as accurate as today.

> **REVISION TIP**
>
> Think about why using multiple sources of evidence is better than relying on one source of evidence.

Shrinking glaciers and melting ice: since 1979, scientists have taken satellite photos of Arctic sea ice. Records show the size of Arctic sea ice is shrinking. Glaciers are also retreating and some may disappear by 2035. This evidence is reliable but does not extend over a long period of time.

Natural causes of climate change

Orbital changes: Milankovitch cycles

Three Milankovitch cycles alter the distance between the Earth and the Sun (**Figure 3**).

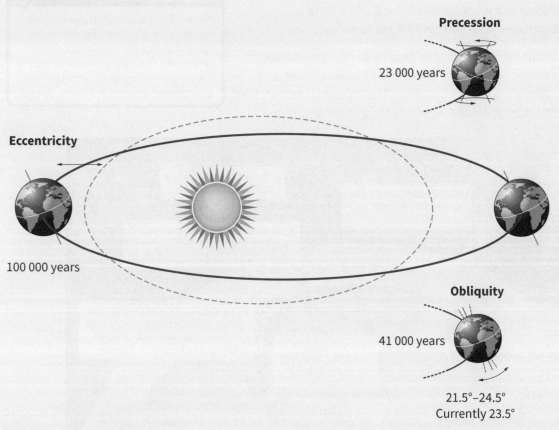

Precession

23 000 years

Eccentricity

100 000 years

Obliquity

41 000 years

21.5°–24.5°
Currently 23.5°

▲ *Figure 3 The Milankovitch cycles*

These cycles combine to cause long-term climate changes between glacial and interglacial periods.

Solar output

Dark spots on the Sun's surface, caused by magnetic storms, release more energy, warming the Earth. Over 11-year cycles, the number of Sun spots increase and decrease again.

Volcanic activity

Large volcanic eruptions release ash and gases like sulphur dioxide into the atmosphere. This ash cloud blocks sunlight reaching the Earth, resulting in cooler temperatures. The effects last for two to three years.

1 **Eccentricity** (orbit): every 100 000 years, the Earth's orbit around the Sun moves from a circle to an oval and back again. This means the Earth is sometimes closer to the Sun.

2 **Obliquity** (tilt): the Earth is tilted on its axis. Over 41 000 years, the Earth tilts more towards the Sun and back to more upright. This changes seasonal temperatures. More tilt equals warmer summers.

3 **Precession** (wobble): as the Earth spins on its axis it wobbles like a spinning top, changing the direction it points to over 23 000 years. This affects how warm or cold different seasons are.

Knowledge

6 The evidence and reasons for climate change

Human causes of climate change

Naturally occurring greenhouse gases like CO_2 and water vapour absorb radiation (heat) that is reflected off the Earth's surface. Without this, the Earth would be too cold for life to exist.

Human activity has put more greenhouse gases into the atmosphere. This creates an enhanced greenhouse effect and global warming (**Figure 4**). Carbon dioxide accounts for 60% of the enhanced greenhouse effect, methane 15%, nitrous oxide 6%, and halocarbons 15%.

> **WATCH OUT**
>
> Pay attention to the difference between the *natural* and *enhanced* greenhouse effect. If an exam question asks specifically about the enhanced effect, it will expect you to discuss how human activity is contributing to climate change.

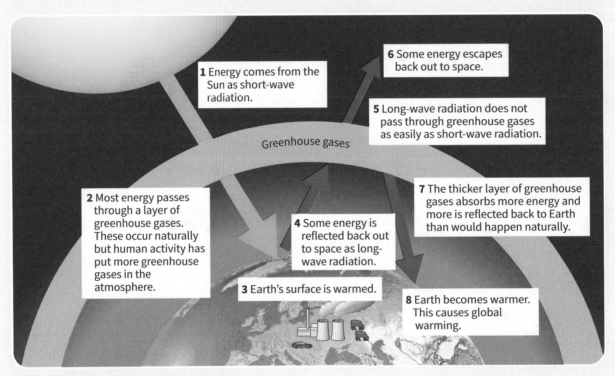

1 Energy comes from the Sun as short-wave radiation.

2 Most energy passes through a layer of greenhouse gases. These occur naturally but human activity has put more greenhouse gases in the atmosphere.

3 Earth's surface is warmed.

4 Some energy is reflected back out to space as long-wave radiation.

Greenhouse gases

5 Long-wave radiation does not pass through greenhouse gases as easily as short-wave radiation.

6 Some energy escapes back out to space.

7 The thicker layer of greenhouse gases absorbs more energy and more is reflected back to Earth than would happen naturally.

8 Earth becomes warmer. This causes global warming.

▲ **Figure 4** *The enhanced greenhouse effect*

Greenhouse gas sources

- **Burning fossil fuels:** coal, oil, and gas are burnt to provide energy for industry, transport, and heating homes, among other uses. This releases CO_2.
- **Agriculture:** livestock and crop farming are a big source of greenhouse gases. Methane is released from animals and rice farming, while nitrous oxide is found in most agricultural fertilisers.
- **Deforestation:** trees absorb CO_2 from the atmosphere and store it. When they are cut down or burnt, they release CO_2.

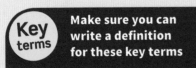

Make sure you can write a definition for these key terms

agriculture   climate change   deforestation   fossil fuels
orbital changes   Quaternary period   solar output
volcanic activity

Learn the answers to the questions below, then cover the answers column with a piece of paper and write down as many as you can. Check and repeat.

Questions | Answers

	Questions	Answers
1	What is the Quaternary period?	the last 2.6 million years
2	What is a glacial period?	a colder period within an ice age lasting for approximately 100 000 years
3	What source of evidence can scientists use to study the Earth's climate up to 800 000 years ago?	ice cores taken from the Arctic and Antarctic
4	Name a gas that scientists study in ice cores to learn about past climates.	carbon dioxide
5	Why do Milankovitch cycles alter the amount of energy the Earth receives from the Sun?	they change the distance between the Sun and the Earth, altering the amount of energy the Earth receives
6	What natural cause of climate change affects the Earth's climate over the shortest period of time?	volcanic eruptions
7	What are Sun spots?	dark spots on the Sun's surface caused by magnetic energy
8	Why do large volcanic eruptions cause temperatures on the Earth to cool?	the ash cloud blocks the Sun's energy
9	What is the enhanced greenhouse effect?	it refers to the additional greenhouse gases humans have put in the atmosphere. Humans have, therefore, 'enhanced' (made bigger) the natural greenhouse effect
10	Which gas contributes the largest percentage towards the enhanced greenhouse effect?	carbon dioxide (it contributes 60% of the enhanced greenhouse effect)
11	Name three ways that human activity has released more greenhouse gases into the atmosphere.	burning fossil fuels; agriculture; deforestation
12	Why do people burn fossil fuels?	to generate energy for activities such as industry, transport, and heating homes

Put paper here

Previous questions

Now go back and use these questions to check your knowledge of previous topics.

Previous questions | Answers

	Previous questions	Answers
1	What is the layer of the Earth on which the crust sits?	the mantle
2	Name two reasons why people continue to live near volcanic hazards.	jobs in tourism; precious minerals; they feel safe; fertile soils; geothermal energy
3	Between what latitudes do tropical storms form?	5°–15° north and south of the equator

Put paper here

Exam-style questions

Study **Figure 1**, a graph showing the area in the Arctic covered by sea ice in September 1979–2014.

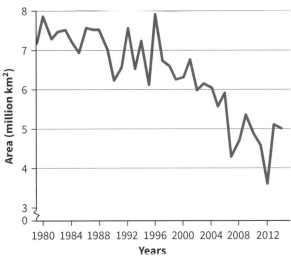

▲ *Figure 1*

1.1 Using **Figure 1**, which of the following statements is true?
Shade **one** circle only. [1 mark]

A In 1984, the area covered in sea ice was 4 million km². ○

B The smallest area covered in sea ice was in 2004. ○

C There was less sea ice in 1996 than in 1990. ○

D The trend shows that the area covered in sea ice is getting smaller. ○

1.2 Describe the change in Arctic sea ice in September, as shown in **Figure 1**. [2 marks]

1.3 Monitoring changes in Arctic sea ice is one piece of evidence for climate change. Outline how **two** other pieces of evidence show that climate change has taken place. [4 marks]

Study **Figure 2**, photographs showing human activity linked to climate change.

▲ *Figure 2*

1.4 Explain how human activity has contributed to climate change Use **Figure 2** and your own knowledge. [6 marks]

1.5 Name **two** pieces of evidence that show climate change has taken place. [2 marks]

6

Study **Figure 3**, a painting showing people holding a fair on a frozen River Thames in 1684.

▲ *Figure 3*

1.6 Suggest why **Figure 3** may be an unreliable source of evidence for climate change. **[2 marks]**

2.1 Explain how orbital changes cause changes in the Earth's climate. **[4 marks]**

2.2 Explain how volcanic activity causes changes in the Earth's climate. **[4 marks]**

2.3 Outline how solar output causes changes in the Earth's climate. **[2 marks]**

2.4 Suggest how agriculture contributes to climate change. **[2 marks]**

2.5 Suggest how deforestation contributes to climate change. **[4 marks]**

> **EXAM TIP**
>
> *Suggest* as a command word means presenting a possible case. It can be similar to the command word 'explain'. But with only two marks available here, you are not expected to write lots of detail.

Study **Figure 4**, a graph showing changes in the Earth's temperature and CO_2 levels over the last 1000 years.

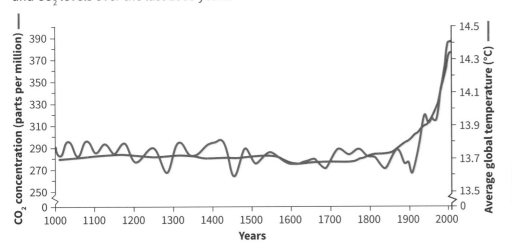

▲ *Figure 4*

2.6 'Climate change since 1850 has been caused by human activity.' To what extent do you agree? Use **Figure 4** and your own knowledge. **[9 marks]** **[+3 SPaG marks]**

> **EXAM TIP**
>
> Try to write developed statements, using connectives such as *however* or *furthermore* to link your ideas together. This will help you access the top marks.

Questions referring to previous content

3.1 Describe the weather conditions in the eye of a tropical storm. **[2 marks]**

3.2 For a tropical storm you have studied, explain how responses to this storm reduced its impact on people. **[4 marks]**

3.3 For a recent extreme weather event in the UK you have studied, assess whether physical causes were more significant than human causes. **[9 marks]** **[+3 SPaG marks]**

> **EXAM TIP**
>
> Make it clear whether you agree or not (though you can qualify your answer using phrases like 'mostly agree' or 'partially disagree').

 Knowledge

7 The effects of climate change and their management

Global effects cause local effects

At a global scale, the environment is affected by rising atmospheric temperatures. Global temperatures are predicted to increase by at least 1.5°C by 2040. Rising temperatures make sea levels rise through melting ice caps and glaciers, and through thermal expansion. Sea levels are predicted to rise by at least 30 cm by 2040.

Global environmental effects then cause local environmental effects, like more intense tropical storms, more severe droughts, coastal flooding, and species extinction. People are affected by things like the impacts of tropical storms, flooding, crop failure, and food shortages.

The effects on the environment and people are different in different places. Some countries are more vulnerable than others. In general, HICs are better able to cope with climate change as they usually have more money and resources.

Selected effects of climate change on people and the environment

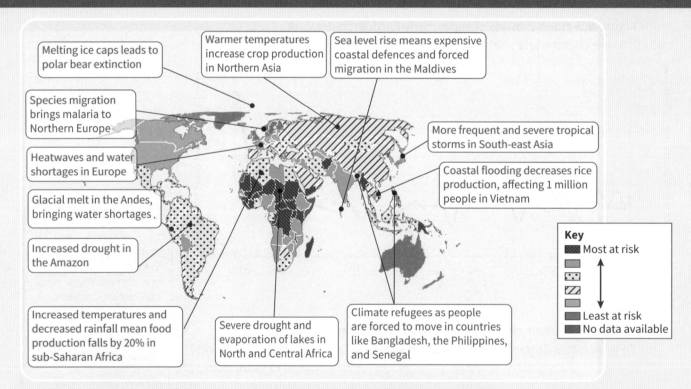

▲ **Figure 1** *Countries most at risk from climate change, and the effects of climate change on people and the environment*

 Key terms **Make sure you can write a definition for these key terms**

adaptation   afforestation   agricultural systems   alternative energy

carbon capture   international agreements   managing water supply

mitigation   rising sea levels

 REVISION TIP

Try to learn at least three specific effects of climate change on people and the environment. An exam question might focus on one of these and examples will help you access the top marks.

Mitigation strategies try to reduce the causes of climate change

Strategy	What is it?	How does this help?	Issues
Alternative energy production	Uses hydroelectric, solar, wind, tidal, and nuclear power to generate energy.	CO_2 emissions reduced because alternative energy sources do not emit many greenhouse gases.	Very effective but switching production takes a long time to implement. Currently more expensive than fossil fuels and nuclear waste is difficult to dispose of.
Carbon capture and storage	Technology is used to capture and store the CO_2 produced in fossil fuel power stations.	CO_2 produced from fossil fuels does not enter the atmosphere.	Very expensive. Critics doubt it will work well enough to have any significant impact.
Planting trees (**afforestation**)	Planting and restoring forested areas.	Trees remove CO_2 from the atmosphere.	Potentially effective but removing 25% of CO_2 needs 1 billion new hectares of trees. This could take 1000 years to plant.
International agreements	Countries commit to limiting climate change. Important agreements include the Paris Agreement (2015) and COP26 (2021).	In Paris, 195 countries signed legally binding agreements to take measures (such as cutting CO_2 emissions) to keep global temperature increase below 2°C.	Climate change can only be tackled through global cooperation but it is difficult to get countries to agree to significant targets.

Adaptation strategies try to adjust and respond to climate change

Strategy	What is it?	How does this help?	Evaluation
Changing **agricultural systems**	Planting drought-resistant crops; using more efficient irrigation.	Food supply will continue in drought-affected areas. Water use is more limited.	Could increase food production successfully but requires educating farmers about the new technology and making it available to them.
Managing water supply	Reducing water usage with aerators on taps; capturing, storing, and recycling water. Water transfer schemes to move water to areas of scarcity.	Reducing water usage will help countries adapt to water shortages.	Can be very effective at reducing water usage but requires investment in new technology. Water transfer schemes are expensive and alter ecosystem characteristics.
Reducing risk from **rising sea levels**	Coastal defence schemes like building sea walls; building houses on stilts.	Allows people to still inhabit areas affected by sea level rise.	Hard engineering works in the medium term but is expensive and has ongoing maintenance costs.

Retrieval

Learn the answers to the questions below, then cover the answers column with a piece of paper and write down as many as you can. Check and repeat.

Questions / Answers

	Questions	Answers
1	Name a global environmental impact of climate change.	rising atmospheric temperatures
2	Why are sea levels rising?	thermal expansion; melting glaciers and ice caps
3	Name an environmental impact of climate change.	e.g., sea level rise; more severe tropical storms; more severe droughts; species extinction
4	Name one way that people are affected by climate change.	e.g., forced migration; the economic cost of coastal defences; increases in disease
5	What is thermal expansion?	when the oceans expand because they are warmer, causing sea levels to rise
6	What is a climate refugee?	someone who is forced to move because of climate change (e.g., moving from an area prone to flooding)
7	What is a drought?	a prolonged period of time with lower than usual rainfall
8	What is meant by a mitigation strategy for managing climate change?	something that tries to reduce the causes of climate change
9	What is meant by an adaptation strategy for managing climate change?	something that tries to respond to climate change by changing current practices
10	Name a mitigation strategy for managing climate change.	alternative energy production; carbon capture; planting trees; international agreements
11	Name an alternative energy source.	hydroelectric power; solar power; wind power; nuclear power
12	What is carbon capture?	when the carbon produced by burning fossil fuels is captured and stored underground
13	Name an adaptation strategy for managing climate change.	changing agricultural systems; managing water supplies; reducing risk from rising sea levels
14	Name one way agricultural systems can be adapted for climate change.	targeted, drip-fed irrigation, or planting drought-resistant crops

Put paper here

Previous questions

Now go back and use these questions to check your knowledge of previous topics.

Previous questions / Answers

	Previous questions	Answers
1	Name a factor that affects the risk that hazards pose.	the wealth of a country; population density; geographical location
2	Name two reasons why people continue to live near volcanic hazards.	jobs in tourism; precious minerals; they feel safe; fertile soils; geothermal energy
3	What evidence is there that the UK is getting hotter?	10 of the hottest years have occurred since 2002

Put paper here

Exam-style questions

Study **Figure 1**, a map showing projected water shortages in 2050.

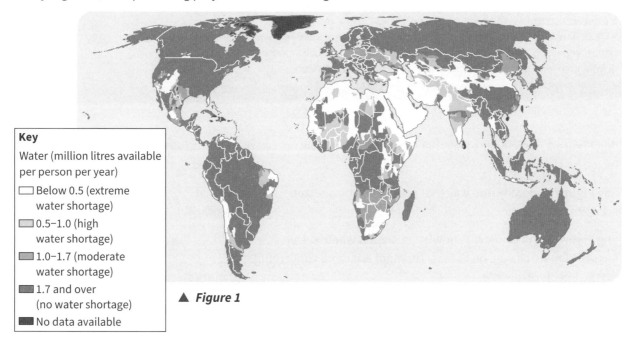

Key

Water (million litres available per person per year)

▢ Below 0.5 (extreme water shortage)

▢ 0.5–1.0 (high water shortage)

▢ 1.0–1.7 (moderate water shortage)

▢ 1.7 and over (no water shortage)

▢ No data available

▲ *Figure 1*

1.1 Using **Figure 1**, which of the following statements is true?
Shade **one** circle only. **[1 mark]**

A	North Africa is projected to have extreme water shortage.	◯
B	Northern Europe is projected to have extreme water shortage.	◯
C	The Middle East is projected to have high water shortage.	◯
D	Most of North America is projected to have extreme water shortage.	◯

1.2 Describe the distribution of countries projected to have extreme water shortage. **[2 marks]**

1.3 Using **Figure 1** and your own understanding, discuss the issues for people caused by climate change. **[6 marks]**

1.4 Outline **two** ways that the environment will be affected by climate change. **[4 marks]**

> **EXAM TIP** ◎
>
> *Discuss* as a command word requires you to present key points about different sides of an argument, issue, or the strengths and weaknesses of an idea.

Study **Figure 2**, a newspaper report about climate change.

Climate change: IPCC report warns of 'irreversible' impacts of global warming

The latest UN report says that many climate change impacts are irreversible. Places may cease to exist and up to 14% of species face a very high risk of extinction. Extreme weather events like floods, droughts, and heatwaves are increasing, and rising sea levels are impacting coastal settlements. The IPCC expects a billion more people to be at risk from coastal-specific climate hazards in the next few decades.

▲ *Figure 2*

1.5 Using **Figure 2**, identify **one** way that the environment will be affected by climate change. **[1 mark]**

> **EXAM TIP**
> Remember you must refer to something in the Figure to get a mark.

1.6 Using **Figure 2**, identify **one** way that people will be affected by climate change. **[1 mark]**

1.7 Using **Figure 2** and your own knowledge, assess whether the effects of climate change on the environment are more concerning than the effects on people. **[9 marks]**
[+3 SPaG marks]

> **EXAM TIP**
> This is where the specific effects on people and environment that you learnt can be used as evidence to back up the points you make.

2.1 Describe the difference between mitigation strategies and adaptation strategies as responses to climate change. **[2 marks]**

2.2 Name **one** mitigation strategy for managing climate change. **[1 mark]**

2.3 Name **one** way societies can adapt to climate change. **[1 mark]**

2.4 Name an alternative energy source and state **one** disadvantage of using this to generate energy. **[2 marks]**

2.5 Explain how alternative energy production and international agreements can help manage climate change. **[4 marks]**

> **EXAM TIP**
> You need to talk about both of these issues to get full marks.

2.6 Explain how carbon capture and planting trees can help manage climate change. **[4 marks]**

2.7 Discuss whether carbon capture and planting trees can be effective in mitigating climate change. **[6 marks]**

3.1 Suggest reasons why some people might disagree with spending money on carbon capture. **[4 marks]**

3.2 Suggest **two** ways that agricultural systems can be adapted to help manage climate change. **[4 marks]**

3.3 Explain how changing agricultural systems and managing water supply can help manage climate change. **[6 marks]**

3.4 Outline how the risk of rising sea levels can be reduced. **[3 marks]**

3.5 'Reducing the causes of climate change through mitigation is more important than adapting to climate change.' To what extent do you agree with this statement? **[9 marks]**
[+3 SPaG marks]

> **EXAM TIP**
>
> Make it clear whether you agree or not (remember you can qualify your answer using phrases like 'mostly agree' or 'partially disagree'). Give evidence for why you believe this.

Questions referring to previous content

4.1 Suggest **one** reason why tropical storms are found in bands 5° to 15° north and south of the equator. **[2 marks]**

4.2 For a recent extreme weather event in the UK you have studied, explain how management strategies are reducing the risk of future events. **[6 marks]**

Knowledge

8 Ecosystems from a local scale to global scale

Components of an ecosystem

An **ecosystem** is a natural system made up of **biotic** (living, e.g., plants) and **abiotic** (non-living, e.g., soil or sunlight) components.

 ### Case study: Small-scale UK ecosystems: a pond

A pond is an example of a small-scale UK ecosystem. Different components perform different functions in an ecosystem:

- **Producers** receive their energy from the Sun and convert this into biomass (e.g., plants).

- **Consumers** receive energy by eating producers or other consumers (e.g., fish).

- **Decomposers** recycle nutrients by breaking down dead plants and animals and returning nutrients to the soil (e.g., fungi and bacteria).

▲ **Figure 1** Pond food web

The biotic and abiotic components interact. **Food chains** and more complex **food webs** (**Figure 1**) show how energy moves through different trophic levels in an ecosystem.

Changing one component in an ecosystem has knock-on effects on all components. If frogs (**Figure 1**) were removed, mayflies could thrive, affecting other parts of the ecosystem.

SPECIFICATION TIP

You need named examples of a small-scale UK ecosystem. An example you may have studied is given here.

Distribution and characteristics of global-scale ecosystems

Tropical rainforests: Roughly 0–10° north and south of the Equator. Hot and wet climate. Lush and diverse vegetation.

Hot deserts: Roughly 15–35° north and south of Equator. Hot and dry climate. Sparse vegetation like cacti.

Temperate grassland: Roughly 25–40° north and south of the Equator. Hot summers and cold winters with wet and dry seasons. Mostly grasses.

Temperate deciduous forest: Roughly 30–60° north of the Equator. Mild and wet climates with four seasons. Broadleaf trees that lose their leaves in winter, like oaks.

Key
- Tundra
- Coniferous forest
- Temperate deciduous forest
- Temperate grassland
- Mediterranean
- Hot desert
- Tropical rainforest
- Tropical grassland (savanna)
- Other biomes (e.g., polar, ice, mountains)

Tropic of Cancer
Equator
Tropic of Capricorn

REVISION TIP

You are going to study tropical rainforests and either hot deserts or tundra in lots of detail, so focus here on the other global-scale ecosystems.

Tropical grassland (savanna): Roughly 10–20° north and south of the Equator. Hot climate with wet and dry seasons. Grasses with occasional trees.

Coniferous forests: Roughly 50–60° north of the Equator. Cold and dry winters and mild summers. Evergreen trees like pines and firs.

Tundra: Roughly 60–75° north of the Equator. Cool summers and cold winters. Low-lying vegetation like mosses and lichens.

◄ **Figure 2** Global-scale ecosystems

Characteristics of a tropical rainforest

The climate in a tropical rainforest is hot all year round. Average temperatures are 27°C. Rainfall is high but it is very high for six months of the year. Rainforests also create their own climate through the water cycle. Heavy rainfall is rapidly returned to the atmosphere through evaporation and transpiration. This then condenses into clouds, leading to more rainfall.

The hot and wet climate provides ideal conditions for plant and animal species to thrive. Tropical rainforests have more **biodiversity** than any other ecosystem, containing half of the Earth's land-based plant and animal species.

The soils in the rainforest have few nutrients because nutrients are leached (washed out) by the heavy rain. However, rapid nutrient recycling means nutrients are stored in the biomass (plants) rather than the soil (**Figure 3**).

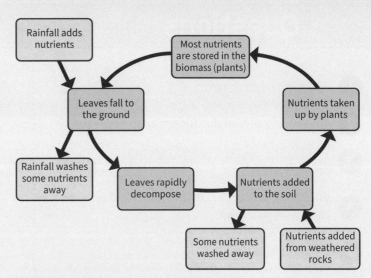

▲ *Figure 3 Rainforest **nutrient cycle***

Rainforest structure and adaptations

Animal adaptations

Many animals, like the leaf-tailed gecko, are camouflaged against predators.

Spider monkeys have long limbs and prehensile (gripping) tails to help move through the trees.

Plant adaptations

Lianas are vines that reach the light by wrapping around trees.

Some plants have waxy drip tip leaves so rainwater runs off easily.

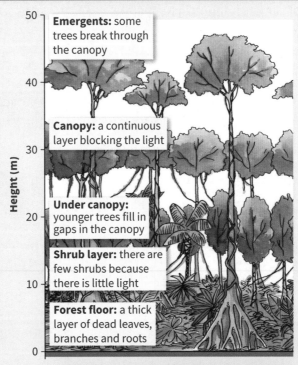

Emergents: some trees break through the canopy

Canopy: a continuous layer blocking the light

Under canopy: younger trees fill in gaps in the canopy

Shrub layer: there are few shrubs because there is little light

Forest floor: a thick layer of dead leaves, branches and roots

Height (m)

◀ *Figure 4 Rainforests have five layers*

Key terms

Make sure you can write a definition for these key terms

abiotic   biodiversity   biotic   consumer   decomposer   ecosystem   food chain   food web   nutrient cycle   producer

Retrieval

Learn the answers to the questions below, then cover the answers column with
a piece of paper and write down as many as you can. Check and repeat.

Questions	Answers
1 What is an ecosystem?	a natural system made up of biotic (living) and abiotic (non-living)components
2 What is the role of producers in an ecosystem?	they convert energy from the Sun into biomass
3 What is the role of decomposers in an ecosystem?	they break down dead plants and animals, and return nutrients to the soil
4 Where do consumers in an ecosystem receive their energy from?	from eating producers or other consumers
5 What is a food chain?	it is a sequence showing how different animals eat each other
6 What global-scale ecosystem is found 10°–20° north and south of the equator?	tropical grassland (savanna)
7 What type of climate is found in tropical grassland ecosystems?	hot with wet and dry seasons
8 Name a global-scale ecosystem found between 25°–40° north and south of the equator.	temperate grasslands
9 What type of climate is found in temperate grassland ecosystems?	hot summers and cold winters with a wet and dry season
10 Between what latitudes are temperate deciduous forests found?	30°–60° north of the equator
11 What is the typical vegetation found in deciduous forests?	broadleaf trees like oaks that lose their leaves in winter
12 At what latitude are coniferous forests found?	50°–60° north of the equator
13 At what latitudes are tropical rainforests found?	0°–10° north and south of the equator
14 What is the climate like in a tropical rainforest?	hot and wet all year round
15 How do tropical rainforests create their own water cycle?	high levels of evaporation and transpiration return moisture to the atmosphere
16 Why do soils in tropical rainforests have few nutrients?	nutrients leach from soils because of heavy rainfall; rapid nutrient recycling means most nutrients are stored in the biomass
17 How have spider monkeys adapted to living in a tropical rainforest?	they have prehensile (gripping) tails so they can move through the trees in the canopy
18 Name a type of plant that has adapted to living in a tropical rainforest.	lianas

Put paper here

Exam-style questions

Study **Figure 1**, a freshwater pond food web.

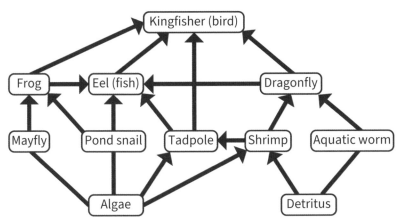

▲ *Figure 1*

1.1 Using **Figure 1**, which of the following statements is true?
Shade **one** circle only. **[1 mark]**

    A   Frogs eat eels.   ◯

    B   Dragonflies eat shrimps.   ◯

    C   Aquatic worms eat shrimps.   ◯

    D   Frogs eat algae.   ◯

1.2 Using **Figure 1**, which of these are secondary consumers?
Shade **two** circles only. **[2 marks]**

    A   Kingfisher   ◯   **D**   Eel   ◯

    B   Algae   ◯   **E**   Dragonfly   ◯

    C   Pond snail   ◯   **F**   Mayfly   ◯

1.3 Using **Figure 1**, identify a producer in this ecosystem. **[1 mark]**

1.4 Using **Figure 1**, suggest what might happen if the algae was
removed from the pond. **[2 marks]**

> **EXAM TIP** 🎯
>
> *Suggest* as a command
> word means presenting a
> possible case, or proposing
> an idea, solution, or answer.
> It can be similar to the
> command word 'explain'.

1.5 Using **Figure 1**, explain how energy moves through the ecosystem. **[4 marks]**

> **EXAM TIP** 🎯
>
> Note there are 4 marks
> available, which means you
> need a detailed explanation.
> Start with producers and
> follow the energy flow right
> through to the end.

Exam-style questions

1.6 Outline the role of decomposers in an ecosystem. **[2 marks]**

1.7 Outline the role of producers in an ecosystem. **[2 marks]**

Study **Figure 2**, a map showing the distribution of large-scale global ecosystems.

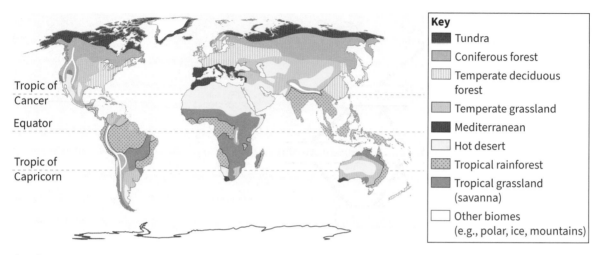

Key
- Tundra
- Coniferous forest
- Temperate deciduous forest
- Temperate grassland
- Mediterranean
- Hot desert
- Tropical rainforest
- Tropical grassland (savanna)
- Other biomes (e.g., polar, ice, mountains)

▲ *Figure 2*

2.1 Using **Figure 2**, which of the following statements is true? Shade **one** circle only. **[1 mark]**

   A   Tropical rainforests are found on the Equator. ◯

   B   Tundra is found on the Tropic of Cancer. ◯

   C   Coniferous forests are found only in the Northern Hemisphere. ◯

   D   There are deserts in Indonesia. ◯

2.2 Using **Figure 2**, describe the distribution of coniferous forest ecosystems. **[2 marks]**

2.3 State **one** characteristic of a tundra ecosystem. **[1 mark]**

2.4 State **one** characteristic of a temperate deciduous forest ecosystem. **[1 mark]**

> **EXAM TIP**
>
> *Describe* as a command word requires you to say where something is and what the pattern is. (No explanation is needed.)

Study **Figure 3**, a climate graph for Manaus in the Amazon rainforest in Brazil.

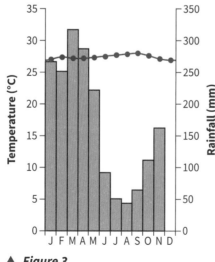

▲ *Figure 3*

3.1 In December there was 210 mm of rainfall. Add a bar to **Figure 3** to add this data to the graph. **[1 mark]**

3.2 Using **Figure 3**, which of the following statements is true? Shade **one** circle only. **[1 mark]**

     A   The temperature fluctuates throughout the year. ◯

     B   The highest temperature is in March. ◯

     C   The highest temperature is in December. ◯

     D   There was 260 mm of rain in January. ◯

3.3 Explain why tropical rainforests receive large amounts of rainfall. **[4 marks]**

Study **Figure 4**, the nutrient cycle in a tropical rainforest.

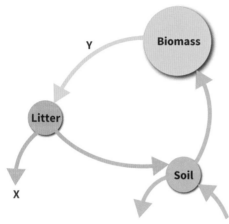

▲ *Figure 4*

3.4 Using **Figure 4**, state a label that could be put at point **X**. **[1 mark]**

3.5 Using **Figure 4**, state a label that could be put at point **Y**. **[1 mark]**

3.6 Using **Figure 4**, suggest why the biomass circle is larger than the soil and litter circles. **[2 marks]**

3.7 Using **Figure 4**, suggest what would happen to the soils if the trees were cut down. **[2 marks]**

4.1 Describe the main characteristics of the tropical rainforest ecosystem. **[4 marks]**

4.2 Name **one** animal species found in a tropical rainforest. **[1 mark]**

Study **Figure 5**, plants and animals in a tropical rainforest.

▲ *Figure 5*

4.3 Using **Figure 5** and your own knowledge, explain how plants and animals have adapted to survive in the tropical rainforest. **[6 marks]**

EXAM TIP ◎

This question is asking you to discuss plants *and* animals.

Knowledge

 Case study: Causes and impacts of deforestation in the Amazon rainforest

Deforestation of the Amazon rainforest

The Amazon is the world's largest rainforest, 60% of which is in Brazil. **Deforestation** has been rapid since the 1970s, with an average of 6000 football pitches cut down every day. Deforestation peaked in 2004, but after a decade of decline has recently been increasing again. The main reason for deforestation is **economic development**. Many people in Brazil want to exploit the Amazon's resources in order to develop.

> **SPECIFICATION TIP**
>
> You need a named example of a tropical rainforest to illustrate the causes and impacts of deforestation. A case study you may have studied is given here.

Causes of deforestation

Logging accounts for about 2% of deforestation. Much of it is illegal. Valuable hardwood trees like mahogany are cut down and exported for furniture.

Subsistence farming accounts for about 25% of deforestation. This is when local Brazilians move into the Amazon to grow food for themselves and their families.

Commercial farming accounts for about 70% of deforestation, mostly due to cattle ranching. Trees are cut down to provide land to rear cattle to supply the beef and leather industries. There are also large commercial farms growing crops like soy.

Road building only accounts for a small amount of deforestation but is significant because it opens up the rainforest to subsistence farming, logging, and other activities.

> **REVISION TIP**
>
> Learn the two biggest percentages so you have some specific detail to add to your exam answers.

Mineral extraction like gold and copper mines produce exports for the global market. The iron ore mine at Carajas is the world's largest mine, employing 3000 people.

Energy development: generating hydroelectric power floods huge areas of land.

Settlement and population growth: towns like Manaus near Carajas grow through migration as people move from other parts of Brazil in search of work.

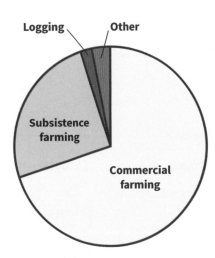

▲ **Figure 1** *Causes of deforestation*

 Key terms Make sure you can write a definition for these key terms

conservation   commercial farming   debt reduction   deforestation
ecotourism   energy development   logging   mineral extraction
selective logging   settlement   subsistence farming   tropical hardwoods

Environmental and economic impacts of deforestation in the Amazon

Local climate change

| Rainforest trees create a local water cycle by releasing moisture through evapotranspiration. | → | Rainforests generate 75% of their own rain this way. | → | Removing trees leads to a drier and hotter environment. | → | Summer temperatures in the Amazon have increased by 3.2°C since 1980. | → | This causes more frequent drought and forest fires, destroying more trees. |

Global climate change

| The Amazon absorbs 25% of global CO_2. | → | The amount it absorbs has reduced 30% since 1990. | → | The Amazon also stores 150 billion tonnes of carbon. | → | Deforestation releases stored carbon, contributing to the enhanced greenhouse effect. | → | Brazil's CO_2 emissions rose by 9.5% in 2020, largely due to deforestation. |

Increased soil erosion

| Trees bind the soil together and protect it from heavy rainfall. | → | Deforestation means the soil is washed away. | → | Nutrients in the soil are also washed (leached) out. | → | Most rainforest nutrients are stored in the vegetation, so the soil quickly becomes infertile. | → | This means more trees need to be cut down for grazing cattle and growing crops. |

Economic growth

| Activities like logging and mining have created wealth for many people in Brazil. | → | 8% of Brazil's GDP comes from the Amazon. | → | This means money can be spent on health, education, and building infrastructure. | → | But deforestation has negative impacts on local and global climates. | → | The estimated cost of global reduced crop yields caused by Amazon deforestation is US$3.6 trillion over the next 30 years. |

The value of tropical rainforests

Rainforests worldwide are important to people and the environment.

- They absorb and store CO_2, reducing the enhanced greenhouse effect.
- They regulate local and regional water cycles, reducing drought.
- They are home to half the world's plant and animal species.
- 25% of the world's medicines come from rainforest plants.
- They provide many resources like fruit, rubber, and hardwood.
- Indigenous tribes live in the rainforest.

REVISION TIP

How might you argue for and against deforestation? How might different people (e.g., unemployed Brazilians or environmental campaigners) think differently about deforestation? Forming an opinion on these issues will help you remember the facts.

Knowledge

9 Managing tropical rainforests sustainably

Strategies to sustainably manage tropical rainforests

	What is it?	Advantages and disadvantages
Selective logging **Example:** heli-logging is used in Malaysia.	Instead of clearing big sections of forest, only specific trees are felled. These are removed by helicopter or dragged out by animals like elephants.	☑ The cycle of destruction is managed and the forest can regenerate. ☒ The amount of timber obtained is reduced.
Replanting **Example:** Conservation International is planting 73 million trees in the Amazon.	Forest seeds grown in nurseries are planted to recreate the original forest.	☑ Some success, especially if done soon after deforestation. ☒ Impossible to recreate the ecosystem.
Conservation **Example:** Corcovado National Park in Costa Rica.	National parks and nature reserves are established to stop deforestation.	☑ Effective at preserving the forest. ☒ Economic development opportunities are reduced.
Education **Example:** the Rainforest Alliance works with farmers in Peru to promote sustainable coffee production.	Local people are taught more sustainable ways to make money from the rainforest. People in HICs are encouraged to stop buying products that damage the rainforest.	☑ Money is earned in a more sustainable way. ☒ Relies on goodwill rather than legal agreements.
Ecotourism **Example:** Monteverde Cloud Forest in Costa Rica.	Small-scale tourism where tourists stay in ecolodges and are educated about the rainforest by local guides.	☑ Local people earn money through conserving the environment. ☒ Too small scale to have a large economic benefit.
International tropical hardwood agreements **Example:** ITTA.	The 2006 International Tropical Timber Agreement (ITTA) promotes the sale of timber from sustainable sources (e.g., selective logging) by registering each tree felled.	☑ Covers 80% of tropical rainforests. ☒ Illegal trade in hardwood difficult to stop.
Debt reduction **Example:** the USA paid US$21 million to Brazil in 2010 in return for rainforest conservation.	Cancelling part of a country's debt in exchange for conservation of the rainforest. This reduces the economic need for deforestation and has become known as 'debt for nature swapping'.	☑ Makes conserving the rainforest economically beneficial. ☒ Has a minimal impact with less than 1% of debt typically affected.

> **REVISION TIP**
>
> Form an opinion on these strategies – do you think they are good or ineffective? Which is the best? And why?

Learn the answers to the questions below, then cover the answers column with
a piece of paper and write down as many as you can. Check and repeat.

Questions | Answers

#	Question	Answer
1	What is the underlying reason for deforestation in the Amazon?	economic development
2	What are the main causes of deforestation in the Amazon?	commercial farming; subsistence farming; logging; road building; mineral extraction; energy development; settlement; population growth
3	What percentage of deforestation in the Amazon is because of commercial farming?	70%
4	Name four impacts of deforestation on the Amazon rainforest.	local climate change; global climate change; soil erosion; economic growth
5	What happens to the local climate when large-scale deforestation takes place?	it becomes drier and hotter
6	Why does deforestation contribute to the enhanced greenhouse effect?	because the trees can no longer remove CO_2 from the atmosphere; CO_2 stored in the trees is released into the atmosphere
7	Why does deforestation for farming tend to lead to more deforestation a few years later?	because most nutrients are in the trees and not the soil — removing trees means the few nutrients in the soil are leached, making the soil infertile
8	What percentage of Brazil's GDP comes from exploiting the Amazon rainforest?	8%
9	How do activities like commercial farming and logging help Brazil to develop?	they create money that can be spent on things like health, education, and infrastructure
10	What percentage of the world's plant and animal species are found in tropical rainforests?	about 50%
11	Name seven strategies used to sustainably manage tropical rainforests.	selective logging; replanting; conservation; education; ecotourism; international hardwood agreements; debt reduction
12	What is a disadvantage of using replanting as a sustainable management strategy?	it is very difficult to recreate the rainforest as it was before deforestation
13	What is a disadvantage of education as a sustainable management strategy?	it relies on goodwill and is not legally enforceable
14	What is a disadvantage of ecotourism as a sustainable management strategy?	it is small-scale, so does not have huge economic benefits
15	What is an advantage of using debt reduction as a sustainable management strategy?	it makes conserving the rainforest economically beneficial

Put paper here

Previous questions | Answers

#	Question	Answer
1	What is an ecosystem?	a natural system made up of biotic (living) and abiotic (non-living) components
2	What type of climate is found in temperate grassland ecosystems?	hot summers and cold winters with a wet and dry season

Put paper here

Practice

Exam-style questions

Study **Figure 1**, a graph showing deforestation in the Brazilian Amazon 1988–2014.

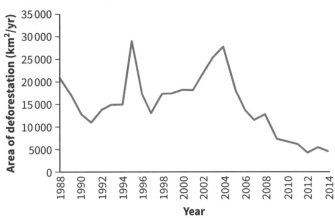

▲ *Figure 1*

1.1 Using **Figure 1**, which of the following statements is true?
Shade **one** circle only. **[1 mark]**

LINK

To understand the skill of reading a line graph, see the Geographical Skills section, page 228.

A   The highest rate of deforestation took place in 1988.   ○

B   The rate of deforestation slowed down between 2004 and 2014.   ○

C   10 000 km² of rainforest was lost in 2012.   ○

D   The rate of deforestation slowed down between 1998 and 2004.   ○

1.2 State **one** reason why deforestation is taking place in tropical rainforests.
[1 mark]

1.3 Explain how commercial farming can cause deforestation.   **[2 marks]**

1.4 Explain how road building can cause deforestation.   **[4 marks]**

EXAM TIP

Explain as a command word requires you to give reasons why something is the case. Note the difference in marks between questions 1.3 and 1.4. You are expected to give more detail on a 4-mark question.

Study **Figure 2**, a table showing the area of tropical rainforest in Brazil and Indonesia.

▼ *Figure 2*

Year	Area of rainforest in Brazil (unit millions of hectares)	Area of rainforest in Indonesia (unit millions of hectares)
2001	343.2	93.8
2010	331.9	90.2
2020	318.7	84.4

1.5 Using **Figure 2**, calculate the area of rainforest lost to deforestation in Brazil between 2001 and 2020.   **[1 mark]**

1.6 Using **Figure 2**, calculate whether Brazil or Indonesia had the largest percentage decrease in the area of tropical rainforest between 2001 and 2020. Show your working.   **[2 marks]**

Study **Figure 3**, a hydroelectric dam and a coal mine in a tropical rainforest.

▲ *Figure 3*

1.7 Using **Figure 3**, assess the causes of deforestation for a tropical rainforest you have studied. **[9 marks]** **[+3 SPaG marks]**

2.1 State **one** reason why tropical rainforests are valuable to the environment. **[1 mark]**

2.2 Explain **two** reasons why tropical rainforests are valuable to people. **[4 marks]**

2.3 Outline the impact deforestation has on soils in the tropical rainforest. **[2 marks]**

2.4 Suggest how deforestation might change the local climate in the rainforest. **[4 marks]**

2.5 Explain how deforestation contributes to global climate change. Refer to a case study in your answer. **[6 marks]**

Exam-style questions

Study **Figure 4**, images showing economic activity in a tropical rainforest.

Logging

Agriculture

▲ *Figure 4*

2.6 'The economic benefits of deforestation outweigh the environmental costs.' To what extent do you agree with this statement? Use **Figure 4** and your own knowledge in your answer. **[9 marks]**
[+3 SPaG marks]

3.1 Name **one** strategy used to manage the rainforest sustainably. **[1 mark]**

3.2 Suggest how international agreements can be used to help manage the rainforest sustainably. **[2 marks]**

3.3 Explain how selective logging and replanting can be used to manage the rainforest sustainably. **[4 marks]**

3.4 Outline **one** disadvantage of using conservation and education to manage the rainforest sustainably. **[2 marks]**

3.5 Explain how debt reduction can be used to manage the rainforest sustainably. **[4 marks]**

EXAM TIP

To what extent as a command requires you to judge the importance or success of something. Use words like 'strongly agree' or 'somewhat agree' to indicate the extent of your agreement. Use evidence and link some ideas to the images.

Study **Figure 5**, an advert for an ecotourism holiday in Costa Rica and photo of an ecotourism lodge.

The Costa Rican rainforest

Visit us

Imagine a place tucked away in the rainforest near the Caribbean Sea. It is so remote that you have to travel there by boat. Monkeys and birds greet you when you arrive rather than crowds and traffic. You'll leave behind the busyness of modern life and live without electricity. Surrounded by nature, you will learn about and really appreciate the rainforest.

▲ *Figure 5*

3.6 Using **Figure 5** and your own knowledge, assess the effectiveness of ecotourism as a strategy to manage the rainforest sustainably. **[6 marks]**

> **EXAM TIP**
>
> *Assess* as a command word requires you to weigh up the evidence and reach an informed conclusion.

Questions referring to previous content

4.1 Outline **one** reason why there are few nutrients in the soil in a tropical rainforest. **[2 marks]**

Study **Figure 6**, a table showing climate data for Manaus in the Amazon rainforest.

▼ *Figure 6*

Month	Jan	Feb	Mar	Apr	May	Jun	Jul	Aug	Sep	Oct	Nov	Dec
Temp (°C)	31	31	31	31	31	31	32	33	33	33	33	32
Rainfall (mm)	249	231	262	221	170	84	58	38	46	107	142	203

4.2 Calculate the average temperature. **[1 mark]**

4.3 Calculate the range of rainfall. **[1 mark]**

4.4 Calculate the inter-quartile range for rainfall. **[2 marks]**

> **LINK**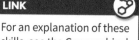
>
> For an explanation of these skills, see the Geographical Skills section, page 232.

Knowledge

10 The physical characteristics of hot desert ecosystems

The hot desert climate

Hot deserts are found between 15° and 35° north and south of the equator, where global atmospheric circulation creates high pressure. They average less than 250 mm of rain a year (rainforests have 2000 mm). Temperatures are very hot, averaging 38°C in the day, but nights can be below 0°C because there is no cloud cover to retain the heat. This gives a large temperature range.

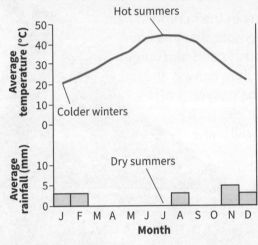

▲ **Figure 1** A **climate** graph for the Sahara Desert

SPECIFICATION TIP

You will have studied either hot deserts or cold environments. So, check carefully if you need to revise this topic.

Characteristics of hot deserts

No cloud cover

Few animals

High atmospheric pressure

Sparse vegetation

Dry soils with few nutrients

▶ **Figure 2** Hot desert characteristics

The different parts of the desert ecosystem are interdependent

- The thin soils are held together by plant roots.
- Leaves provide shade, keeping moisture in the soil.
- Long root systems draw water deep from the soil.
- Animals depend on plants and other animals for food.

- Dead animals and vegetation put nutrients back in the soil.
- Nomadic people move from place to place to graze cattle. If overgrazing takes place, it can lead to desertification.

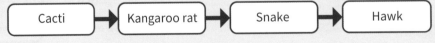

Cacti → Kangaroo rat → Snake → Hawk

▲ **Figure 3** A simple food chain in a hot desert

Biodiversity in hot deserts

The harsh conditions and poor soils in hot deserts mean there is low biodiversity. Some areas are more diverse than others. Plant and animal life is more diverse around temporary water sources and on the edges of the desert.

Plant adaptations

Cacti are **xerophytes**, which means they are well adapted to desert environments that have little water (**Figure 4**).

Other plants adapt through having very short life cycles, so they die before the harsh summers arrive. Their seeds can lie **dormant** for years before being activated by water.

Cacti are succulents (store water in their stem).

Cactus spines deter predators looking for water.

Waxy skin reduces transpiration.

Cactus spines help provide shade and reduce evaporation.

No leaves prevent water loss through photosynthesis.

Cacti have a wide root system to access water.

▶ **Figure 4** *A cactus is well adapted to the hot desert environment*

Animal adaptations

Camels are well adapted to the **physical conditions** in hot desert ecosystems (**Figure 5**).

Other animals adapt through being nocturnal and avoiding hot temperatures in the day.

A fatty hump to store and release energy. Camels can go months without food

Leathery mouth to eat spiky plants

Thick fur to keep warm at night

Long eyelashes and hairy ears to block out the sand

Little water lost through sweating and urination

Wide feet that don't sink in the sand

▶ **Figure 5** *A camel has adaptations to cope with its environment*

Key terms

Make sure you can write a definition of these key terms

adaptation   climate   dormant
interdependent   physical characteristic
physical conditions   xerophytes

REVISION TIP

Think about how the adaptations are linked specifically to the climate and conditions in hot deserts.

Retrieval

Learn the answers to the questions below, then cover the answers column with a piece of paper and write down as many as you can. Check and repeat.

Questions / Answers

	Questions	Answers
1	Where are hot deserts found?	between 15° and 35° north and south of the equator, where global atmospheric circulation creates high pressure
2	What is the average annual rainfall in a hot desert?	less than 250 mm
3	Why are hot deserts cold at night?	there is no cloud cover to retain the heat
4	What are the characteristics of soils in hot deserts?	dry with few nutrients
5	Do hot deserts have high or low atmospheric air pressure?	high pressure
6	How are soils, plants, and animals interdependent in a hot desert?	plants bind the soils together, animals eat the plants, dead animals and animal waste return nutrients to the soils
7	What is the name given to a plant adapted to survive in environments with limited water supply?	xerophyte
8	What is a succulent plant?	a plant that stores water in its stem
9	Why do cacti have waxy skins?	it reduces water loss through transpiration
10	Why do cacti have spines?	they deter predators looking for water
11	Why do cacti have wide root systems?	to access water from a wide area
12	Why do camels have humps?	the humps are a store of fat, which gives them energy when food is scarce
13	Why do camels have long eyelashes and hairy ears?	to prevent sand getting in their eyes and ears
14	Why do camels have wide feet?	so they do not sink in the sand

Put paper here

Previous questions / Answers

	Previous questions	Answers
1	What is the role of producers in an ecosystem?	they convert energy from the Sun into biomass
2	Why do soils in tropical rainforests have few nutrients?	leaching of nutrients from soils because of heavy rainfall; rapid nutrient recycling means most nutrients are stored in the biomass
3	Why does deforestation contribute to the enhanced greenhouse effect?	because the trees can no longer remove CO_2 from the atmosphere; CO_2 stored in the trees is released into the atmosphere

Put paper here

Exam-style questions

Study **Figure 1**, a map showing the location of the world's hot deserts.

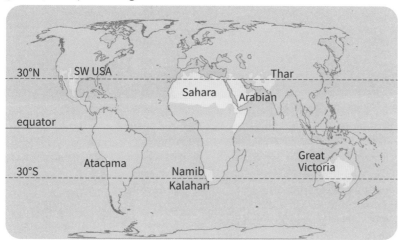

▲ *Figure 1*

1.1 Which of the following statements is correct?
Shade **one** circle only.   **[1 mark]**

A   The majority of hot deserts are found between 30°N and
       30°S of the equator.   ◯

B   The majority of hot deserts are found in South America.   ◯

C   Most hot deserts are found in continental interiors away
       from coastlines.   ◯

D   Hot deserts are found in all continents.   ◯

Study **Figure 2**, an image showing global atmospheric circulation.

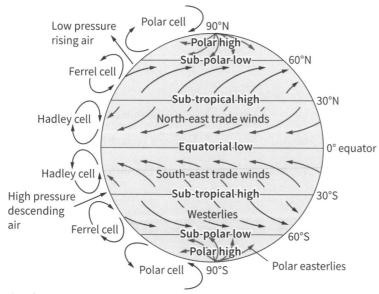

▲ *Figure 2*

1.2 Using **Figure 2**, explain the distribution of deserts.   **[4 marks]**

> **LINK**
>
> This question is linking
> the hot desert topic to
> the global atmospheric
> circulation model on
> page 14.

Exam-style questions

Study **Figure 3**, a climate graph for a hot desert in Salah, Algeria.

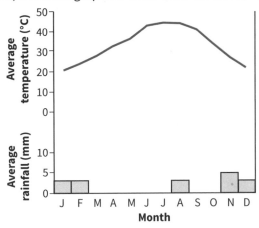

▲ *Figure 3*

1.3 Using **Figure 3**, complete the following paragraph. **[3 marks]**

Rainfall in Salah is low throughout the year. The highest rainfall is in
.... when there is .... mm of rain.
There is no rainfall between March and July, and September and October.
The maximum temperature is high throughout the year, reaching
a peak of 41°C in ....

Study **Figure 4**, climate data for a hot desert.

▼ *Figure 4*

	Jan	Feb	Mar	Apr	May	Jun	Jul	Aug	Sep	Oct	Nov	Dec
Temperature (°C)	29	28	30	32	35	36	36	36	35	34	31	28
Precipitation (mm)	25	2	4	4	0	0	0	0	0	3	26	15

1.4 Which month recorded the highest temperature? **[1 mark]**

1.5 Using **Figure 4**, calculate the temperature range for this hot desert environment. **[1 mark]**

LINK

For help understanding means and ranges, see the Geographical Skills section, pages 232.

1.6 Using **Figure 4**, calculate the inter-quartile range for temperature. Show your working. **[2 marks]**

1.7 Using **Figure 4**, calculate the mean precipitation. **[1 mark]**

1.8 Using **Figure 4**, calculate the total annual rainfall. **[1 mark]**

1.9 Suggest why hot deserts can be cold at night. **[1 mark]**

2.1 State **one** physical characteristic of a hot desert. **[1 mark]**

2.2 Outline the features of soil in hot desert environments. **[2 marks]**

2.3 Suggest how soils, plants, and animals are interdependent in a hot desert. **[4 marks]**

2.4 Describe the physical characteristics of hot desert environments. **[2 marks]**

EXAM TIP

Suggest as a command word means presenting a possible case or proposing an idea. It can be similar to the command word 'explain'.

2.5 'There are a variety of factors that influence biodiversity.' Explain this statement using your own knowledge of hot desert environments. **[4 marks]**

2.6 Outline **one** way in which animals have adapted to survive in hot deserts. **[2 marks]**

EXAM TIP

Outline as a command word means to set out the main characteristics of something; give a brief account or summary. Here, there is one mark for identifying an adaptation and one mark for outlining how this helps the animal to survive in hot deserts.

Study **Figure 5**, a picture of a jerboa and a cactus.

▲ *Figure 5*

2.7 Using **Figure 5** and your own knowledge, discuss how plants and animals adapt to hostile hot desert environments. **[9 marks]**
[+ 3 SPaG marks]

EXAM TIP

When presented with stimulus material you must include some reference to that material in your answer. For example, as part of your answer here, specifically mention how cacti have adapted to hot desert environments.

Questions referring to previous content

3.1 State **one** characteristic of tundra ecosystems. **[1 mark]**

3.2 Describe the challenges facing plants as they grow in the tropical rainforest ecosystem. **[4 marks]**

3.3 Outline how subsistence agriculture is causing deforestation in the tropical rainforest. **[2 marks]**

⚙ Knowledge

11 Opportunities and challenges in hot deserts

 Case study: The Thar Desert

Opportunities for development in the Thar Desert

- **Mineral extraction:** mines in the desert extract minerals like **gypsum** (used for making concrete) and **phosphorite** (used in fertiliser). Quarries extract marble used in the construction industry.

- **Energy:** renewable electricity is generated in **solar farms** and India's largest wind farm at Jaisalmer. There are also coal mines and oil reserves.

- **Farming:** the Indira Gandhi Canal brings water into parts of the desert, irrigating 3500 km² of land near Jodhpur. This allows **commercial agriculture,** growing wheat, cotton, and maize.

- **Tourism:** the Desert National Park in Rajasthan brings many tourists who enjoy activities like desert safaris, where they explore the desert on camels.

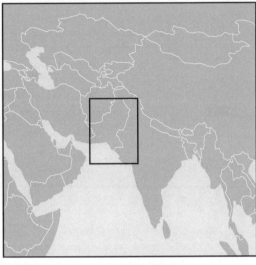

▲ *Figure 1 The Thar Desert in north-west India and Pakistan is an example of a hot desert*

Challenges of development in the Thar Desert

- **Extreme temperatures:** daily temperatures can reach 50°C. This makes it difficult for people to work, and hinders industry and development in the area. The limited water supply has high evaporation rates.

- **Water supply:** the low rainfall means little water for people, industry, and agriculture. There are occasional natural ponds (*tobas*) and human-made ponds (*johads*) around which people live.

- **Inaccessibility:** the desert is 200 000 km² (about the size of England and Scotland combined). It has a limited transport **infrastructure** with few roads and only four railways. Most places beyond the main cities like Jaisalmer are only accessible by camel.

> **SPECIFICATION TIP**
>
> You will have studied either hot deserts or cold environments. So, check carefully if you need to revise this topic.

> **SPECIFICATION TIP**
>
> You need a named example of a hot desert to illustrate development opportunities and challenges. A case study you may have studied is given here.

> **REVISION TIP**
>
> Remember to learn some specific facts about your case study. Learn specific names and places (e.g., Jaisalmer for the location of a wind farm). Specific details help you access the higher marks in exams.

> **REVISION TIP**
>
> What do you think is the biggest problem of living in the Thar Desert? Forming an opinion on this will help you remember the facts.

Causes and management of desertification

Desertification is the gradual change of fertile land into desert. Areas on the fringes of hot deserts are at risk of desertification. One billion people live in areas at risk of desertification.

Climate change is one reason for desertification. Parts of the world are receiving less rainfall, which makes the soil infertile. Desertification is also accelerated by local human activity.

Human activity causing desertification

Over-cultivation

More people can cause the soil to become over-farmed, destroying nutrients and turning the soil to dust.

Overgrazing

More people often means more animals. They eat the vegetation and erode the soil with their hooves, turning it to dust.

Population growth caused by high birth rates and in migration

Removal of firewood

Local people cut down trees for firewood for cooking. This exposes the soil to wind and rain erosion.

Soil erosion

Overgrazing, farming, and removal of trees means there is little or no vegetation to hold the soil together. It is dry and dusty, and easily eroded by the wind or rain.

Reducing the risk of desertification

Water and soil management

Water can be gathered and stored in small earth dams during the wet season, then be used to irrigate the land. Stone lines **(Figure 2)** can be laid along slope contours to prevent water washing the soil away.

Tree planting

Planting trees, especially drought-resistant ones like Acacia trees, can help bind the soil together (reducing erosion) and provide shade. The leaves also put nutrients back in the soil.

Appropriate technology

Digging water pits and laying stone lines are examples of **appropriate technology** (cheap and easy to use) to combat desertification. Other examples include solar ovens that cook using the Sun's energy, resulting in less need for firewood.

▲ *Figure 2 Stone lines stop water washing the soil away*

Key terms Make sure you can write a definition for these key terms

appropriate technology   commercial agriculture   desertification   erosion   gypsum   inaccessibility   infrastructure   mineral extraction   over-cultivation   phosphorite   solar farm

Retrieval

Learn the answers to the questions below, then cover the answers column with a piece of paper and write down as many as you can. Check and repeat.

Questions | Answers

#	Question	Answer
1	Name three factors that make development in the Thar Desert difficult.	extreme temperatures; limited water supply; inaccessibility
2	How hot does it get in the Thar Desert?	daily temperatures can reach 50°C
3	What development opportunities are there in the Thar Desert?	mineral extraction; energy production; farming; tourism
4	What minerals are mined in the Thar Desert?	gypsum; phosphorite; marble
5	How is renewable energy generated in the Thar Desert?	solar energy in solar farms, and wind energy at Jaisalmer in India's largest wind farm
6	How is farming made possible in the Thar Desert?	the Indira Gandhi Canal brings water into the desert
7	Name a crop grown in commercial agriculture in the Thar Desert.	wheat; cotton; maize
8	What is the name of a national park in the Thar Desert?	Desert National Park
9	What is desertification?	the gradual change of fertile land into desert
10	Name five reasons for desertification.	population growth; over-cultivation; overgrazing; removal of firewood; soil erosion
11	What are 'stone lines'?	a management strategy for desertification: stones are laid along contour lines to prevent water washing soil away
12	How can drought-resistant trees help reduce the risk of desertification?	they bind the soil together and provide shade
13	How can solar ovens reduce the risk of desertification?	they stop people cutting down trees for cooking

Put paper here

Previous questions | Answers

#	Question	Answer
1	What is the role of decomposers in an ecosystem?	they break down dead plants and animals, and return nutrients to the soil
2	Why do cacti have spines?	they deter predators looking for water
3	What are the characteristics of soils in hot deserts?	dry with few nutrients

Put paper here

Exam-style questions

1.1 Outline **one** challenge of developing hot desert environments. **[2 marks]**

1.2 Suggest why extreme temperatures and water supply provide a challenge to developing hot desert environments. **[4 marks]**

> **EXAM TIP**
>
> This question asks about extreme temperatures *and* water supply. You must mention both to get full marks.

1.3 Outline how inaccessibility provides a challenge to developing hot desert environments. **[2 marks]**

1.4 'Extreme temperatures are the biggest challenge for economic development in hot desert environments.' Using a case study, discuss whether you agree with this statement. **[6 marks]**

> **EXAM TIP**
>
> *Discuss* as a command word requires you to give key points about different sides of an argument or issue or the strengths and weaknesses of an idea. For this question, discuss other challenges like inaccessibility too.

1.5 Explain how energy production provides an opportunity for development in hot deserts. **[4 marks]**

1.6 Suggest how farming provides an opportunity for development in hot deserts. **[4 marks]**

Study **Figure 1**, photographs of economic opportunities in hot deserts.

> **EXAM TIP**
>
> Note the word 'successful' in the question. In your answer you must comment on whether economic development has been successful.

▲ *Figure 1*

1.7 'Hot deserts offer many opportunities for successful economic development.' To what extent do you agree with this? Use **Figure 1** and your own knowledge. **[9 marks]** **[+3 SPaG marks]**

> **EXAM TIP**
>
> 'And your own knowledge' requires you to include information from your case study.

2.1 Define 'desertification'. **[1 mark]**

Exam-style questions

Study **Figure 2**, a map showing areas at risk from desertification.

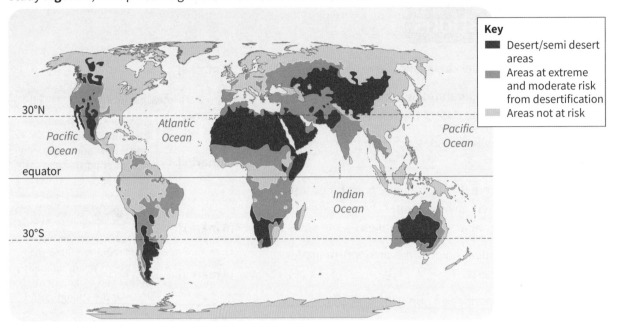

▲ *Figure 2*

2.2 Using **Figure 2**, describe the distribution of areas at extreme and moderate risk of desertification. **[3 marks]**

2.3 State **one** reason for desertification. **[1 mark]**

2.4 Explain how overgrazing and the need for firewood cause desertification in areas on the fringes of hot deserts. **[4 marks]**

2.5 Explain how population growth can cause desertification in areas on the fringes of hot deserts. **[6 marks]**

2.6 To what extent are physical factors the cause of desertification in areas on the fringes of hot deserts? **[6 marks]**

3.1 Suggest how **one** strategy can reduce the risk of desertification. **[2 marks]**

3.2 Explain how tree planting can reduce the risk of desertification. **[4 marks]**

Study **Figure 3**, some strategies put in place to manage desertification.

▲ *Figure 3*

3.3 'A variety of strategies is needed if desertification is to be successfully managed.' Use **Figure 3** and your own understanding to discuss this statement.

[9 marks]

[+3 SPaG marks]

Questions referring to previous content

Study **Figure 4**, a diagram showing the structure of a rainforest.

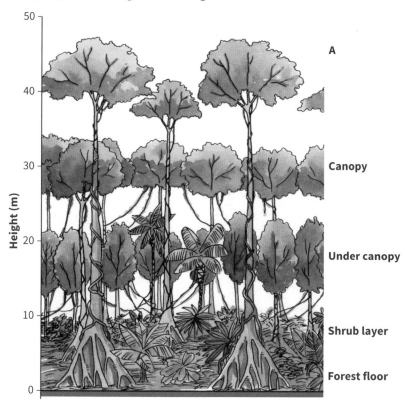

▲ *Figure 4*

4.1 What label should be written at **A**? [1 mark]

4.2 Outline the characteristics of the forest floor. [2 marks]

4.3 Explain why there is high biodiversity in a tropical rainforest. [4 marks]

Study **Figure 5**, a map showing the location of the world's hot deserts.

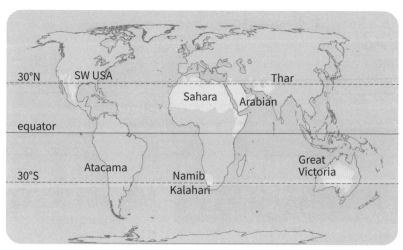

▲ *Figure 5*

5.1 Using **Figure 5**, describe the distribution of the world's hot deserts. [2 marks]

12 The characteristics of cold environments: polar and tundra

Comparing polar and tundra environments

Polar ecosystems are found in the Arctic and Antarctic. Tundra is found just south of the Arctic at 60° to 70° north.

SPECIFICATION TIP

You will have studied either hot deserts or cold environments. So, check carefully if you need to revise this topic.

▼ **Figure 1** Climate graphs for polar (left) and tundra (right) ecosystems

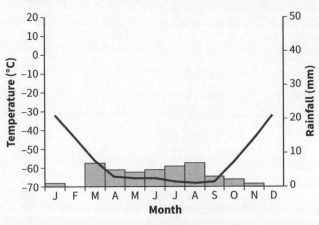
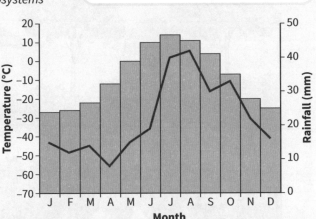

	Polar	Tundra
Climate	• Winter temperatures fall below −50°C • Low precipitation	• Winter temperatures fall to −20°C • Warmer summers • Some precipitation, especially in coastal areas
Soils	• Land is covered in ice so no soil is exposed	• Soils frozen (**permafrost**) but top layer (active layer) melts in the summer • Can become waterlogged • Infertile and acidic
Plants	• Little vegetation • Mosses and lichens on rocks	• Low-growing plants and mosses • Low bushes and small trees in warmer regions
Animals	• Very low biodiversity • Too cold for most animals • Few insects • Polar bears, penguins, whales, and seals live in the ocean and on the fringes of the ice	• Low biodiversity • More food options for animals • Reindeer, foxes, hares, and birds like ptarmigans • Insects like midges and mosquitoes, especially in the summer
People	• Some **indigenous people** • No permanent residents in Antarctica – only scientists	• Indigenous people and settlements built around mineral (coal/oil) extraction

Issues related to biodiversity

The cold **climate** and harsh conditions mean that cold environments have low biodiversity. When the ecosystem is damaged, it takes a long time to recover because the growing seasons are short. Global warming is melting sea ice and threatening many species like polar bears, walruses, and seals.

REVISION TIP

Learn some specific similarities and differences between these environments so you can give detail in your exam answers.

Interdependence in cold environments

All parts of an ecosystem are linked. Changes in one part have knock-on effects on other parts. Nutrient recycling is slow because of the cold temperatures.

Soils: permanently frozen (permafrost). Few nutrients.

Animals: the climate and limited food allow low diversity. Herbivores live off plants. Carnivores live off herbivores.

Climate: very cold, harsh, and windy. Little precipitation.

Plants: the climate allows little diversity. Slow **decomposition** when plants die.

People: too cold for most humans. No agriculture and few food sources. Difficult to build in frozen ground.

▲ *Figure 2* *Cold environment ecosystems*

Animal adaptations to cold environments

Animals like polar bears (**Figure 3**), arctic foxes, and hares have adapted to the cold environment.

REVISION TIP

Think about how the animal and plant adaptations are linked specifically to the climate and conditions in cold environments.

Thick fur to keep warm

White fur for camouflage

Strong sense of smell to find food

Black nose to absorb sunshine

Wide feet and large claws to grip on ice

Insulating fat

▶ *Figure 3* *Polar bears have adapted to the harsh environment*

Plant adaptations to cold environments

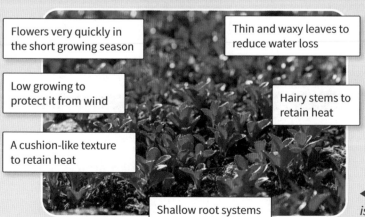

Flowers very quickly in the short growing season

Thin and waxy leaves to reduce water loss

Low growing to protect it from wind

Hairy stems to retain heat

A cushion-like texture to retain heat

Shallow root systems in frozen ground

Key terms **Make sure you can write a definition for these key terms**

adaptation   climate   decomposition
indigenous people   interdependence
permafrost

◀ *Figure 4* *The bearberry plant is adapted to a cold environment*

Retrieval

Learn the answers to the questions below, then cover the answers column with
a piece of paper and write down as many as you can. Check and repeat.

Questions | Answers

	Questions	Answers
1	Where are polar and tundra cold environments found?	polar environments are found in the Arctic and Antarctic; tundra is just south of the Arctic at 60° to 70° north
2	How cold are polar and tundra environments?	they are both very cold, but polar environments are colder with temperatures as low as −50°C
3	What is permafrost?	soil that is permanently frozen; in tundra environments the top layer may defrost in the summer and is known as the active layer
4	How does biodiversity compare between polar and tundra environments?	both have low biodiversity, but polar environments have less biodiversity because the conditions are even more extreme
5	Why is nutrient recycling slow in cold environments?	decomposition of dead material is slow in the very cold temperatures
6	Name an animal found in polar environments.	polar bears; penguins; whales; seals
7	Name an animal found in tundra environments.	reindeer; foxes; hares; birds like ptarmigans
8	Why do polar bears have white fur?	to act as camouflage
9	Why do polar bears have a strong sense of smell?	to help find food in an ecosystem with very low biodiversity
10	How is climate change having an impact on polar bear habitats?	melting sea ice means that polar bear habitats are being lost, threatening them with extinction
11	Why are plants in cold environments very low-growing?	to protect them from the wind
12	Why do plants in cold environments produce flowers very quickly?	because it is only warm enough to have a growing season for a very short period of time
13	Why do plants in cold environments often have hairy stems?	to help them retain heat
14	Name a plant that has adapted to the tundra cold environment.	bearberry plant

Put paper here

Previous questions | Answers

	Previous questions	Answers
1	What is the role of producers in an ecosystem?	they convert energy from the Sun into biomass
2	Why do soils in tropical rainforests have few nutrients?	leaching of nutrients from soils because of heavy rainfall; rapid nutrient recycling means most nutrients are stored in the biomass
3	Why does deforestation contribute to the enhanced greenhouse effect?	because the trees can no longer remove CO_2 from the atmosphere; CO_2 stored in the trees is released into the atmosphere

Put paper here

12 The characteristics of cold environments: polar and tundra

Exam-style questions

Study **Figure 1**, a map showing the location of cold environments.

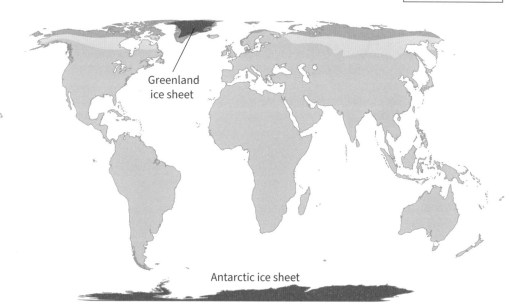

Key
■ polar ▨ tundra

Greenland
ice sheet

Antarctic ice sheet

▲ *Figure 1*

1.1 Using **Figure 1**, describe the distribution of tundra environments. **[2 marks]**

1.2 Which of the following statements are true?
Shade **two** circles only. **[2 marks]**

A Polar environments are colder than tundra environments. ◯

B Polar and tundra environments have high rates of precipitation. ◯

C Tundra environments have less biodiversity than
polar environments. ◯

D Reindeer are found in polar environments. ◯

E Polar environments are areas with high atmospheric pressure. ◯

F There is no vegetation in polar environments. ◯

Study **Figure 2**, a climate graph of Fairbanks, Alaska.

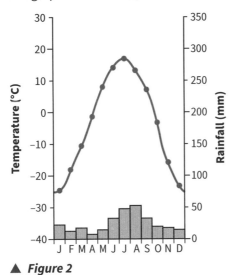

▲ *Figure 2*

1.3 Using **Figure 2**, complete the following paragraph. **[3 marks]**

Precipitation in Fairbanks is quite low throughout the year. The highest precipitation
is in .... when there is .... mm of precipitation.
The temperature varies considerably with a low of −25°C in December and a high of
16°C in ....

Study **Figure 3**, climate data for Spitzbergen, Svalbard.

▼ *Figure 3*

	Jan	Feb	Mar	Apr	May	Jun	Jul	Aug	Sep	Oct	Nov	Dec
Temperature (°C)	−7	−7	−9	−5	−1	4	7	6	3	−1	−3	−6
Precipitation (mm)	26	25	24	15	20	19	25	40	36	39	37	31

1.4 Which month recorded the highest temperature? **[1 mark]**

1.5 Using **Figure 3**, calculate the temperature range for
this cold environment. **[1 mark]**

1.6 Using **Figure 3**, calculate the inter-quartile range for
temperature. Show your working. **[2 marks]**

1.7 Using **Figure 3**, calculate the mean precipitation. **[1 mark]**

1.8 Using **Figure 3**, calculate the total annual precipitation. **[1 mark]**

1.9 Suggest why polar environments have very low precipitation. **[2 marks]**

LINK

For help understanding
means and ranges, see the
Geographical Skills section,
pages 232.

LINK

Think about the global
atmospheric circulation
model you studied on
page 14.

2.1 State **one** physical characteristic of a tundra environment. **[1 mark]**

2.2 Outline the features of soils in tundra environments. **[2 marks]**

2.3 Suggest how soils, plants, and animals are interdependent in the tundra environment. **[4 marks]**

> **EXAM TIP**
>
> *Suggest* as a command word means presenting a possible case or proposing an idea. It can be similar to the command word 'explain'.

2.4 Describe the physical characteristics of polar environments. **[4 marks]**

2.5 'There are a variety of factors that influence biodiversity.' Explain this statement using your own knowledge of cold environments. **[4 marks]**

2.6 Outline **one** way in which animals have adapted to survive in cold environments. **[2 marks]**

> **EXAM TIP**
>
> *Outline* as a command word means to give a brief account or summary. Here there is one mark for identifying an adaptation and one mark for outlining how it helps animals survive in cold environments.

Study **Figure 4**, photographs of an Arctic fox and a bearberry plant.

▲ *Figure 4*

2.7 Using **Figure 4** and your own knowledge, discuss how plants and animals adapt to hostile cold environments. **[9 marks]**
[+3 SPaG marks]

> **EXAM TIP**
>
> When presented with stimulus material, you must include some reference to that material in your answer. For example, specifically mention here how bearberry plants have adapted to cold environments.

Questions referring to previous content

3.1 State **one** characteristic of rainforest ecosystems. **[1 mark]**

3.2 Describe the challenges facing plants as they grow in the tropical rainforest ecosystem. **[4 marks]**

3.3 Outline how subsistence agriculture is causing deforestation in the tropical rainforest. **[2 marks]**

Knowledge

13 Challenges and opportunities in cold environments

 Case study: Svalbard islands

Challenges of development in Svalbard

- **Extreme temperatures:** daily temperatures can be as low as −30°C. This makes it difficult for people to work outside and for machinery to operate.

- **Provision of buildings and infrastructure:** building on permafrost means buildings need to be raised above ground level so the heat they give off does not melt the land underneath (**Figure 2**). Buildings sink (suffer from subsidence) and topple over if the permafrost melts. Roads are built on gravel to stop the permafrost melting and heated water pipes are also kept off the ground.

- **Inaccessibility:** Svalbard is very remote with only one main airport. There are few roads outside of Longyearbyen and most people use snowmobiles or 4x4s.

▲ **Figure 1** *The Svalbard Islands are nine Norwegian islands in the Arctic Circle*

> **SPECIFICATION TIP**
>
> You need a named example of a cold environment to illustrate **development opportunities** and **challenges** relating to these. A case study you may have studied is given here.

> **REVISION TIP**
>
> What do you think is the biggest barrier to development in Svalbard? Forming an opinion on this will help you to remember the facts.

stilts

▲ **Figure 2** *Houses in Svalbard are set above the ground to stop the permafrost melting*

Opportunities for development in Svalbard

- **Mineral extraction:** coal mining was once the most important economic activity and still employs around 300 people.

- **Energy:** burning coal is controversial because of climate change. All of Svalbard's energy is provided by the coal-fired power station at Longyearbyen. Solar energy in the summer months (when there is 24 hours of sunlight a day) or geothermal energy might provide greener alternatives in the future.

- **Fishing:** fish stocks are plentiful in the Barents Sea off Svalbard. Cod and herring are popular and fishing is controlled jointly by Norway and Russia.

- **Tourism:** in 1990 there was virtually no tourism in Svalbard but it is now the biggest employer. 2018 saw 85 000 visitors and a further 45 000 on cruise ships coming for attractions like the Northern Lights, dog sled trips, and ice cave visits. Large visitor numbers can damage fragile ecosystems.

Managing economic development in cold environments

Indigenous people like the Inuit live there, depending on the fragile ecosystem for their way of life.

Untouched **wilderness** environments are important for scientific study.

Why do cold environments need to be protected?

Many plant and animal species only live in cold environments, so need protecting.

The white snow and ice reflect the Sun's energy back to space. If the snow and ice melts, global warming will quicken.

Permafrost is a big store of methane. If melting gets quicker, then lots of methane will be released, adding to the enhanced greenhouse effect.

Strategies to balance economic development with conservation

- **Use of technology:** the Trans-Alaska pipeline allows the oil in the Arctic to be transported without using ships. It is raised above the ground to prevent the hot oil melting the permafrost and to allow caribou to move underneath it when they migrate (**Figure 3**).

- **Role of governments:** governments can create laws to protect the environment. The Arctic National Wildlife Refuge in Alaska was established in 1960 and protects 19 million acres from economic development.

- **International agreements:** the 1959 Antarctic Treaty prevents economic development and controls tourism in Antarctica. The Arctic Council is an international organisation of eight countries who collaborate to manage the Arctic in a sustainable way.

- **Conservation groups:** Greenpeace campaigns for a ban on oil drilling and large-scale fishing in the Arctic. The World Wildlife Fund helps protect Arctic environments.

 Key terms Make sure you can write a definition for these key terms

conservation group development challenges
development opportunities
extreme temperature fragile environment
infrastructure inaccessibility tourism
wilderness

▲ **Figure 3** *The Trans-Alaska pipeline is raised above the permafrost*

Retrieval

Learn the answers to the questions below, then cover the answers column with a piece of paper and write down as many as you can. Check and repeat.

Questions

	Questions	Answers
1	Name three factors that make development in Svalbard difficult.	extreme cold temperatures; providing buildings and infrastructure; its inaccessibility
2	How cold does it get in Svalbard?	daily temperatures can be as low as −30°C
3	Why is it difficult to build in Svalbard?	because the ground is permanently frozen (permafrost)
4	Why are houses built off the ground in Svalbard?	so the heat they give off does not melt the permafrost, which would make the buildings topple over
5	Name three industries that provide economic opportunities in Svalbard.	mineral extraction; energy production; tourism
6	What was the most important economic activity that drove economic development in Svalbard?	coal mining
7	How many people are employed in coal mining in Svalbard?	around 300
8	What alternative energy sources might be used for energy production in Svalbard in the future?	solar power in the summer and geothermal energy
9	How many tourists visited Svalbard in 2018?	85 000 visitors plus another 45 000 on cruise ships
10	Why are cold environments important in preventing global warming?	the white snow and ice reflect a lot of the Sun's energy; and permafrost is a store of methane that will be released if it melts
11	Why is the Trans-Alaska oil pipeline raised above the ground?	so the permafrost does not melt and migration routes of the caribou are not blocked
12	How many acres of land are protected by the Arctic National Wildlife Refuge in Alaska?	19 million
13	What is the Arctic Council?	an organisation of eight countries that collaborate to sustainably manage the Arctic
14	Name a conservation group trying to protect the Arctic.	Greenpeace; the World Wildlife Fund

Put paper here

Previous questions

	Previous questions	Answers
1	What is the role of decomposers in an ecosystem?	they break down dead plants and animals, and return nutrients to the soil
2	How does biodiversity compare between polar and tundra environments?	both have low biodiversity, but polar environments have less biodiversity because the conditions are even more extreme
3	Name a plant that has adapted to the tundra cold environment	bearberry plant

Put paper here

Exam-style questions

1.1 Outline **one** challenge of developing cold environments. **[2 marks]**

1.2 Suggest why extreme temperatures and inaccessibility provide a challenge to developing cold environments. **[4 marks]**

> **EXAM TIP**
> This question asks about extreme temperatures *and* inaccessibility. You must mention both to get full marks.

1.3 Outline why it is difficult to build buildings and infrastructure in cold environments. **[2 marks]**

1.4 'Extreme temperatures pose the biggest challenge for economic development in cold environments.' Using a case study, discuss whether you agree with this statement. **[6 marks]**

> **EXAM TIP**
> *Discuss* as a command word requires you to give the points on both sides of an argument and come to a conclusion. For this question, discuss other challenges like inaccessibility too.

1.5 Explain how energy production provides an opportunity for development in cold environments. **[4 marks]**

1.6 Suggest how fishing provides an opportunity for development in cold environments. **[4 marks]**

Study **Figure 1**, photographs of economic opportunities in cold environments.

▲ *Figure 1*

> **EXAM TIP**
> 'And your own knowledge' requires you to include information from your case study.

1.7 'Cold environments offer many opportunities for successful economic development.' To what extent do you agree with this? Use **Figure 1** and your own knowledge. **[9 marks]**
[+3 SPaG marks]

> **EXAM TIP**
> Note the word 'successful' in the question. In your answer you must comment on whether economic development has been successful.

2.1 Define 'wilderness areas'. **[2 marks]**

2.2 Explain why cold environments are considered fragile environments. **[4 marks]**

2.3 Suggest why melting permafrost might quicken global warming. **[2 marks]**

2.4 Explain **two** ways that cold environments can be harmed by economic development. **[4 marks]**

> **EXAM TIP**
> *Justify* as a command word means support your argument with evidence – give detailed reasons for an idea.

2.5 'Cold environments are more valuable if left intact rather than being developed economically.' Do you agree? Justify your answer. **[6 marks]**

Exam-style questions

3.1 Suggest how **one** strategy can reduce damage to cold environments caused by economic development. **[2 marks]**

3.2 Explain how action by governments can balance the needs of economic development with conservation in cold environments. **[6 marks]**

3.3 Outline how technology can balance the needs of economic development with conservation in cold environments. **[4 marks]**

Study **Figure 2**, a news article about internet access in the Arctic and an image of Greenpeace trying to prevent whaling in the Arctic.

The double-edged sword of technology for development in the Arctic

The Arctic submarine cable project is bringing high-speed internet into remote Arctic regions. This improves health care and allows access to economic opportunities, but also attracts foreign companies wanting to exploit natural resources. Organisations like the Arctic Council can give indigenous communities a voice in development decisions and help manage these new development opportunities.

▲ *Figure 2*

3.4 'A variety of strategies are needed to balance the needs of economic development and conservation in cold environments.'
Use **Figure 2** and your own understanding to discuss this statement. **[9 marks]**
[+3 SPaG marks]

Questions referring to previous content

Study **Figure 3**, a diagram showing the structure of a rainforest.

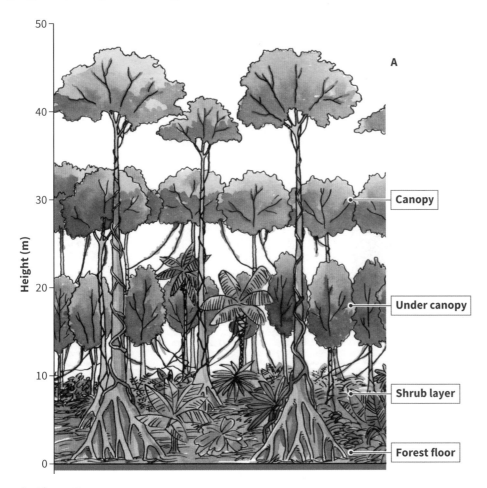

▲ *Figure 3*

4.1 What label should be written at **A**? [1 mark]

4.2 Outline the characteristics of the forest floor. [2 marks]

4.3 Explain why there is high biodiversity in a tropical rainforest. [4 marks]

Knowledge

14 The UK's diverse landscapes

Upland and lowland landscapes

A **landscape** is an area whose character has been shaped by the interaction of physical and human processes. The UK's landscapes are broadly divided by the Tees–Exe line running from the mouth of the River Tees in north-east England to the mouth of the River Exe in south-west England. North of this line are **upland** landscapes; south of this line are **lowland** landscapes. These landscapes are created by physical processes and human activity.

Upland landscapes

- Scotland, north and west England, Wales, and Northern Ireland
- Hard, resistant rocks like granite and slate
- In the north, Wales, and in Northern Ireland, glacial features like aretes, pyramidal peaks and U-shaped valleys

Lowland landscapes

- South and east of England
- Less resistant rocks like clays and chalk
- Rolling hills and flat fens

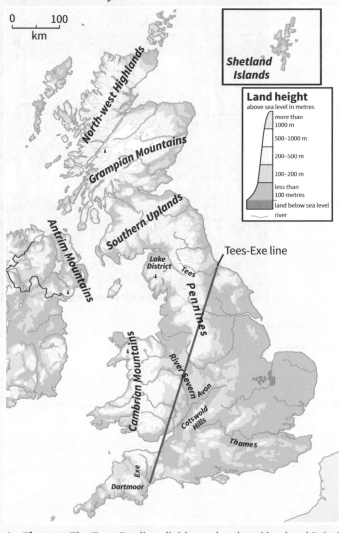

▲ **Figure 1** The Tees-Exe line divides upland and lowland Britain

The UK's river systems

The UK has an extensive system of interconnected rivers. The longest river is the River Severn, which starts in the Cambrian Mountains in Wales, flows into England where it is joined by the River Avon, and then flows into the Bristol Channel.

 Key terms Make sure you can write a definition for these key terms

landscape   lowland landscape
river system   upland landscape

 WATCH OUT

Make sure that you understand the distinction between the British Isles and the United Kingdom or UK (made up of England, Scotland, Wales, and Northern Ireland, shown on **Figure 1**).

Learn the answers to the questions below, then cover the answers column with a piece of paper and write down as many as you can. Check and repeat.

Questions

Answers

	Questions		Answers
1	Define the word 'landscape'.	Put paper here	an area whose character has been shaped by the interaction of physical and human processes
2	Name a mountain range found in upland UK.		Cambrian Mountains; Pennines; Southern Uplands; Grampian Mountains; North-west Highlands; Antrim Mountains
3	Name a hard rock found in upland areas of the UK.	Put paper here	granite; slate
4	Name a soft rock found in lowland areas of the UK.		clay; chalk
5	Name the longest river in the UK.	Put paper here	the River Severn

 ## Practice

Exam-style questions

Study **Figure 1**, a map of the UK.

1.1 Which of these places are in lowland UK? Shade **one** circle only. **[1 mark]**

A	Cotswold Hills ○	**C**	Grampian Mountains ○
B	Dartmoor ○	**D**	Lake District ○

1.2 Describe the distribution of upland areas of the UK. **[2 marks]**

1.3 Which of these is a description of the Grampian Mountains?
Shade **one** only. **[1 mark]**

A A mountain range running from the north of Wales to the south of Wales ○

B A mountain range running from the west coast of Scotland to the east coast of Scotland south of Loch Lomond ○

C A mountain range on the east coast of Northern Ireland ○

D A mountain range running from the west coast of Scotland to the east coast of Scotland south of the River Dee ○

1.4 Which of the following is a description of the River Thames?
Shade **one** circle only. **[1 mark]**

A A river with its source in the Pennines and its mouth in the North Sea ○

B A river running from the Cambrian Mountains to the Bristol Channel ○

C A river in the north-west of England ○

D A river with its source in the Cotswold Hills and its mouth in the North Sea ○

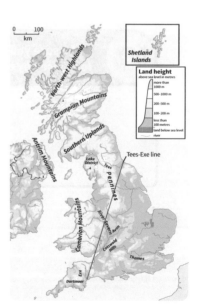

▲ *Figure 1*

Knowledge

15 Physical processes shaping coastal landscapes

Two types of weathering

Weathering is the breaking down or dissolving of rocks on the Earth's surface.

Mechanical weathering is the breaking down of rocks into smaller pieces without changing their chemical composition. Freeze-thaw is an example:

- Water collects in cracks in the rock.
- At night it freezes and expands, forcing the rock apart.
- The freeze-thaw cycle is repeated; over time, fragments of rock break off as **scree**.

Chemical weathering is when rocks are broken down by changes in their chemical composition. For example, when acidic rainwater containing CO_2 dissolves limestone.

> **SPECIFICATION TIP**
>
> You will have studied any two of coastal, river, or glacial landscapes. So, check carefully if you need to revise this topic.

> **Key terms** **Make sure you can write a definition for these key terms**
>
> coastal processes   constructive wave
> deposition   destructive wave
> erosion   longshore drift   mass movement
> transportation   weathering

Mass movement

Cliffs can collapse through **mass movement** when large amounts of rocks or soil move all at once. There are three types of mass movement:

- **Rockfalls:** when fragments of rock broken down by mechanical weathering break off a cliff face.
- **Landslides:** when blocks of rock slide along bedding planes.
- **Slumping/rotational slip:** when heavy, saturated soil suddenly slips in a rotational movement.

Rockfall

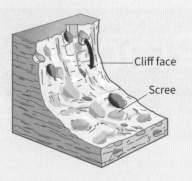

Landslide

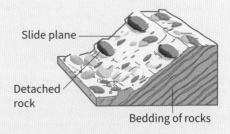

Slumping/rotational slip

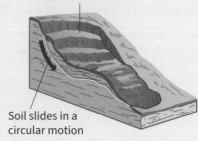

▲ *Figure 1 Three types of mass movement*

Types of waves

The coastline is affected by the action of waves. The strength of a wave depends on the strength of the wind and the fetch. The fetch is the distance over which the wind has blown.

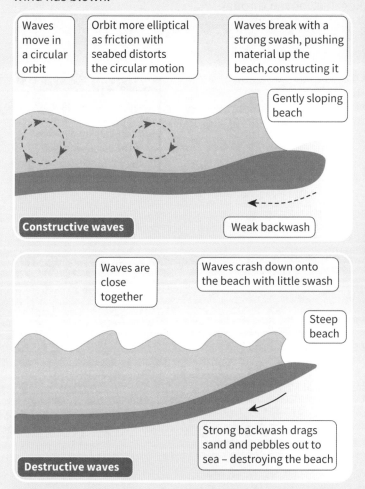

Constructive waves:

- Strong swash
- Weak backwash
- Less frequent
- Deposit material (constructing beach)
- Long, gently sloping beaches

Destructive waves:

- Weak swash
- Strong backwash
- More frequent
- Crashes downwards
- Erodes material (destroying beach)
- Steep beaches

▲ **Figure 2** *Constructive and destructive waves*

Coastal erosion

Erosion is the wearing away and removal of rocks on the coastline. There are four types of erosion:

Hydraulic power	The force of the waves hitting a cliff. The waves also compress air into cracks in the cliff, forcing it apart.
Abrasion	Waves throw sand, rocks, and pebbles at the cliff.
Solution	Slightly acidic seawater dissolves the cliff face.
Attrition	Rocks within the water knock into each other, becoming smaller and rounder.

The speed of erosion depends on:

- the strength of the waves
- the geology (rock type) of the coastline.

WATCH OUT

Attrition is an erosion process that does not affect the cliff face or coastline. It affects rocks in the water.

⚙ Knowledge

15 Physical processes shaping coastal landscapes

Transportation

The sea transports eroded material along the coastline. It is moved through a process called **longshore drift (Figure 3)**.

Material is transported in four different ways (**Figure 4**).

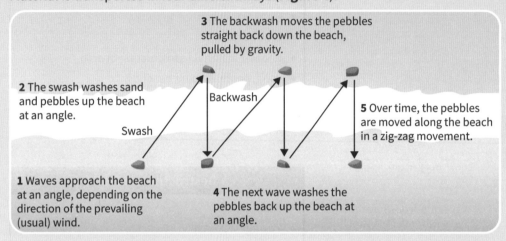

2 The swash washes sand and pebbles up the beach at an angle.

Swash

3 The backwash moves the pebbles straight back down the beach, pulled by gravity.

Backwash

5 Over time, the pebbles are moved along the beach in a zig-zag movement.

1 Waves approach the beach at an angle, depending on the direction of the prevailing (usual) wind.

4 The next wave washes the pebbles back up the beach at an angle.

> **WATCH OUT** ⓘ
>
> 'Solution' is the name of a transportation process *and* an erosional process. It is the same word for different processes.

▲ **Figure 3** Longshore drift

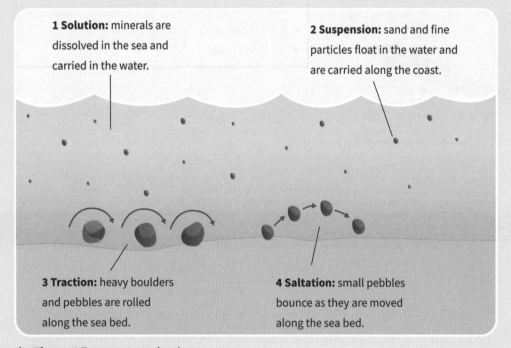

1 Solution: minerals are dissolved in the sea and carried in the water.

2 Suspension: sand and fine particles float in the water and are carried along the coast.

3 Traction: heavy boulders and pebbles are rolled along the sea bed.

4 Saltation: small pebbles bounce as they are moved along the sea bed.

▲ **Figure 4** Transport mechanisms

Deposition

When the material is transported along the coast, eventually it is deposited somewhere new. Material is deposited when the water slows down and loses energy.

Learn the answers to the questions below, then cover the answers column with a piece of paper and write down as many as you can. Check and repeat.

Questions | Answers

#	Question	Answer
1	Name four physical processes that shape coastal landscapes.	weathering; mass movement; erosion; transportation; deposition
2	Name a type of mechanical weathering.	freeze-thaw weathering
3	Name three types of mass movement.	rockfalls; landslides; slumping
4	Which type of wave has a strong swash?	constructive
5	Which type of wave creates long, gently sloping beaches?	constructive
6	Which type of wave removes material from beaches?	destructive
7	Name four types of erosion.	hydraulic power; abrasion; solution; attrition
8	Which type of erosion involves the sea throwing sand and pebbles against a cliff?	abrasion
9	Which type of erosion is caused by the force of the waves smashing into a cliff?	hydraulic power
10	What is the name of the process through which the sea transports eroded material along the coastline?	longshore drift
11	What determines the direction that longshore drift will transport material along the coastline?	the direction of the prevailing wind
12	Name four ways that material is transported in the sea.	traction; saltation; suspension; solution
13	Which type of transportation involves small pebbles bouncing as they are moved?	saltation
14	Which type of transportation moves minerals that are dissolved in the seawater?	solution
15	What happens to material being transported when the sea's movement slows down?	it is deposited

Put paper here

Practice

1.1 State **two** differences between destructive and constructive waves. **[2 marks]**

1.2 Complete the sentences about waves by writing the correct words in the spaces. **[3 marks]**

There are two types of waves found at the coast. .... waves have a strong ...., which removes material from the beach. .... waves build up the beach due to the large amounts of sediment they carry and their powerful swash.

1.3 Define the 'fetch' of a wave. **[1 mark]**

1.4 Name the type of wave that deposits material on a beach. **[1 mark]**

1.5 Define 'mechanical weathering'. **[2 marks]**

1.6 Define 'chemical weathering'. **[2 marks]**

> **EXAM TIP**
> *Define* as a command word means you need to state the meaning of a term. No explanation is needed.

1.7 Read the following definition: 'The downward movement of material under the influence of gravity.' Which term does this best describe? Shade **one** circle only. **[1 mark]**

    A   Deposition   ◯

    B   Erosion   ◯

    C   Weathering   ◯

    D   Mass movement   ◯

1.8 Outline the mass movement process of sliding. **[2 marks]**

Study **Figure 1**, the coastline at Holbeck Hall, Scarborough.

▲ *Figure 1*

1.9 Explain how mass movement has had an impact on the coastline shown in **Figure 1**. [4 marks]

2.1 Define the term 'erosion'. [1 mark]

2.2 Outline how geology affects the rate of erosion on a stretch of coastline. [2 marks]

2.3 There are several different processes of coastal erosion. Define 'hydraulic power'. [2 marks]

2.4 There are several different processes of coastal erosion. Define 'abrasion'. [2 marks]

2.5 There are several different processes of coastal erosion. Define 'attrition'. [2 marks]

2.6 Read the following definition: 'When rock fragments that are being carried by the sea knock into each other, resulting in smaller and more rounded rocks and pebbles.' Which process of erosion does this definition best describe? Shade **one** circle only. [1 mark]

    A   Hydraulic power   ◯

    B   Abrasion   ◯

    C   Attrition   ◯

    D   Solution   ◯

2.7 Explain the process of longshore drift. [4 marks]

2.8 Define 'deposition'. [1 mark]

2.9 Outline **one** reason why the sea might deposit sediment. [2 marks]

2.10 Describe the characteristics of coastlines where deposition is common. [2 marks]

⚙ Knowledge

16 Coastal landforms

The **geological structure** and **rock type** on a coastline influence the development of coastal landforms.

Landforms resulting from coastal erosion

Headlands and bays

A **bay** is an inlet where the coastline curves inward. A **headland** is where the land sticks out into the sea. Headlands and bays are formed because of different geology along the coastline (**Figure 1**).

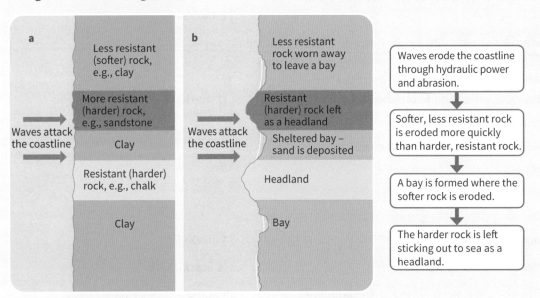

Waves erode the coastline through hydraulic power and abrasion.

↓

Softer, less resistant rock is eroded more quickly than harder, resistant rock.

↓

A bay is formed where the softer rock is eroded.

↓

The harder rock is left sticking out to sea as a headland.

REVISION TIP ☑

Make sure you name specific erosion processes when explaining the formation of coastal landforms.

▲ **Figure 1** Headland and bay formation

Cliffs and wave-cut platforms

- Waves erode the base of the **cliff** to create a wave-cut notch.
- The notch deepens until the cliff above it collapses.
- The cliff retreats, leaving behind a **wave-cut platform**.

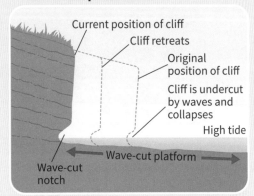

▲ **Figure 2** Cliff and wave-cut formation

Caves, arches, stacks, and stumps

These landforms are found in headlands.

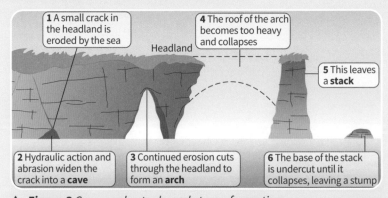

1 A small crack in the headland is eroded by the sea

4 The roof of the arch becomes too heavy and collapses

Headland

5 This leaves a **stack**

2 Hydraulic action and abrasion widen the crack into a **cave**

3 Continued erosion cuts through the headland to form an **arch**

6 The base of the stack is undercut until it collapses, leaving a stump

▲ **Figure 3** Cave, arch, stack, and stump formation

Key terms Make sure you can write a definition for these key terms

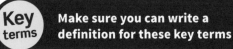

arch   bar   bay   beach   cave   cliff   geological structure
headland   rock type   sand dune   spit   stack   wave-cut platform

Landforms created by deposition

Beaches and sand dunes

Beaches

Beaches are formed by constructive waves when material is deposited. Sandy beaches typically form in sheltered bays, and pebble beaches where the waves have more energy.

Sand dunes

Sand dunes form when the wind blows sand onshore.

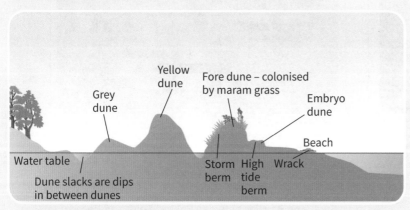

▲ **Figure 4** Sand dune formation

An embryo dune develops where a small obstacle, like a piece of wood, traps some sand.

↓

Vegetation like sea lyme grass starts to grow, holding the dune together.

↓

More sand is trapped and vegetation like marram grass grows. The dunes grow in size, becoming fore dunes.

↓

More vegetation stabilises the dune as it becomes a yellow dune.

↓

The vegetation that dies adds nutrients, forming more fertile soils and leading to grey dunes with a wide range of vegetation.

Spits and bars

A **spit** is a long expanse of sand attached to the land at one end. It is formed when longshore drift transports material along a coastline and there is a sudden change in the direction of the coastline. When a spit grows right across a bay, it is called a **bar**.

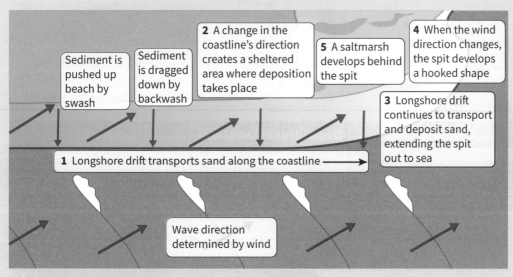

▲ **Figure 5** Longshore drift

Case study: Landforms on the Swanage coastline

Coastal landforms at Swanage

Old Harry Rocks is the name given to the stack off a chalk headland near Swanage. There are also cliffs, caves, and arches.

Studland Bay is a sand spit formed by longshore drift moving sand from south to north. It also has sand dunes and a salt marsh.

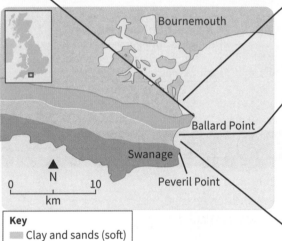

Bournemouth

Ballard Point

Swanage

Peveril Point

0 — 10
N
km

Key
- Clay and sands (soft)
- Chalk (hard)
- Limestone (hard)

Discordant coastline Note how the alternating bands of rock are perpendicular to the coastline. This is called a discordant coastline and creates headlands and bays.

Swanage Bay lies between Ballard Point and Peveril Point. It has formed because the clay bay has eroded more quickly than the chalk headland to the north (Ballard Point) and the limestone headland to the south (Peveril Point). The sheltered bay has a broad, sandy beach.

▲ **Figure 6** *The Swanage coastline*

Summary of coastal landforms

Erosional landform	Where?	Depositional landform	Where?
Headland	Ballard Point, Peveril Point	Beach	Swanage Bay, Studland Bay
Bay	Swanage Bay	Spit	Studland Bay
Cliffs, caves, arches, stack, stump	Old Harry Rocks	Sand dunes	Studland Bay

SPECIFICATION TIP

You need a named example of a section of coastline in the UK to identify its major landforms of erosion and deposition. A case study you may have studied is given here.

WATCH OUT

Studland Bay is not a bay caused by erosion between two headlands. It should be used as an example of a spit.

Retrieval

Learn the answers to the questions below, then cover the answers column with a piece of paper and write down as many as you can. Check and repeat.

Questions	Answers
1 Name a coastal landform created by erosion.	headland; bay; cliff; wave-cut platform; cave; arch; stack; stump
2 What is a bay?	an inlet where the coastline curves inward
3 Are bays formed from hard or soft rock?	soft rock
4 Are headlands formed from hard or soft rock?	hard rock
5 What happens to a cliff to create a wave-cut platform?	the cliff retreats (moves backwards) and leaves a wave-cut platform behind
6 Put these landforms in the order in which they are formed: stack, arch, crack, stump, cave.	crack, cave, arch, stack, stump
7 Are stacks formed from soft rock or hard rock?	hard rock
8 Name four landforms created by deposition.	beaches; sand dunes; spits; bars
9 What type of wave creates beaches?	constructive waves
10 Put these types of dune in the order in which they are formed: yellow dune, embryo dune, grey dune, fore dune.	embryo dune, fore dune, yellow dune, grey dune
11 What is the first stage in the formation of sand dunes; a very small pile of sand that has been trapped by an obstacle and vegetation has started to grow?	an embryo dune
12 What is the type of grass that is very common in fore dunes and yellow dunes?	marram grass
13 What is a spit?	a long expanse of sand attached to the land at one end
14 What has to happen to the coastline for a spit to start forming?	it has to suddenly change direction or shape
15 What transportation process has to be taking place for spits to form?	longshore drift

Put paper here

Previous questions	Answers
1 What type of erosion is caused by the force of the waves smashing into the cliff?	hydraulic power
2 What is the name of the process through which the sea transports eroded material along the coastline?	longshore drift

Put paper here

Exam-style questions

Study **Figure 1**, a 1:50 000 Ordnance Survey map extract of Swanage coast.

LINK

Questions 1–10 test a variety of map-reading skills. See pages 225–226 for an overview of map-reading skills.

1.1 Using **Figure 1**, what is the distance between Peveril Point and Ballard Point? Shade **one** circle only. **[1 mark]**

A 2.75 km ○

B 3.5 km ○

C 4 km ○

D 4.25 km ○

1.2 Using **Figure 1**, which of these grid squares has land with the steepest gradient? Shade **one** circle only. **[1 mark]**

A 0381 ○

B 0183 ○

C 0280 ○

D 0277 ○

1.3 Using **Figure 1**, identify the coastal landform shown in grid square 0478.
 [1 mark]

1.4 Using **Figure 1**, suggest a reason for the formation of the feature shown in grid square 0478. **[1 mark]**

1.5 The middle of Swanage Bay is located in grid square 0379. Suggest how Swanage Bay was formed. **[4 marks]**

1.6 Using **Figure 1**, identify the 6-figure grid reference for the information centre in Swanage.
Shade **one** circle only. **[1 mark]**

A 024 782 ○

B 017 798 ○

C 031 790 ○

D 033 821 ○

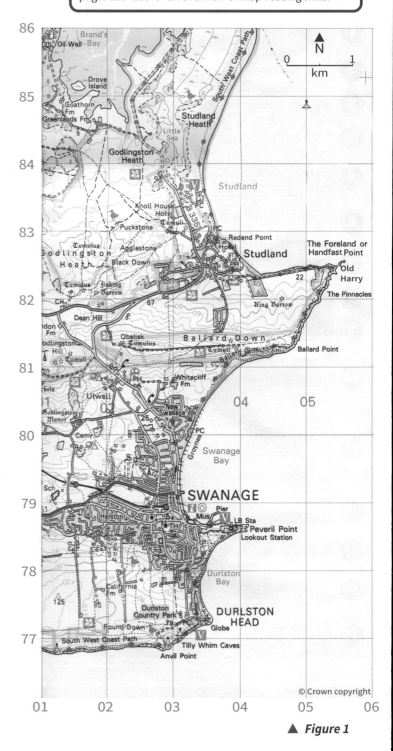

▲ *Figure 1*

1.7 Using **Figure 1**, identify the direction that Durlston Head is in from the town of Swanage.
Shade **one** circle only. **[1 mark]**

A North ○   C South ○

B North-east ○   D East ○

Study **Figure 2**, a photograph of Old Harry in grid square 055 826.

1.8 State in which direction the photographer was standing when **Figure 2** was taken. [1 mark]

▶ *Figure 2*

1.9 Explain how erosion has led to the formation of the landforms shown in **Figure 2**. [6 marks]

1.10 Using an example of a stretch of UK coastline you have studied, assess the role of geology in the formation of its landforms. [9 marks]
[+3 SPaG marks]

 EXAM TIP

The question specifically highlights 'erosion'. You would be expected to name and explain some erosion processes in your answer.

2.1 Explain how wave-cut platforms are formed. [4 marks]

EXAM TIP

Examiners are particularly interested in seeing a clear sense of sequence when you explain how landforms are formed (but do not write in bullet points).

Study **Figure 3**, a photograph of coastal landforms in Wales.

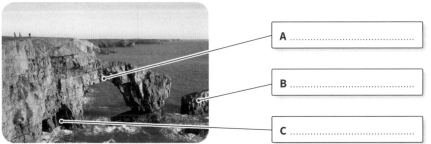

A ....

B ....

C ....

▲ *Figure 3*

2.2 Label the features **A–C** on **Figure 3**. [3 marks]

2.3 Using **Figure 3**, suggest how this landform might change over time. [4 marks]

2.4 Explain how a beach is formed. [4 marks]

2.5 Explain how a spit is formed. Use one or more diagrams in your answer. [4 marks]

2.6 Outline **two** conditions required for the formation of sand dunes. [2 marks]

2.7 Explain how a sand dune is formed. Use one or more diagrams in your answer. [4 marks]

EXAM TIP

Diagrams should be clearly drawn and have labels or annotations illustrating key processes. Labels are words identifying features, while annotations include some explanation.

2.8 Using an example of a stretch of UK coastline you have studied, assess the importance of erosion and deposition in the formation of the major landforms. [9 marks]

Questions referring to previous content

3.1 Identify **two** factors that influence the strength of a wave. [2 marks]

3.2 Which of these is a way that material is transported along a stretch of coastline? Shade **one** circle only. [1 mark]

| **A** | Attrition | ○ | **C** | Hydraulic power | ○ |
| **B** | Abrasion | ○ | **D** | Traction | ○ |

Knowledge

17 Coastal management strategies

Approaches to coastal management

- **Hard engineering:** when structures are built to prevent erosion taking place.
- **Soft engineering:** when strategies are put in place to reduce erosion by working alongside natural processes.
- **Managed retreat:** a sustainable strategy where land is allowed to flood and human activity is moved away from the coastline.

Hard engineering

	Sea walls	Groynes	Rock armour	Gabions
How does it work?	• A physical barrier preventing the sea from hitting the coastline. Recurved sea walls reflect wave energy back out to sea.	• Wooden or concrete barriers built to trap sediment moved by longshore drift. This builds a protective beach that absorbs wave energy.	• Large boulders in front of the coastline absorb the wave energy.	• Wire cages filled with stones that absorb wave energy when placed in front of the coastline.
Costs	• Very expensive to build. • Ongoing repair costs. • Interrupts natural erosion, which can increase erosion elsewhere.	• Interrupting longshore drift leads to increased erosion elsewhere.	• Expensive. • Ugly and restricts beach access. • Interrupts natural erosion, which can increase erosion elsewhere.	• Short lifespan where cages rust after 5–10 years.
Benefits	• Very effective. • Can be attractive and used as promenades.	• Relatively cheap. • Builds beaches for tourism.	• Effective. • Can look natural.	• Relatively cheap. • Can be disguised with vegetation.

WATCH OUT

Remember that groynes *reduce* longshore drift; they do not stop it.

WATCH OUT

'Cost' does not only mean a financial cost. It is closer in meaning to 'disadvantages'.

Soft engineering

	Beach nourishment and reprofiling	Dune regeneration
How does it work?	Sand dredged from offshore is added to beaches. The beaches are then shaped (reprofiled) to make them higher and wider, protecting the coastline behind.	Sand dunes are regenerated to act as a natural barrier to erosion. Marram grass is planted to stabilise dunes and they are fenced off from human activity.
Costs	• Medium initial costs but has to be repeated as the new sand is removed by longshore drift.	• Requires regular monitoring and management. • Takes a long time.
Benefits	• Natural looking and good for tourism.	• Very cheap. • Maintains an attractive natural environment.

Managed retreat

	Coastal realignment
How does it work?	The land is allowed to flood, meaning that human activity retreats inland. This is normally low-value farmland.
Costs	Land floods, which can mean people lose their homes or farmers lose land.
Benefits	• A natural equilibrium is reached with no negative impacts elsewhere. • New habitats like salt marshes are formed.

WATCH OUT

Different stakeholders will have different views about which forms of management are best. For example, coastal residents may want secure hard engineering solutions. Environmentalists, fearing for natural habitats, might prefer soft engineering or managed retreat.

 ## Case study: Coastal management of Lyme Regis, Dorset

Reasons for coastal management

• Lyme Regis (a small coastal town in Dorset) is important to Dorset's £800 million tourist economy.
• Much of the town is built on unstable cliffs that might collapse.
• Rapid erosion has seen many properties destroyed.
• Existing defences have been breached many times.

SPECIFICATION TIP

You need a named example of a coastal management scheme in the UK. A case study you may have studied is given here.

 Key terms Make sure you can write a definition for these key terms

beach nourishment and reprofiling   coastal realignment   dune regeneration   gabions
groynes   hard engineering   managed retreat   rock armour   sea wall   soft engineering

Knowledge

17 Coastal management strategies

Coastal management scheme

A management scheme started in the 1990s and was completed in 2015. It used both hard and soft engineering and was divided into four phases. The total cost was over £43 million.

Phases 1 and 2 (1990s–2007)

- Cliffs were drained, stabilised, and nailed together.
- New sea walls and a promenade were built.
- Beach feeding created a wide beach to absorb wave energy.
- Rock armour was built to absorb sea energy from destructive waves from the south-west.

Phase 3

- Not undertaken.

Phase 4 (2013–2015)

- Another sea wall built and cliff stabilisation undertaken.

REVISION TIP

Remember to learn specific aims, dates, and costs from your case study.

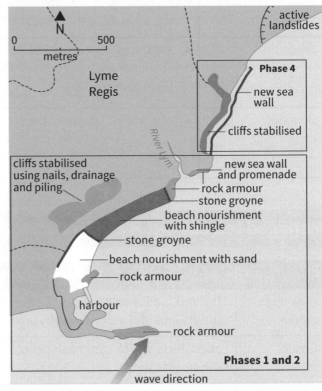

▲ *Figure 1* Coastal management in Lyme Regis

Effects and conflicts

Positive effects
• The new beaches have attracted more tourists. This has boosted local businesses.
• 480 homes have been protected.
• The defences have withstood stormy winters.
• The harbour is better protected.

Negative effects
• There is increased traffic and congestion.
• Preventing cliff movement has stopped fossils being revealed.
• The defences affect the look of the natural landscape.
• The defences interfere with natural processes, affecting other places along the coast.

Conflicts between stakeholders

- Businesses might enjoy the extra trade.
- Some residents might dislike the congestion.
- Some residents might feel better protected.
- Fishermen like the harbour being protected.
- Environmentalists worry about disrupting natural processes.

Learn the answers to the questions below, then cover the answers column with a piece of paper and write down as many as you can. Check and repeat.

Questions | Answers

	Questions	Answers
1	What is hard engineering?	an approach to coastal management that builds physical structures to try to stop erosion taking place
2	What is managed retreat?	a sustainable approach to coastal management that allows land to flood and moves human activity away from the coastline
3	Name four hard engineering coastal management techniques.	sea wall; rock armour; groynes; gabions
4	Name two soft engineering coastal management techniques.	beach nourishment and reprofiling; dune regeneration
5	How do recurved sea walls prevent coastal erosion?	they prevent the sea hitting the coastline and reflect wave energy back out to sea
6	What is a benefit of using groynes to manage erosion?	they are relatively cheap; they create beaches, which is good for tourism
7	What are gabions?	wire cages filled with stones
8	What is beach nourishment?	when sand is added to beaches to protect the coastline
9	What is a disadvantage of beach nourishment?	it needs to be repeated as sand is removed from the beach by longshore drift
10	How does planting marram grass help with dune regeneration?	it helps to stabilise and bind the dune together
11	What is a benefit of dune regeneration?	it is cheap; it maintains a natural-looking environment
12	What is a benefit of coastal realignment?	it does not have negative impacts in other places; new habitats might form
13	Give four reasons why Lyme Regis needed coastal management.	it is important to Dorset's economy; the town is built on unstable cliffs; erosion has destroyed many properties; existing defences are inadequate
14	How much did the coastal management at Lyme Regis cost?	over £43 million
15	What were the key strategies used at Lyme Regis?	cliffs drained and stabilised; new sea walls; beach feeding; rock armour
16	Name a positive effect of the coastal management scheme.	new beaches attracted more tourists; 480 homes protected; the harbour is protected

Put paper here

Previous questions | Answers

	Previous questions	Answers
1	Name four physical processes that shape coastal landscapes.	weathering; mass movement; erosion; transportation; deposition
2	Name four types of erosion.	hydraulic power; abrasion; solution; attrition
3	Name a coastal landform created by erosion.	headland; bay; cliff; wave-cut platform; cave; arch; stack; stump

Put paper here

Practice

Exam-style questions

1.1 Define 'hard engineering coastal management'. [1 mark]

1.2 Define 'soft engineering coastal management'. [1 mark]

1.3 Define 'managed retreat'. [1 mark]

1.4 Outline **one** difference between soft and hard engineering coastal management strategies. [2 marks]

1.5 Outline how rock armour protects the coastline. [2 marks]

1.6 Outline how gabions protect the coastline. [2 marks]

1.7 Outline how groynes protect the coastline. [2 marks]

1.8 Outline **one** cost of using sea walls to protect the coastline. [2 marks]

1.9 Outline **one** cost of using rock armour to protect the coastline. [2 marks]

1.10 Outline **one** cost of using gabions to protect the coastline. [2 marks]

1.11 Outline **one** cost of using groynes to protect the coastline. [2 marks]

Study **Figure 1**, a photograph of sea defences on a stretch of UK coastline.

▲ *Figure 1*

1.12 Explain how the sea defences shown in **Figure 1** can help protect the coastline. [4 marks]

1.13 Discuss whether the benefits of protecting the coastline with the defences shown in **Figure 1** outweigh the costs. [6 marks]

> **EXAM TIP**
>
> *Discuss* as a command word requires you to present key points about different sides of an argument, issue, or the strengths and weaknesses of an idea.

Study **Figure 2**, a photograph of an area protected by coastal defences.

▲ *Figure 2*

▲ *Figure 3*

2.1 Using **Figure 2**, suggest **two** reasons why coastal areas are chosen for hard engineering coastal management strategies. **[4 marks]**

2.2 Using **Figure 2**, **Figure 3**, and your own knowledge, explain why some areas receive coastal defences and others do not. **[6 marks]**

2.3 Suggest why hard engineering strategies can cause conflicts in coastal areas. **[4 marks]**

2.4 Outline how beach nourishment and reprofiling can protect the coastline. **[2 marks]**

2.5 Outline how managed retreat can protect the coastline. **[2 marks]**

2.6 Outline **one** cost of using beach nourishment and reprofiling to protect the coastline. **[2 marks]**

2.7 Outline **one** cost of using sand dune regeneration to protect the coastline. **[2 marks]**

2.8 Outline **one** cost of using managed retreat to protect the coastline. **[2 marks]**

Study **Figure 4**, photographs of coastal management on the UK coast.

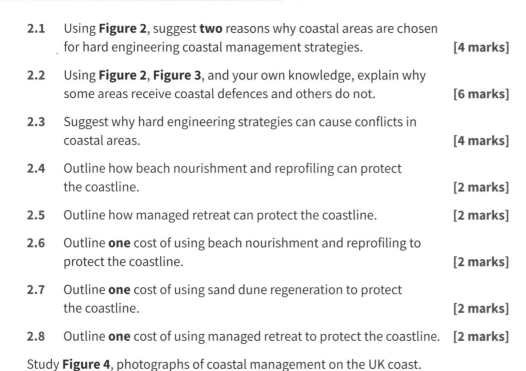

▲ *Figure 4*

3.1 Explain how the management strategies shown in **Figure 4** can help protect the coastline. **[4 marks]**

3.2 Explain the costs and benefits of the management strategies shown in **Figure 4**. **[6 marks]**

3.3 Explain **two** benefits of using managed retreat to manage some coastlines in the UK. **[4 marks]**

3.4 Suggest why some people might not be in favour of using managed retreat as a coastal management strategy. **[2 marks]**

3.5 For a UK coastal management scheme you have studied, describe the reasons why management was required and the key features of a scheme that has been introduced to solve these issues. **[6 marks]**

3.6 Describe **two** positive effects of a UK coastal management scheme you have studied. **[4 marks]**

3.7 'Coastal management schemes often cause conflict.' Explain this statement using a UK coastal management scheme you have studied. **[6 marks]**

Questions referring to previous content

4.1 Using a diagram, explain the process of freeze-thaw weathering. **[4 marks]**

4.2 Explain the formation of a bar. **[4 marks]**

Knowledge

18 River processes and landforms

The long profile and cross profile

The **long profile** of a river illustrates how the gradient of the land changes as a river flows from its source in the mountains to its mouth on the coast. The **cross profile** illustrates how the shape of the valley changes as the river flows downstream.

SPECIFICATION TIP

You will have studied any two of coastal, river, or glacial landscapes. So, check carefully if you need to revise this topic.

Upper course	Middle course	Lower course

Long profile

Steep gradient Mostly vertical erosion

Lateral erosion and **deposition**

Gentle gradient Mostly deposition

Cross profile

Narrow V-shaped valley

Wider valley and river

Very wide river Very wide and flat valley

▶ *Figure 1 Long and cross profiles*

Fluvial processes: erosion

Erosion is the wearing away of the river bed and banks. Rivers erode vertically (downwards) and laterally (side to side).

There are four types of erosion:

Hydraulic action	The force of the water hitting the river banks. Faster flowing water has more hydraulic power.
Abrasion	Stones carried by the river scrape away at the river bed and banks.
Solution	Slightly acidic river water dissolves alkaline rocks like limestone.
Attrition	Stones within the water knock into each other and become smaller and rounder.

LINK

These definitions are similar but not identical to those studied in coastal landscapes.

WATCH OUT

Attrition is an erosion process that does not affect the river bank or bed. It affects stones in the water.

Fluvial processes: transportation

Solution: minerals are dissolved in water carried by the river.

Suspension: mud and fine particles float in the water and are carried by the river.

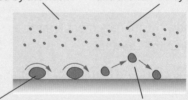

Traction: heavy boulders are rolled along the river bed.

Saltation: small stones bounce as they are moved by the river.

▲ *Figure 2 Transportation processes*

WATCH OUT

'Solution' is the name of a transportation process *and* an erosional process. It is the same word for different processes.

Fluvial processes: deposition

A river deposits the load it is carrying when the flow of the water slows down. For example:

- when it meets an obstacle
- when it meanders (bends)
- when it meets the sea.

River landforms caused by erosion

Interlocking spurs are formed in the upper course, when a river winds around bands of more resistant rock **(Figure 3)**.

Figure 4 shows how waterfalls and gorges form.

▲ *Figure 3* Interlocking spurs

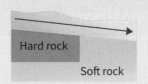

1 A river meets a band of softer, less resistant rock.

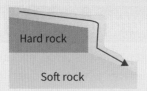

2 The softer, less resistant rock erodes more quickly through abrasion and hydraulic action.

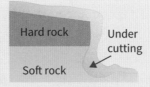

3 A plunge pool is formed, and there is undercutting of the hard cap rock.

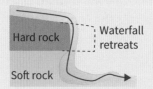

4 The cap rock collapses and the waterfall retreats upstream, forming a gorge.

▲ *Figure 4* Waterfall formation

River landforms caused by erosion and deposition

Meanders are bends in the river. They form when a river moves away from a straight course because of an obstacle, or shallow and deep sections, in the river channel. More erosion takes place where the water flows faster, and this becomes the outside of a meander. The line of fastest flow is called the thalweg.

Deposition takes place where the water flow is slowest, forming the inside of the meander.

Continued erosion on the outside and deposition on the inside means the bend in the river gets bigger over time.

Ox-bow lakes are horseshoe-shaped lakes. They are formed when a meander is cut off from a river. This is because erosion takes place on the outside of a meander.

How meanders exaggerate over time

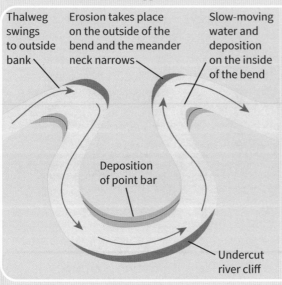

Ox-bow lake

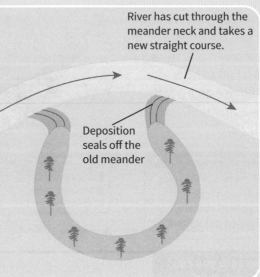

▲ *Figure 5* Ox-bow lake

18 River processes and landforms

Landforms created by deposition

Flood plains are large, flat areas of land either side of the river where the river floods. When it floods the river deposits fine sediment called alluvium that gradually builds up the flood plain.

Levées are natural embankments either side of the river. They are formed when the river floods and deposits the coarse (large) material it is carrying next to the river channel. With repeated floods, two banks build up either side of the river.

Estuaries are the part of the river where it meets the sea and freshwater mixes with saltwater. They often have mudflats that are visible at low tide. These form where the river deposits sediment when it is slowed by the incoming sea.

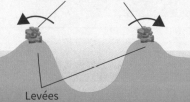

Coarse sediment deposited first as river floods and velocity slows

Alluvium is deposited, building up the flood plain

Flood plain on either side of the river

Levées

▶ **Figure 6** *Formation of flood plains and levées*

📖 Case study: Landforms on the River Tees

The River Tees is in the north-east of England. Its source is at Cross Fell in the Pennines, where it receives over 2000 mm of rainfall a year.

There are interlocking spurs in the upper course, south of Cow Green Reservoir. The Tees also has a waterfall and gorge at High Force Waterfall.

There are many meanders in the middle and lower courses. The town of Yarm is enclosed by a meander. In the lower course south of Darlington, there are ox-bow lakes and levées. The Tees has a large estuary with mudflats where it meets the sea east of Middlesborough.

High Force is 20 m high.

A layer of hard rock (dolerite) lies on top of softer rock (limestone).

High Force has retreated, leaving a gorge.

▲ **Figure 7** *High Force Waterfall on the River Tees*

SPECIFICATION TIP

You need a named example of a river valley in the UK. A case study you may have studied is given here.

REVISION TIP

Learn the specific names of the hard (dolerite) and softer (limestone) rocks in High Force Waterfall. Use these when explaining its formation.

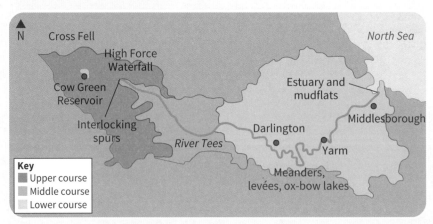

Cross Fell

High Force Waterfall

North Sea

Cow Green Reservoir

Estuary and mudflats

Middlesborough

Interlocking spurs

River Tees

Darlington

Yarm

Key
- Upper course
- Middle course
- Lower course

Meanders, levées, ox-bow lakes

▲ **Figure 8** *The River Tees*

Key terms — Make sure you can write a definition for these key terms

abrasion   attrition   cross profile   deposition   erosion
fluvial processes   hydraulic action   landform   long profile
saltation   solution   suspension   traction   transportation

Learn the answers to the questions below, then cover the answers column with a piece of paper and write down as many as you can. Check and repeat.

Questions | Answers

	Questions		Answers
1	What does the long profile of a river illustrate?		how the gradient of the land changes from source to mouth
2	What is the difference between vertical and lateral erosion?		vertical erosion is downwards and lateral erosion is side to side
3	Where on the long profile is vertical erosion the main process?		in the upper course
4	What is a cross profile of a river?		it illustrates the shape of the river valley
5	How does the cross profile change along the course of a river?		it starts off with narrow and steep sides, and becomes wider and flatter
6	Name four processes of erosion.		hydraulic action; abrasion; solution; attrition
7	Which process of erosion is when stones in the water knock into each other, becoming smaller and rounder?		attrition
8	Name four ways a river transports its load.		traction; saltation; suspension; solution
9	What type of transportation is when mud and fine particles float in the water as they are carried by the river?		suspension
10	When will a river deposit its load?		when it slows down
11	Name three landforms caused by erosion.		interlocking spurs; waterfalls; gorges
12	When are interlocking spurs formed?		when a river winds round bands of more resistant rock
13	Name two landforms created from both erosion and deposition taking place.		meanders; ox-bow lakes
14	Where does erosion take place on a meander?		on the outside of the bend
15	Name three landforms created by deposition.		flood plains; levées; estuaries
16	What are levées?		natural embankments on either side of the river channel
17	What is the name of the waterfall on the River Tees?		High Force Waterfall

Put paper here

Practice

Exam-style questions

1.1 State how the river's gradient changes along the long profile, moving from the river's source to its mouth. **[1 mark]**

1.2 Suggest how the size and shape of the river's load changes from the upper to lower course. **[2 marks]**

1.3 Outline **one** fluvial process through which rivers erode the landscape. **[2 marks]**

1.4 Define 'hydraulic action'. **[2 marks]**

1.5 Define the erosion process of solution. **[2 marks]**

1.6 Define the process of abrasion. **[1 mark]**

1.7 Outline **one** cost of using sea walls to protect the coastline. **[2 marks]**

1.8 Which of the following statements about rivers transporting material is true? Shade **one** circle only. **[1 mark]**

   A   Traction takes place in times of high discharge.   ◯

   B   A large amount of material is transported through suspension in the upper course.   ◯

   C   Large material is transported through saltation.   ◯

   D   Solution is more likely to happen in the upper course.   ◯

1.9 Suggest **one** reason why a river might deposit its load. **[1 mark]**

Study **Figure 1**, a photograph of a river valley.

1.10 Using **Figure 1**, identify a landform resulting from river erosion. **[1 mark]**

Study **Figure 2**, a 1:50 000 Ordnance Survey map extract of the River Tees.

> **EXAM TIP**
>
> Processes of erosion, transportation, and deposition are called 'fluvial processes' on the specification.

> **EXAM TIP**
>
> If a definition question is worth 2 marks, then you must give a bit of extra detail in your answer.

> **LINK**
>
> If you have also studied coasts, then these processes are very similar, but don't use the words 'waves' or 'sea' when describing *river* erosion.

▲ *Figure 1*

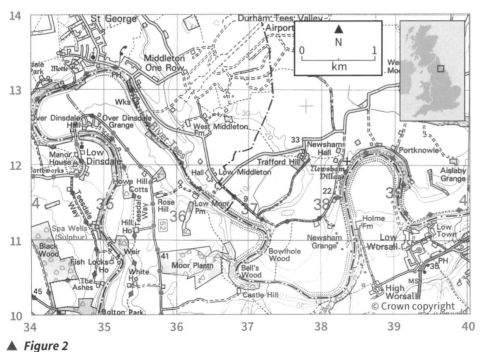
▲ *Figure 2*

2.1 Using **Figure 2**, what is the length of Moor Plantation (grid squares 3510 and 3610)? Shade **one** circle only. **[2 marks]**

A	0.5 km	◯	**C**	1 km	◯
B	0.8 km	◯	**D**	2 km	◯

2.2 Using **Figure 2**, describe the relief in grid square 3712. **[3 marks]**

2.3 Using **Figure 2**, identify a river landform found in grid square 3412. **[1 mark]**

2.4 Using **Figure 2**, what is found at 395 107? **[1 mark]**

2.5 Using **Figure 2**, what height above sea level is the highest point in grid square 3811? **[1 mark]**

LINK

Questions 2.1–2.5 test a variety of map-reading skills. See page 224 in the Geographical Skills section for help with this.

3.1 Explain the formation of interlocking spurs. **[2 marks]**

3.2 Explain how a waterfall is formed. **[6 marks]**

Study **Figure 3**, a photograph of a meander in a river.

3.3 Explain the formation of meanders like the one seen in **Figure 3**. **[4 marks]**

3.4 Using **Figure 3**, suggest how this landscape may change in the future. **[4 marks]**

EXAM TIP

Do not just write 'erosion' – name specific erosion processes, like hydraulic action, to add detail to your explanations.

Study **Figure 4**, a diagram of a meandering river.

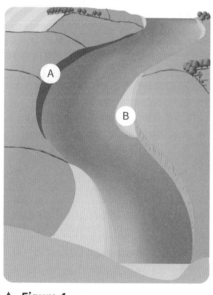

▲ *Figure 4*

▲ *Figure 3*

3.5 Using **Figure 4**, state what fluvial process is taking place at point **A**. **[1 mark]**

3.6 Using **Figure 4**, state what fluvial process is taking place at point **B**. **[1 mark]**

3.7 Describe the key features of a flood plain. **[2 marks]**

3.8 Outline how levées are formed. **[4 marks]**

3.9 Suggest why deposition takes place in a river estuary. **[2 marks]**

3.10 For a river valley you have studied, explain the formation of its major landforms. **[9 marks]**
[+3 SPaG marks]

EXAM TIP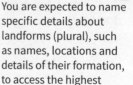

You are expected to name specific details about landforms (plural), such as names, locations and details of their formation, to access the highest marks.

Knowledge

19 River flooding and management

Physical factors affecting flood risk

- **Precipitation:** heavy rainfall increases the chance of flooding because rain will eventually drain into rivers through surface run-off, throughflow, and groundwater flow.

- **Geology** (rock type): impermeable rocks do not absorb rainwater, meaning soils become saturated, leading to increased surface run-off and a risk-of flooding.

- **Relief:** steep hillsides allow water to run off quickly into rivers, increasing the risk of flooding. Very flat land can also increase the risk of flooding because the water does not flow away.

Human factors (land use) affecting flood risk

- **Urbanisation:** urban areas replace natural surfaces like fields with largely impermeable surfaces like concrete. Rainwater cannot soak into the soil and runs off quickly into rivers, increasing flood risk.

- **Deforestation:** trees intercept precipitation (they stop rain from reaching the ground). Water on their leaves evaporates into the atmosphere. They also use water as they grow. Removing trees means that more water enters rivers, increasing the risk of flooding.

- **Agriculture:** when trees, bushes, and grass are removed to grow crops there is less vegetation to intercept rainwater, especially when fields are bare soil. This means more surface run-off and increases the risk of flooding.

Flood hydrographs

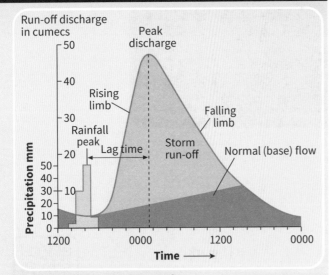

▲ *Figure 1 Flood **hydrograph***

A flood hydrograph (**Figure 1**) shows how a river changes after rainfall. It displays:

- rainfall as a bar graph in mm

- **discharge** (how much water is in the river) as a line graph in m³ per second or cumecs

- lag time – the time between peak rainfall and peak discharge

- base flow – the 'normal' discharge of the river.

Factors affecting hydrograph shape

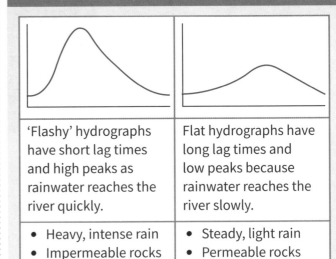

'Flashy' hydrographs have short lag times and high peaks as rainwater reaches the river quickly.	Flat hydrographs have long lag times and low peaks because rainwater reaches the river slowly.
• Heavy, intense rain • Impermeable rocks • Steep slopes • Urban areas	• Steady, light rain • Permeable rocks • Gentle slopes • Forested areas

 Key terms — **Make sure you can write a definition for these key terms**

> benefit   cost   discharge   geology
> hard engineering   hydrograph   land use
> precipitation   relief   soft engineering

Hard engineering (structures built to prevent flooding)

	Dams and reservoirs	Channel straightening	Embankments	Flood relief channel
What is it?	A dam is a physical barrier built across a river. The lake created behind a dam is called a reservoir.	Meanders are cut off and a straight river channel is built.	Walls or mud embankments are built either side of the river.	An extra river channel is built to divert water from urban areas.
Benefits	• The flow of water in the river can be controlled, preventing floods. • Can be combined with projects like hydroelectric power.	• Straightening the river channel means that water flows more quickly, so it is moved out of the area before flooding can occur.	• The river can hold more water, reducing flood risk. • Can be natural looking.	• Diverts water from flood prone areas. • Can create new recreational spaces.
Costs	• Very expensive. • A large area of land is flooded behind the dam, destroying natural ecosystems.	• Expensive with ongoing maintenance costs. • Flood risk is increased downstream.	• Flood risk is increased downstream. • Expensive; ongoing maintenance costs.	• Expensive. • Increases flood risk where the relief channel rejoins the main river.

Soft engineering (management strategies working with natural processes to reduce flooding)

	Flood warning and preparation	Flood plain zoning	Afforestation	River restoration
What is it?	Potential flooding is monitored, with warnings and flood forecasts given out.	Land next to the river is organised into zones, with different **land use** in each zone moving away from the river.	Trees are planted in the drainage basin.	Rivers are restored to their natural state by removing artificial embankments and recreating meanders.
Benefits	• People can prepare with sandbags or temporary flood gates, and move valuables upstairs. • Cheap	• Valuable land and economic activity is located in areas unlikely to flood. • No interference with natural processes.	• Trees intercept and absorb precipitation, reducing run off. • Cheap. • Adds to biodiversity and creates new recreational spaces.	• Impact of human interference is removed, which can reduce flooding in some places. • Natural habitats are recreated.
Costs	• Does not stop flooding. • High clean-up costs. • People might ignore warnings.	• Difficult to do retrospectively. • Does not stop flooding.	• Takes a long time to have any effect. • May not reassure people like hard engineering schemes do.	• Land that used to flood will flood again. • Expensive.

19 River flooding and management

 ## Case study: Flood management in Banbury

Why was a flood management scheme needed in Banbury?

- Banbury is a town 50 km north of Oxford, built on the flood plain of the River Cherwell. It has a long history of flooding.

- Flooding in 1998 caused damage worth £12.5 million, shutting the railway station and affecting 150 homes and businesses.

- Banbury experienced flooding again in 2007.

Banbury flood alleviation scheme

The following strategies were used to reduce the risk of flooding:

- A flood storage reservoir upstream of Banbury.

  o 2.9 km embankment built to create a storage reservoir for floodwater, preventing water entering the town **(Figure 2)**.

  o Two flow control structures to regulate the flow of water from the rivers into Banbury.

- Road raising – the A361 that runs through the reservoir area was raised.

- Local defences downstream of the reservoir.

  o Embankments at Wildmere and Prodrive Industrial Estates, and at Banbury United Football Club.

- A pumping station protecting 400 houses in the Grimsbury area of Banbury.

As part of the Biodiversity Action Plan, the Borrow Pit (which provided the material for the embankment) was converted into a country park with new trees, hedgerows, and ponds.

> **SPECIFICATION TIP**
>
> You need a named example of a flood management scheme in the UK. A case study you may have studied is given here.

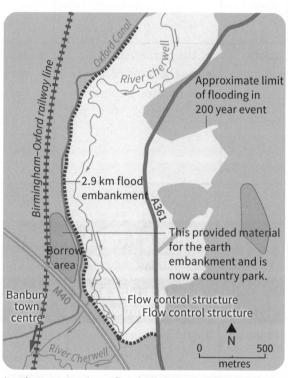

▲ *Figure 2 Banbury flood alleviation scheme*

> **REVISION TIP**
>
> Learn some key facts and statistics to use in case study questions.

Social, economic, and environmental issues

Social	Economic	Environmental
• New recreation space created in Banbury Country Park. • A361 can remain open during floods. • People can have more confidence that their houses will not be flooded.	• Cost of scheme was £18.5 million. • 441 houses and 73 businesses (value of £100 million) protected. • Key donors were the Environment Agency and Cherwell District Council.	• Flood control structures are 'passive'. They operate automatically without electricity or staff. • Earth embankment was built from material excavated locally in the Borrow area. • Borrow area converted to a reservoir and Country Park as part of the Biodiversity Action Plan.

Learn the answers to the questions below, then cover the answers column with a piece of paper and write down as many as you can. Check and repeat.

Questions   Answers

	Questions	Answers
1	State three physical factors affecting flood risk.	precipitation; geology; relief
2	How does geology affect flood risk?	some rocks are impermeable, meaning soils become saturated and surface run-off increases
3	How does deforestation affect flood risk?	trees intercept and absorb water, so removing trees means more water reaches rivers
4	How does urbanisation affect flood risk?	there are more impermeable surfaces like pavements, meaning rainwater runs off quickly into rivers
5	What is shown by a line graph on a flood hydrograph?	the discharge of the river (how much water is in the river)
6	What is the lag time?	the time between the peak rainfall and peak discharge in a flood event
7	Name four factors that would make a flood hydrograph 'flashy'.	intense rainfall; urbanisation; steep relief; impermeable geology
8	What is the difference between hard and soft engineering?	hard engineering builds structures to try to stop flooding, soft engineering tries to use natural processes to adapt to flooding
9	Name four hard engineering flood management strategies.	dams and reservoirs; channel straightening; embankments; flood relief channels
10	Name four soft engineering flood management strategies.	flood warning and preparation; flood plain zoning; afforestation; river restoration
11	What is flood plain zoning?	when land next to the river is zoned so that land use next to the river has low economic value (e.g., a park) and houses are built away from the river
12	Name a disadvantage of flood warning and preparation as a flood management strategy.	it does not stop flooding; clean-up costs can be high; people might ignore warnings
13	Name a cost (disadvantage) that channel straightening, embankments, and flood relief channels all share.	they can all potentially increase the risk of flooding further downstream

Put paper here

Previous questions   Answers

	Previous questions	Answers
1	Name four processes of erosion.	hydraulic action; abrasion; solution; attrition
2	Name two landforms created from both erosion and deposition taking place.	meanders; ox-bow lakes

Put paper here

Practice

Exam-style questions

1.1 Which of these is a physical factor that affects flood risk?
Shade **one** circle only. **[1 mark]**

A   Arable farming   ◯

B   Urbanisation   ◯

C   Precipitation   ◯

D   Afforestation   ◯

1.2 Explain how geology **and** relief can affect flood risk. **[4 marks]**

> **EXAM TIP**
> *Explain* as a command word requires you to set out purposes or reasons – say why or how.

Study **Figure 1**, photographs of deforestation in the UK and an urban area.

▲ *Figure 1*

> **EXAM TIP**
> Remember to use connectives like 'This means that…' and 'Because of this…' to help develop your explanations.

1.3 Using **Figure 1** and your own knowledge, explain how changes to land use can increase the risk of flooding. **[6 marks]**

1.4 'Flooding is a natural hazard.' Do you agree? Explain your answer. **[9 marks]**
[+3 SPaG marks]

> **EXAM TIP**
> Make it clear whether you agree or not, but remember you can qualify your answer using phrases like 'mostly agree' or 'partially disagree'.

2.1 Define 'river discharge'. **[1 mark]**

Study **Figure 2**, a flood hydrograph for a storm event in different drainage basins.

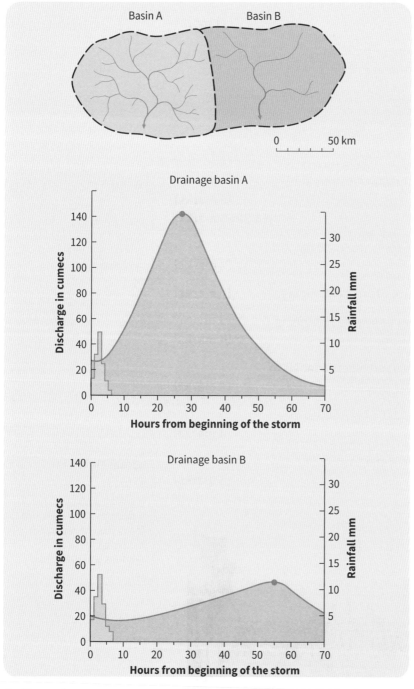

▲ *Figure 2*

2.2 Using **Figure 2**, describe how the river's discharge in drainage basin A changed during the storm event. Use data in your answer. **[3 marks]**

2.3 Using **Figure 2**, which of the following statements is true for drainage basin A?
Shade **one** circle only. **[1 mark]**

A The lag time was 24 hours. ○

B The lag time was 27 hours. ○

C Peak discharge was 50 cumecs. ○

D Rainfall lasted for 10 hours. ○

Exam-style questions

2.4 Using **Figure 2**, state the peak discharge in drainage basin B. **[1 mark]**

2.5 Using **Figure 2**, state the lag time in drainage basin B. **[1 mark]**

2.6 Using **Figure 2**, which of the following statements is true?
Shade **one** circle only. **[1 mark]**

A The discharge of the river in drainage basin B rose
more quickly than the river in drainage basin B. ◯

B Peak rainfall was higher in drainage basin A than in drainage basin B. ◯

C After 50 hours the river levels were rising in drainage basin B. ◯

D The lag time was longer in drainage basin A. ◯

2.7 Using **Figure 2**, suggest reasons why the flood hydrographs have
different shapes. **[9 marks]**
[+3 SPaG marks]

EXAM TIP ⊚

Suggest as a command
word requires you to
present a possible case, to
propose an idea, solution,
or answer.

3.1 Define what is meant by a hard engineering approach to
flood management. **[2 marks]**

3.2 Outline how dams and reservoirs reduce the risk of flooding. **[2 marks]**

3.3 Outline the costs and benefits of using channel straightening
to manage the risk of flooding. **[4 marks]**

3.4 Explain the costs and benefits of using flood relief channels to
reduce the risk of flooding. **[4 marks]**

3.5 Suggest reasons why some people might be opposed to
river restoration. **[4 marks]**

3.6 Assess the benefits of using flood plain zoning as a river
management strategy. **[6 marks]**

Study **Figure 3**, a photograph of a flood barrier.

EXAM TIP ⊚

Assess as a command word
is asking you to make a
judgement. The question
focus is on benefits, but
assessing these also
requires you to discuss
the costs.

▲ *Figure 3*

3.7 Using **Figure 3**, evaluate the costs and benefits of using hard engineering
strategies to manage rivers. **[6 marks]**

EXAM TIP ⊚

Note the question asks
about strategies (plural).
You must talk about more
than one strategy, but
you must also ensure you
discuss flood barriers as
shown in Figure 3.

Study **Figure 4**, a plan for flood plain zoning.

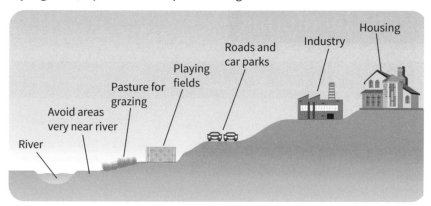

▲ *Figure 4*

3.8 'Rivers need to be managed through a range of strategies.'
Do you agree? Explain your answer referring to **Figure 3**,
Figure 4, and your own knowledge.

[9 marks]
[+3 SPaG marks]

Study **Figure 5**, a photograph of floods in Cockermouth in 2009.

▲ *Figure 5*

4.1 Using **Figure 5**, identify one possible environmental impact
of the flood. **[1 mark]**

4.2 Using **Figure 5**, suggest a social impact of the flood. **[2 marks]**

4.3 Using **Figure 5**, suggest an economic impact of the flood. **[4 marks]**

4.4 For a flood management scheme in the UK you have studied,
outline why the management scheme was needed. **[4 marks]**

4.5 For a flood management scheme in the UK you have studied,
explain how the scheme will reduce flood risk in the future. **[4 marks]**

4.6 For a flood management scheme in the UK you have studied,
outline the social and economic issues arising from the scheme. **[4 marks]**

4.7 Outline the environmental issues caused by a flood management
scheme in the UK that you have studied. **[4 marks]**

4.8 For a flood management scheme in the UK you have studied,
to what extent has the scheme been successful? **[6 marks]**

Questions referring to previous content

5.1 Define the river erosion process of abrasion. **[2 marks]**

5.2 Explain the role of geology in the formation of a waterfall. **[4 marks]**

> **EXAM TIP**
>
> Questions 4.1 to 4.3 are
> similar but have different
> marks. The higher the
> marks, the more detail and
> development is needed.

> **EXAM TIP**
>
> Make sure you refer to
> specific details and name
> the place of your example.

> **EXAM TIP**
>
> Commenting on
> social, economic, and
> environmental issues can
> help when judging the
> extent to which a scheme
> has been successful.

Knowledge

20 Glacial processes and landforms

Glacial extent in the UK

During the last ice age, glaciers covered all of Scotland, most of northern England and most of Wales. Glacial activity shaped the land, creating distinctive landforms.

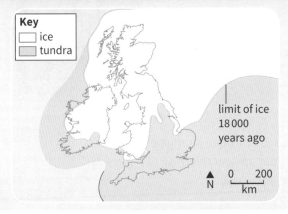

Key
- ☐ ice
- ▨ tundra

limit of ice 18 000 years ago

N 0   200
        km

▶ **Figure 1** *Maximum ice cover in the UK during the last glacial period*

SPECIFICATION TIP

You will have studied any two of coastal, river, or glacial landscapes. So, check carefully if you need to revise this topic.

Weathering processes

Freeze-thaw weathering takes place in glacial environments.

- Water collects in cracks in the rock.
- The water freezes and expands, forcing the rock apart.
- Over time this is repeated and fragments of rock break off as scree.

Weathering provides material for **abrasion** and weakens rocks, making them more likely to be removed by **plucking**.

Glacial movement and transportation

Glaciers move slowly downhill, transporting eroded material as they move (**Figure 2**). Glaciers move:

- through ice deformation when gravity pulls the glacier downhill
- through basal slip when meltwater at the base of the glacier works as a lubricant, helping it slide
- through **rotational slip** where the landscape is curved.

As glaciers move, rocks and debris are transported on top of or inside the glacier. At the front, debris is pushed along in a process called **bulldozing**.

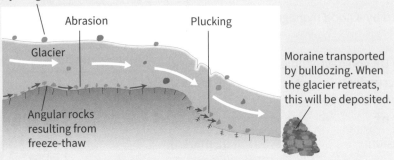

Debris transported by the glacier

Abrasion

Plucking

Glacier

Angular rocks resulting from freeze-thaw

Moraine transported by bulldozing. When the glacier retreats, this will be deposited.

▲ **Figure 2** *Glacial **erosion** and **transportation***

Glacial erosion

Glaciers erode the landscape in two ways:

- Abrasion – when rocks frozen into the glacier scrape and scour away at the valley floor and sides.
- Plucking – when the glacier freezes onto a loose piece of rock and then plucks (pulls) it away as it moves.

Glacial deposition

When a glacier melts, it deposits material called glacial **till** (a loose collection of jagged rock fragments).

Glacial till at the glacier's snout is washed away by meltwater. Larger rocks are deposited close to the glacier, and finer sand and gravel called outwash is deposited much further away.

Erosional landforms

Corries, arêtes, and pyramidal peaks are formed in similar ways.

Corries are armchair-shaped hollows at the top of a glacial valley. They are formed when:

- Snow gathers in hollows and is compressed into ice.
- Freeze-thaw weathering adds rock fragments into the ice.
- Gravity starts pulling the ice down the valley, aided by rotational slip.
- The glacier's rotation and abrasion at the base deepens the hollow.
- Plucking at the back of the glacier steepens the back wall.
- When the ice melts, an armchair-shaped hollow is left, which sometimes contains a lake called a tarn.

Most glaciers move along pre-existing river valleys and change these valleys as they move. They form in hollows, scouring corries and leaving arêtes and pyramidal peaks as they move downhill. Moving into river valleys they then create glacial troughs, truncated spurs, ribbon lakes, and hanging valleys.

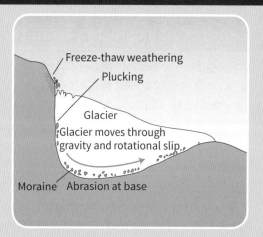

▲ *Figure 3* *Formation of a corrie*

REVISION TIP

Take extra time to understand how corries are formed, because they form the basis for arêtes and pyramidal peaks.

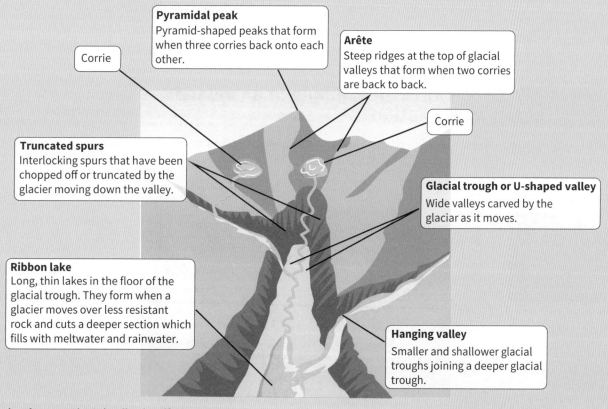

Pyramidal peak
Pyramid-shaped peaks that form when three corries back onto each other.

Arête
Steep ridges at the top of glacial valleys that form when two corries are back to back.

Corrie

Corrie

Truncated spurs
Interlocking spurs that have been chopped off or truncated by the glacier moving down the valley.

Glacial trough or U-shaped valley
Wide valleys carved by the glaciar as it moves.

Ribbon lake
Long, thin lakes in the floor of the glacial trough. They form when a glacier moves over less resistant rock and cuts a deeper section which fills with meltwater and rainwater.

Hanging valley
Smaller and shallower glacial troughs joining a deeper glacial trough.

▲ *Figure 4 Glacial valley landforms*

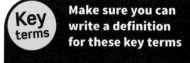

Key terms — Make sure you can write a definition for these key terms

abrasion   bulldozing   deposition   erosion
freeze-thaw weathering   glacial landform   glacial processes
plucking   rotational slip   till   transportation

20 Glacial processes and landforms

Landforms resulting from transportation and deposition

A moraine is material left behind by a moving glacier. It is composed of glacial till and there are four types of moraine.

Drumlins are egg-shaped hills made of glacial till. They form when material at the base of a glacier hits an obstruction and is deposited. The glacier continues to move over the deposited till, sculpting it into drumlin shapes. Drumlins have a blunt end and a tapered end, showing the direction the glacier was moving.

Erratics are large boulders left behind by glaciers that are a different geology (rock type) to the geology of the place where they have been deposited.

Lateral moraine
A ridge of material on the edges of a glacial trough. It is mostly scree that has fallen onto the glacier through freeze-thaw weathering

Medial moraine
A ridge in the middle of a glacial trough formed when two glaciers merge

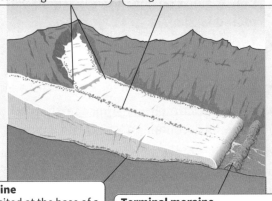

Ground moraine
Moraine deposited at the base of a glacier. It covers a wide area and is the most common moraine

Terminal moraine
A mound at the glacier's snout that has been bulldozed along

▲ **Figure 5** Moraines resulting from **deposition**

Direction of ice flow

Blunt end   Tapered end

◀ **Figure 6** Drumlins resulting from deposition

📖 Case study: Cadair Idris: an example of an upland area affected by glaciation

Cadair Idris is a mountain in Snowdonia in North Wales, with various glacial features (**Figure 7**).

SPECIFICATION TIP

You need a named example of an upland area in the UK affected by glaciation. A case study you may have studied is given below.

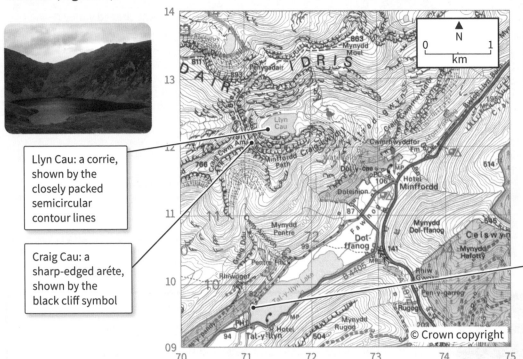

Llyn Cau: a corrie, shown by the closely packed semicircular contour lines

Craig Cau: a sharp-edged aréte, shown by the black cliff symbol

Tal-y-llyn lake: a ribbon lake in the glacial trough

© Crown copyright

◀ **Figure 7** Cadair Idris

Learn the answers to the questions below, then cover the answers column with
a piece of paper and write down as many as you can. Check and repeat.

Questions

Answers

	Questions	Answers
1	Which parts of the UK were glaciated during the last glacial period?	all of Scotland, most of northern England, and most of Wales
2	How do glaciers move?	through gravity, basal slip, and rotational slip
3	What is abrasion?	when rocks frozen in the glaciers scrape against the valley floor and sides
4	What is plucking?	when the glacier freezes onto loose rock and pulls it away as it moves
5	How do glaciers transport material?	debris is carried within the ice, on top of the ice, and in front of the ice
6	What is bulldozing?	the way glaciers transport rocks, debris, and boulders in front of them as they move
7	When do glaciers deposit the material they are transporting?	when they melt
8	What is a corrie?	an armchair-shaped hollow at the top of a glacial valley formed by erosion
9	What physical processes are involved in the formation of a corrie?	precipitation; freeze-thaw weathering; abrasion; plucking; rotational slip
10	What is an arête?	a sharp ridge formed when two corries are back to back
11	What is a glacial trough?	a deep, wide valley carved by a glacier
12	What is a hanging valley?	a glacial valley that meets a deeper glacial valley
13	What is a moraine?	material left behind by a moving glacier, composed of glacial till
14	List four types of moraine.	ground moraine; lateral moraine; medial moraine; terminal moraine
15	Where do you find medial moraine?	in the middle of where two glaciers merge
16	What is a drumlin?	an egg-shaped hill composed of glacial till
17	What is an erratic?	a large boulder deposited by a glacier that is a different type of rock to the place where it has been deposited

Put paper here

Practice

Exam-style questions

1.1 Name **one** type of mechanical weathering that affects glaciated landscapes. **[1 mark]**

Study **Figure 1**, a scree slope composed of rock fragments in upland Britain.

▲ **Figure 1**

1.2 Explain how the landscape in **Figure 1** has been affected by weathering processes. **[4 marks]**

1.3 Outline the glacial erosion process of plucking. **[2 marks]**

1.4 Outline the glacial erosion process of abrasion. **[2 marks]**

1.5 Explain how a glacier moves. **[4 marks]**

1.6 Define glacial bulldozing. **[1 mark]**

1.7 Other than bulldozing, outline **one** way a glacier transports its load. **[1 mark]**

2.1 Which of the **two** following landforms result from erosion? Shade **two** circles only. **[2 marks]**

A	Glacial trough	○	**D**	Hanging valley	○
B	Erratic	○	**E**	Medial moraine	○
C	Terminal moraine	○	**F**	Drumlin	○

2.2 Explain the formation of a corrie. **[4 marks]**

Study **Figure 2**, a photograph of a glacial trough with truncated spurs.

▲ **Figure 2**

2.3 Explain how glacial processes have created the landforms in **Figure 2**. **[6 marks]**

> **EXAM TIP**
>
> *Outline* as a command word means to give a brief account or summary. There are two marks available, so you should aim to write at least two sentences, or one sentence with connectives (e.g., 'because of this...').

> **EXAM TIP**
>
> *Explain* as a command word requires you to set out purposes or reasons – say why or how.

> **EXAM TIP**
>
> Your answer should discuss physical processes like abrasion and should give an accurate sequence of formation.

> **EXAM TIP**
>
> You need to discuss glacial processes (plural) and landforms (plural) to achieve full marks.

2.4 Glacial troughs sometimes contain ribbon lakes. Explain how ribbon lakes are formed. **[4 marks]**

Study **Figure 3**, a photograph showing different moraines.

2.5 Label the moraines marked A and B in **Figure 3**. **[2 marks]**

2.6 For an upland area in the UK affected by glaciation that you have studied, name a glacial landform found in this area and explain its formation. **[4 marks]**

▲ *Figure 3*

Study **Figure 4**, a 1:50 000 Ordnance Survey map extract of Cadair Idris.

3.1 Using **Figure 4**, describe the relief in grid square 7210. **[2 marks]**

3.2 Using **Figure 4**, identify the landform at 711 122.
Shade **one** circle only. **[1 mark]**

A	Corrie	○	**C**	Pyramidal peak ○
B	Glacial trough	○	**D**	Drumlin ○

LINK

To understand the skill of interpreting an Ordnance Survey map, see the Geographical Skills section, page 225.

3.3 Using **Figure 4**, identify the landform at 707 136. **[1 mark]**

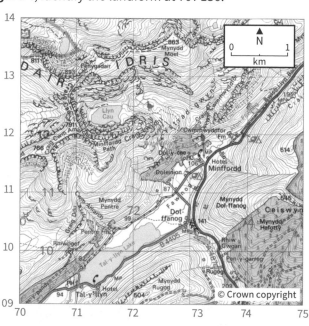

▶ *Figure 4*

▲ *Figure 5*

Study **Figure 5**, a photograph of Tal-y-llyn lake in grid squares 7109 and 7210.

3.4 Using **Figure 4** and **Figure 5**, state the direction the photographer was looking when they took this photograph. **[1 mark]**

3.5 Using **Figure 4**, what is the length of lake Tal-y-llyn in grid squares 7109 and 7210?
Shade **one** circle only. **[1 mark]**

A	2 km	○	**C**	1.45 km ○
B	1 km	○	**D**	1.65 km ○

3.6 Using **Figure 4**, identify the highest point above sea level in grid square 7411. **[1 mark]**

Knowledge

21 Economic activities, conflict, and the management of tourism in glaciated upland areas

Economic activity in glaciated upland areas

- **Farming:** poor soils, mountainous terrain, and a cold and wet climate mean many glaciated areas are only suitable for sheep farming.
- **Forestry:** coniferous trees are suited to the acidic soils. They are grown on plantations and sold as timber.
- **Quarrying:** quarries extract valuable rocks, like slate (used for roofing) and granite (used for kitchen worktops). Limestone is also quarried and is widely used in the construction industry.
- **Tourism:** glaciated landscapes offer spectacular scenery and outdoor activities like walking, climbing, and mountain biking. Tourism employs more people than any other industry in glaciated areas.

Different land uses cause conflicts in glaciated upland areas

Farmers can come into conflict with tourists if walkers leave gates open or trample on crops.

Land used for forestry cannot be used for farming.

Conflicts in upland glaciated areas

Quarrying causes noise, dust, and traffic, and can affect the tranquillity for which many people come to the area.

Tourism brings many people into the area who can be noisy and may not always respect local ways of life.

Conflicts between development and conservation

Tourism in the Lake District National Park is worth £1.4 billion, farming employs 2500 people, and quarrying 450 people. **Economic activity** brings wealth to glaciated upland areas but at a cost to the environment.

- Quarries create noise and dust pollution, scar the landscape, and destroy natural ecosystems in the area.
- Forestry often reduces biodiversity.
- Farming maintains an artificial landscape, preventing diverse ecosystems developing.
- Ecosystems are damaged by large numbers of tourists and infrastructure like roads, visitor centres, and car parks.

 Key terms Make sure you can write a definition for these key terms

conservation   economic activity
farming   forestry
quarrying   tourism

📖 Case study: A glaciated upland area in the UK used for tourism

Tourism in the Lake District

The Lake District is in north-west England and attracts 15.8 million tourists each year.

- Breathtaking landscapes and scenery
- Walking and mountain biking
- History and culture like the homes of Beatrix Potter and William Wordsworth

Lake District tourist attractions

- Water sports and fishing in lakes like Lake Windermere
- Adventure activities like abseiling and rock climbing
- Historic sites like Muncaster Castle

Social, economic, and environmental impacts of tourism

Social	Economic	Environmental
✗ 20% of housing is used for tourism, meaning many local people cannot afford housing.	✗ Traffic congestion slows down business communications.	✗ In 'honeypot' centres like Keswick there is overcrowding, footpath erosion, and litter.
✗ In tourist centres most businesses, like outdoor equipment shops and cafes, cater for tourists and there are few services for local people.	✗ Jobs in tourism are seasonal and poorly paid.	✗ Mountain bike trails and 4×4 off-roading are damaging ecosystems.
✓ Improvements to infrastructure for tourists benefits local people.	✓ 15 000 jobs in tourism supporting the local economy.	✗ Pollution from cars and boats.
	✓ Tourists spend £1000 million supporting local hotels, cafes, and shops.	✓ Some income from tourism is spent on environmental projects.

Strategies to manage the impact of tourism

Traffic congestion

- Dual carriageways on main routes.
- Public transport has been improved, with extra seasonal services like the Honister Rambler.
- Park and ride schemes with 'park and explore' tickets that combine parking with bus travel.

Footpath erosion

- Numerous schemes like the Fix the Fells project, which restores and maintains eroded footpaths using hard-wearing local stone.

Affordable housing

- The Lake District National Park Authority reserves new houses for local people.
- Local councils make builders reserve some houses for local people and sell them at more affordable prices.

Retrieval

Learn the answers to the questions below, then cover the answers column with a piece of paper and write down as many as you can. Check and repeat.

Questions	Answers
1 Name four economic activities in glaciated upland areas.	farming; forestry; quarrying; tourism
2 Name a rock that is quarried in glaciated upland areas.	slate; granite; limestone
3 Why is sheep farming the main type of farming in glaciated upland areas?	because of the steep mountainous terrain, poor soil quality, and cold and wet climate
4 Why can farmers come into conflict with tourists?	tourists might trample on crops and leave gates open, or their dogs might attack sheep
5 Why might quarrying be in conflict with the tourism industry?	quarrying causes noise, dust, and traffic, and can affect the tranquillity for which many people come to the area
6 How many people are employed in farming in the Lake District?	2500
7 Why might forestry conflict with the need for conservation?	because single crops of trees are planted, which reduces biodiversity
8 Why might tourist developments conflict with the need for conservation?	tourists can damage ecosystems by walking in fields, and the infrastructure also damages ecosystems
9 Name three attractions of the Lake District for visitors.	the scenic landscape; walking; mountain biking; adventure activities; history and culture
10 How much money is the tourism industry worth to the Lake District economy?	£1.4 billion
11 State a positive social impact of tourism in the Lake District.	infrastructure improvements also benefit local people
12 State a negative environmental impact of tourism in the Lake District.	footpath erosion; litter; ecosystem damage by off-road vehicles; pollution from cars and boats
13 How is footpath erosion in the Lake District being managed?	footpaths are being restored with local stone through the 'Fix the Fells' project
14 What is the Lake District 'local occupancy scheme'?	a scheme where new houses are only available to local people

Put paper here

Previous questions · Answers

Previous questions	Answers
1 How do glaciers move?	through gravity, basal slip, and rotational slip
2 What is plucking?	when the glacier freezes onto loose rock and pulls it away as it moves
3 What is a corrie?	an armchair-shaped hollow at the top of a glacial valley formed by erosion

Put paper here

21 Economic activities, conflict, and the management of tourism in glaciated upland areas

Exam-style questions

1.1 Name an economic activity that takes place in glaciated upland areas. **[1 mark]**

1.2 Outline the economic opportunities that forestry brings to glaciated upland areas. **[2 marks]**

1.3 Outline the economic opportunities that farming brings to glaciated upland areas. **[2 marks]**

1.4 Outline the economic opportunities that quarrying brings to glaciated upland areas. **[2 marks]**

1.5 Compare the opportunities offered by farming and tourism for glaciated upland areas. **[4 marks]**

Study **Figure 1**, photographs showing farming and tourism in glaciated upland areas.

EXAM TIP

Outline as a command word requires you to summarise the key points, so keep your answer 'punchy' (but always take note of the number of marks available).

EXAM TIP

Compare as a command word requires you to identify similarities and differences.

▲ *Figure 1*

1.6 Using **Figure 1** and your own knowledge, explain how glaciated upland areas provide opportunities for economic activity. **[6 marks]**

2.1 Outline **one** conflict between different land uses in glaciated upland areas. **[2 marks]**

2.2 Using **Figure 1** and your own knowledge, suggest why there are conflicts between different land uses in glaciated upland areas. **[6 marks]**

2.3 Outline **one** way that development in glaciated upland areas conflicts with the need for conservation. **[2 marks]**

EXAM TIP

You are expected to use the stimulus material in your answer, so discuss farming and/or tourism in your answer.

EXAM TIP

Suggest as a command word means presenting a possible case, or proposing an idea, solution, or answer. It can be similar to the command word 'explain'.

2.4 Explain how quarrying and forestry can conflict with the need for conservation in glaciated upland areas. **[4 marks]**

Study **Figure 2**, a newspaper article about tourism in the Lake District and a photograph of a quarry in Yorkshire.

Lake District authority accused of turning region into 'theme park'

Angry residents and campaigners have accused the Lake District National Park Authority of turning the region into a theme park after a ban on recreational off-road vehicles was overturned. Campaigners said the vehicles devastate farm tracks, churn up soil, and along with other cycle tracks are damaging the natural beauty of the area.

▲ *Figure 2*

2.5 Using **Figure 2**, identify **one** environmental impact of tourism. **[1 mark]**

2.6 Using **Figure 2** and your own knowledge, evaluate whether the need for conservation outweighs the benefits of economic development in glaciated upland areas. **[9 marks]**
[+3 SPaG marks]

3.1 For a named example of a glaciated upland area, describe the attractions of this area for tourists. **[4 marks]**

3.2 Outline a social **and** economic benefit of tourism in glaciated upland areas. **[4 marks]**

3.3 Suggest reasons why some people might be opposed to tourist development in glaciated upland areas. **[4 marks]**

3.4 For an example of an upland glaciated area you have studied, explain **one** strategy for managing the impact of tourism. **[4 marks]**

3.5 'With good management, the benefits of tourism in glaciated upland areas outweigh the negative impacts.' Do you agree? Explain your ideas. **[9 marks]**
[+3 SPaG marks]

> **EXAM TIP** @
>
> If you are using the examples in this revision guide, you have the management of traffic congestion, footpath erosion, and second home ownership as examples. Think carefully which **one** of these will allow you to access full marks.

> **EXAM TIP** @
>
> Include some statistics in your answer.

Questions referring to previous content

4.1 Define the term 'erratic'. **[1 mark]**

4.2 Explain how a pyramidal peak is formed. **[4 marks]**

4.3 Explain how a drumlin is formed. **[4 marks]**

Knowledge

22 Urbanisation: issues and challenges

What is urbanisation?

Urbanisation is the proportional increase in the number of people living in built-up, urban areas (towns and cities). **Urban growth** is the physical expansion of built-up areas.

- Rates of urbanisation differ globally, and always have (**Figure 1**). For example, the UK was one of the first countries in the world to become urbanised.

- Nowadays, urban populations are growing more quickly in less developed regions than in more developed regions.

- The greatest rates of urbanisation are found in **low-income countries (LICs)** and **newly emerging economies (NEEs)**.

- In some **high-income countries (HICs)** rates of urbanisation have slowed markedly, with reversals in some cases (**counter-urbanisation**).

> **WATCH OUT** !
>
> *Urban growth* is not the same as *urbanisation*, but usually comes with it. So, make sure you understand the difference and use each term appropriately.

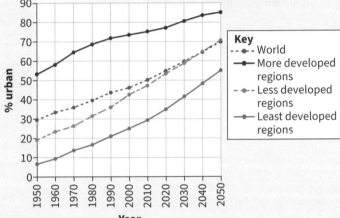

▲ *Figure 1* Graph of urban population, 1950–2050

Why do cities grow?

Around 70% of the world's population is expected to live in urban areas by 2050. There are two main reasons:

Natural increase (births minus deaths). This is higher in LICs and some NEEs because:

- there are higher proportions of (fertile) young adults aged 18–35

- improvements in health care have significantly lowered death rates.

Rural–urban migration. This is caused by push and pull factors.

Push factors (drive people from the countryside)	Pull factors (attract people to towns and cities)
• Farming is hard, prone to hazards, and poorly paid. • Poverty is widespread, especially in LICs. • Rural areas are more isolated, often with limited services (e.g., electricity, water, schools, health care).	• Employment opportunities mean a higher standard of living is possible. • Better services, including shops, entertainments, and transport **infrastructure**. • Friends and family may already be living there.

What are megacities?

A recent trend associated with urbanisation has been the growth of **megacities** (cities with a population of over 10 million). There are over 30 today – most in less developed regions – and 50 might be expected by 2050. There are three main types:

Type	Features	Examples
Slow-growing	No **squatter settlements**	Often in HICs
Growing	Under 20% of population in squatter settlements	Often in NEEs
Rapid-growing	Over 20% of population in squatter settlements	Often in NEEs or LICs

Case study: Urban growth in Rio de Janeiro

Where is Rio?

Rio is located on the south-east Atlantic coast of Brazil, with most of the city built around Guanabara Bay (**Figure 3**).

SPECIFICATION TIP

You need a named example of one major city's urban growth in an LIC or NEE. A case study you may have studied is given here.

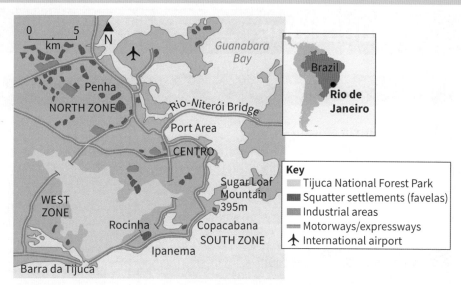

Key
- Tijuca National Forest Park
- Squatter settlements (favelas)
- Industrial areas
- Motorways/expressways
- ✈ International airport

▲ *Figure 3*

Why is Rio important?

Regional	National	International
• Major manufacturing centre (chemicals, pharmaceuticals, and clothing) • Major service centre (company headquarters, finance, education, tourism, and retail) • Stunning natural surroundings	• Brazil's arts and cultural capital (including the world-famous annual carnival) • Major port (exporting coffee, sugar, and iron ore) and transport hub (international airport)	• A UNESCO World Heritage Site (including the iconic Christ the Redeemer statue) • 2016 Olympic/Paralympic Games and 2014 World Cup host

Why has Rio grown?

- Mainly owing to regional, national, and international migration, but also its youthful population, Rio has a rapidly growing population. It has trebled between 1950 and 2020 to 6.7 million people in the city itself and 13.5 million including the surrounding area. Pull factors include:

- employment, economic development, and business opportunities

- access to services (health care and education)

- access to resources (water supply and energy).

 Key terms — **Make sure you can write a definition for these key terms**

> counter-urbanisation   HICs   infrastructure   LICs   megacities   NEEs
> squatter settlements   urban growth   urbanisation

Retrieval

Learn the answers to the questions below, then cover the answers column with a piece of paper and write down as many as you can. Check and repeat.

Questions	Answers
1 What is urbanisation?	the proportional increase in the number of people living in towns and cities
2 What is urban growth?	the physical expansion of urban areas
3 What are low-income countries (LICs)?	poorer countries with mainly primary jobs such as farming and mining (e.g., Bangladesh and Mali)
4 What are newly emerging economies (NEEs)?	countries experiencing higher rates of economic development, with a rapid growth of industrialisation
5 What are high-income countries (HICs)?	richer countries with lots of industry and service jobs (e.g., the UK and Japan)
6 What sorts of countries demonstrate the greatest rates of urbanisation?	low-income countries (LICs) and newly emerging economies (NEEs)
7 What proportion of the world's population already live in urban areas?	more than half
8 What is meant by push and pull factors?	migrants are either driven to cities from hardships in the countryside (push) or attracted to cities by social and economic opportunities (pull)
9 What is a megacity?	city with a population of over 10 million
10 What is a key feature of a rapid-growing megacity?	over 20% of the population living in squatter settlements
11 What is a squatter settlement?	unplanned area of (often illegal) poor-quality housing, lacking in services such as water supply, sewerage, and electricity
12 What is Rio de Janeiro's regional importance?	a major manufacturing centre and major service centre
13 What is Rio de Janeiro's national importance?	it is Brazil's arts and cultural capital a major port; and transport hub with international airport
14 What is Rio de Janeiro's international importance?	a UNESCO World Heritage Site (including the iconic Christ the Redeemer statue); the 2016 Olympic/Paralympic Games and 2014 World Cup host
15 Why has Rio's population more than trebled since 1950?	natural increase and especially migration – pull factors including employment, economic development, and business opportunities, and access to services and resources

Put paper here

Exam-style questions

1.1 What is the correct definition of the term 'urbanisation'?
Shade **one** circle only.   **[1 mark]**

A   A built-up area ○

B   Growth of an urban area ○

C   Growth in urban population ○

D   Growth in the proportion of urban population ○

1.2 Use the data in **Figure 1** to complete the graph.   **[1 mark]**

▼ *Figure 1*

Country	% urban population (1950)
UK	79
Nigeria	10
Botswana	3

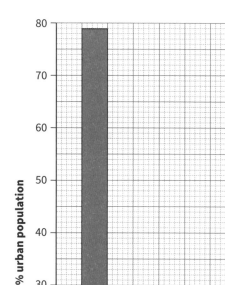

EXAM TIP

Accuracy is essential, so plot graphs in pencil so you can correct mistakes when you check your answers.

LINK

To understand the skill of constructing and reading a bar graph, see the Geographical Skills section, page 227.

1.3 Suggest how this graph might look today.   **[2 marks]**

1.4 Outline how trends in the world's population living in urban areas differ between HICs and LICs.   **[3 marks]**

EXAM TIP

In the exam there will be lines to write on. Use the number of lines given as a guide to how much you might be expected to write.

EXAM TIP

Outline as a command word requires you to summarise the key points – so keep the answer 'punchy'.

Knowledge

 Case study: Economic development opportunities in Rio

What are the economic development opportunities in Rio?

Rio's diverse industries and services support:

- further development of new industries to support the supply chain (**multiplier effect**)
- high levels of income per head (for Brazil)
- growing number of jobs in public services, and the service and **quaternary sectors**
- promotion of Rio as a tourist destination.

> **SPECIFICATION TIP**
>
> You need a named example of one major city's urban growth in an LIC or NEE. A case study you may have studied is given here.

What are the social and economic challenges facing Rio?

Life expectancy, **literacy**, and **infant mortality** rates are better in Rio than in Brazil as a whole, but the city faces many challenges.

	Challenges	Solutions creating opportunities
Health care	Health care and hospital access is better in the wealthier south and west zones (**Figure 3**, page 129).	Community-based 'family health teams' have improved vaccination programmes and health cover from 4% to 70% in some **favelas** (such as Santa Marta).
Education	Only about half of children continue their education beyond the age of 14, owing to: • insufficient schools and teachers • the distance needed to travel to school • a need for teenagers to work to support their families.	• Non-governmental organisations (**NGOs**) such as Schools of Tomorrow work with favela communities to improve education provision • local government grants are provided to help children remain in school • Rocinha favela has opened a university.
Water supply	Water supply and sanitation provision for all is essential – particularly in the densely populated favelas.	Since 1998, seven new treatment plants and 300 km of new water pipes have been built. 96% of the city now has safe piped water.
Energy provision	Overloaded electricity supplies lead to frequent power cuts. Many poorer people are forced to tap into the main supply, which is dangerous and illegal.	New power lines and an HEP station have been installed. A third nuclear power plant is due to open in 2023.
Unemployment	About 3.5 million workers are employed in the **informal economy** (with no contracts, pensions, insurance, or tax contributions). Female (18% in 2019) and youth unemployment rates are particularly high.	Solutions centre on education initiatives.
Crime	Murder, drug trafficking, kidnapping, and armed assaults occur regularly in Rio.	In 2013, Pacifying Police Units (UPPs) were established to reduce crime in favelas and take greater control.

Other urban challenges and solutions in Rio
Housing: the Favela Bairro Project

Over 100 000 in-migrants arrive in Rio each year. Many live in **favelas** – often in hazardous environments (e.g., steep hillsides). The Favela Bairro Project has upgraded many favelas, with infrastructure and **site and service** provision.

But there are still problems:

- the newly built infrastructure is not always maintained by the government
- some residents lack the skills and resources to make repairs
- more education and training are needed to improve literacy and employment.

The Favela Bairro Project provided:

- basic sanitation, plumbing, and electricity
- new leisure, health care, and education facilities
- secured hillsides to prevent landslides
- paved roads.

Most favelas have retail facilities, including bars, travel agents, and restaurants.

Favelas are not always slums or ghettos: residents often take pride in their homes and in making improvements.

More and more houses are brick-built with electricity, running water, sewerage systems, and internet access.

▲ *Figure 1 Rocinha, Rio's largest and oldest favela*

Pollution

The main environmental challenges in Rio relate to air, water, and land pollution.

	Issues	Solutions
Air	High crime levels mean many people prefer to drive. This increases traffic congestion and **smog**.	• Expansion of the metro system (cutting car use). • New toll roads. • Making coast roads one-way during rush hours.
Water	Guanabara Bay is polluted by sewage, industrial waste, oil spills, and ship ballast.	• New sewage works and pipes installed. • Ship owners are fined for illegal discharges.
Land	Waste collection is infrequent in favelas, encouraging rats and causing diseases.	Every year, 3.5 million tonnes of waste go to landfill. A power plant converts landfill biogas (LFG) to generate electricity.

Key terms Make sure you can write a definition for these key terms

favela   infant mortality   informal economy   literacy
multiplier effect   NGO   quaternary sector
site and service   smog

Learn the answers to the questions below, then cover the answers column with a piece of paper and write down as many as you can. Check and repeat.

Questions / Answers

#	Questions	Answers
1	What is meant by the multiplier effect?	when new industry generates taxation revenue for investment into infrastructure, training, and services, which encourages further growth in supply industries and other industrial sectors
2	What is the quaternary sector?	jobs in research, information technology, and the media
3	What is the informal economy?	employment outside the official knowledge of the government (unregulated and contributing no tax revenue)
4	What is meant by site and service provision?	the local authority provides land and services (water, sanitation, power) for residents to build homes
5	What are the economic development opportunities in Rio?	formal-economy jobs in tourism; new industries to support the supply chain; and a growing number of jobs in public services, and the service and quaternary sectors
6	What are the social challenges facing Rio?	access to services (e.g., health care and education); access to resources (e.g., water supply, sanitation, and energy); high crime rate
7	What are the economic challenges facing Rio?	high unemployment; around one third of the workforce working in the informal economy (unregulated and contributing no tax revenue); traffic congestion
8	What are the three main environmental challenges facing Rio?	air pollution (smog), water pollution, and waste disposal

Put paper here

Previous questions / Answers

#	Previous questions	Answers
1	What is urbanisation?	the proportional increase in the number of people living in towns and cities
2	What is urban growth?	the physical expansion of urban areas
3	What sorts of countries demonstrate the greatest rates of urbanisation?	low-income countries (LICs) and newly emerging economies (NEEs)
4	What proportion of the world's population already live in urban areas?	more than half (56% in 2021)
6	What is meant by push and pull factors?	migrants are either driven to cities from hardships in the countryside (push) or attracted to cities by social and economic opportunities (pull)

Put paper here

Exam-style questions

1.1 Give **one** example of a service industry in which a major city in an LIC/NEE is internationally important. **[1 mark]**

1.2 Suggest **two** push factors that drive people to move to cities. **[2 marks]**

1.3 Outline what a squatter settlement is. **[2 marks]**

1.4 Describe how migration has affected the growth of a city in an LIC/NEE. **[3 marks]**

EXAM TIP

This question focuses on push factors only. But if the question asks for push *and* pull factors, make sure that you don't simply write opposites (e.g., 'there are low-paid jobs' *and* 'there are well-paid jobs'). Instead, make sure the factors you write about are different.

Study **Figures 1** and **2**, showing the population of Rio de Janeiro (1950–2020).

▼ *Figure 1*

Year	1950	1960	1970	1980	1990	2000	2010	2020
Population (millions)	3	4.5	6.8	8.8	9.7	11.3	12.4	13.5

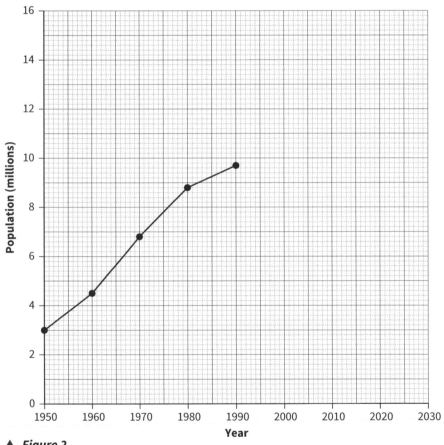

▲ *Figure 2*

1.5 Use the data in **Figure 1** to plot population totals for 2000, 2010 and 2020 on **Figure 2**. **[2 marks]**

1.6 Calculate the percentage change of population between 2010 and 2020. **[1 mark]**

1.7 Assuming the rate of change stays the same, calculate the expected population in 2030. **[1 mark]**

1.8 Plot this extrapolated value on **Figure 2** to complete the graph. **[1 mark]**

1.9 Describe the trend of population growth (1950–2030). **[3 marks]**

LINK

To understand the skill of constructing and reading a line graph, see the Geographical Skills section, page 228.

EXAM TIP

Calculate means work out. How to calculate a percentage is explained in the Geographical Skills section, page 232.

Study **Figure 3**, slum housing in Rio de Janeiro, Brazil

▲ *Figure 3*

2.1 Using the evidence shown in **Figure 3** and your own understanding, describe the housing challenges faced by many cities in LICs and NEEs. **[3 marks]**

2.2 Using a case study of an LIC/NEE, explain how urban growth has created challenges. **[6 marks]**

2.3 Use the data in **Figure 4** to complete the graph. **[1 mark]**

> **EXAM TIP**
>
> *Explain* as a command word requires you to set out purposes or reasons – say why or how.

▼ *Figure 4*

Year	% world urban population expected
2040	65
2050	70

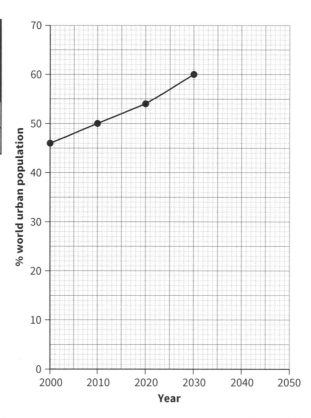

2.4 Define the term 'megacity'. **[1 mark]**

2.5 Explain reasons for the difference in the rate of urbanisation in HICs, NEEs and LICs. **[6 marks]**

2.6 Which of the following is **not** likely to be faced by a worker in the informal sector? Shade **one** circle only. [1 mark]

    A   Working long hours   ○

    B   Paying into a pension fund   ○

    C   Having little job security   ○

    D   Irregular earnings   ○

Study **Figure 5**, Kershar's story.

My name is Kershar. Last year my parents, sister Sundra and I moved from our village to live in Belgachia. This is a district in Kolkata, West Bengal, India. Our house only has two rooms, but we have electricity. My father works as a labourer, but his work is not regular. Kolkata is crowded, noisy and very, very busy! Outside our house people wash laundry, mend clothes, and flatten tin cans to sell and recycle. There are thousands of small workshops here. But it is very smelly, with open sewers. Sundra and I like to walk to Eden Gardens Park where it is beautiful, but we haven't been inside the nearby cricket ground. We go to school every morning and learn maths and literacy. In the afternoon we scavenge for useful scrap which my father can sell. We also help my mother in the house whenever she asks.

▲ *Figure 5*

2.7 What evidence in **Figure 5** suggests that Kershar's family is poor? [3 marks]

> **EXAM TIP** 🎯
>
> When answering this type of question, you should use quotes from the text to support your statements.

2.8 Using a case study of an LIC/NEE, suggest the main challenges facing the management of squatter settlements. [4 marks]

> **EXAM TIP** 🎯
>
> *Suggest* as a command requires you to present a possible case, to propose an idea, solution or answer.

2.9 Using a case study of an LIC/NEE, evaluate the management issues faced by the city authorities. [9 marks] [+3 SPaG marks]

> **EXAM TIP** 🎯
>
> *Evaluate* as a command word requires you to judge from evidence, weighing up both sides of an argument.

> **EXAM TIP** 🎯
>
> A useful trick for high-mark questions is to run through the 5Ws: What, Where, When, Why, and Who? This will help you answer the question in enough depth to access the marks available.

Questions referring to previous content

3.1 For a major city in an LIC/NEE, outline its regional importance. [2 marks]

3.2 For a major city in an LIC/NEE, explain the reasons for its growth. [4 marks]

Knowledge

24 Urban change in the UK: where do people live?

How is the UK population distributed?

- The UK is one of the most urbanised countries in the world.

- Its population is unevenly distributed – the highest densities are focused in the major city regions.

- 84% of people live in urban areas (towns and cities).

- One in seven of those live in London and the south-east of England.

- Many highland regions are very sparsely populated – upland areas are remote and can experience harsh weather (**Figure 1**).

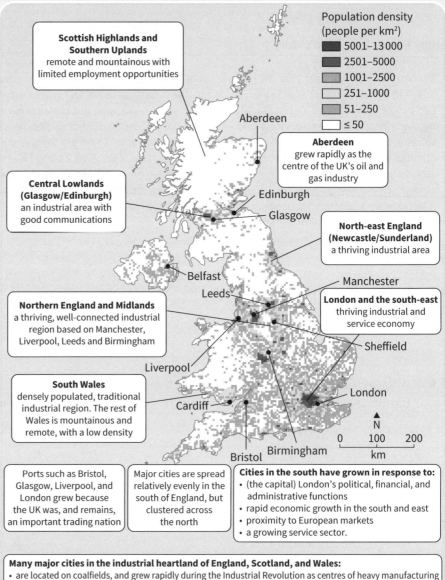

Scottish Highlands and Southern Uplands
remote and mountainous with limited employment opportunities

Population density (people per km²)
- 5001–13 000
- 2501–5000
- 1001–2500
- 251–1000
- 51–250
- ≤ 50

Aberdeen
grew rapidly as the centre of the UK's oil and gas industry

Central Lowlands (Glasgow/Edinburgh)
an industrial area with good communications

North-east England (Newcastle/Sunderland)
a thriving industrial area

Northern England and Midlands
a thriving, well-connected industrial region based on Manchester, Liverpool, Leeds and Birmingham

London and the south-east
thriving industrial and service economy

South Wales
densely populated, traditional industrial region. The rest of Wales is mountainous and remote, with a low density

Aberdeen
Edinburgh
Glasgow
Belfast
Leeds
Manchester
Sheffield
Liverpool
Cardiff
London
Bristol
Birmingham

N
0   100   200
km

Ports such as Bristol, Glasgow, Liverpool, and London grew because the UK was, and remains, an important trading nation

Major cities are spread relatively evenly in the south of England, but clustered across the north

Cities in the south have grown in response to:
- (the capital) London's political, financial, and administrative functions
- rapid economic growth in the south and east
- proximity to European markets
- a growing service sector.

Many major cities in the industrial heartland of England, Scotland, and Wales:
- are located on coalfields, and grew rapidly during the Industrial Revolution as centres of heavy manufacturing
- now demonstrate slow population growth owing to **deindustrialisation**.

▶ **Figure 1** The distribution of the UK population

How might this distribution change?

- There has been a general population drift towards London and south-east England.

- Net immigration (**immigration** minus **emigration**) has declined since 2015, but immigrants generally settle in larger cities where there are more job opportunities.

- There has recently been a movement from urban to rural areas. This **counter-urbanisation** includes older people choosing to retire near the coast or in the country.

Key terms

Make sure you can write a definition for these key terms

counter-urbanisation
deindustrialisation   emigration
immigration

Learn the answers to the questions below, then cover the answers column with a piece of paper and write down as many as you can. Check and repeat.

Questions

Answers

1	How is the UK population distributed?	unevenly – high densities in major city regions, very sparsely in upland areas
2	What proportion of the UK population lives in urban areas?	84%
3	What is counter-urbanisation?	the proportional increase in the number of people living in rural areas – the reverse process of urbanisation
4	What is deindustrialisation?	the decline of a country's traditional manufacturing industry due to exhaustion of raw materials, loss of markets, and competition from NEEs
5	What is emigration?	the act of leaving your own country to settle permanently in another – in short, moving abroad
6	What is immigration?	moving into a new country with the intention of staying and living there

Put paper here

Previous questions

Answers

1	What is a megacity?	city with a population of over 10 million
2	What is a squatter settlement?	unplanned area of (oft en illegal) poor-quality housing, lacking in services such as water supply, sewerage, and electricity
3	What sorts of countries demonstrate the greatest rates of urbanisation?	low-income countries (LICs) and newly emerging economies (NEEs)
4	What proportion of the world's population already live in urban areas?	more than half (56% in 2021)
5	What is meant by push and pull factors?	migrants are either driven to cities from hardships in the countryside (push) or attracted to cities by social and economic opportunities (pull)
6	What is a key feature of a rapid-growing megacity?	over 20% of the population living in squatter settlements

Put paper here

Exam-style questions

Study **Figure 1**, a map showing the distribution of the UK population.

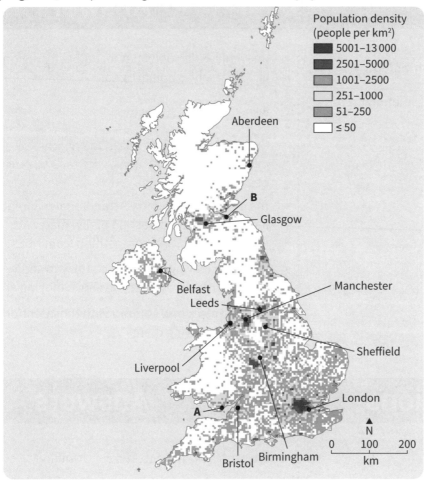

▲ *Figure 1*

1.1 Name the cities labelled **A** and **B** on **Figure 1**. [2 marks]

1.2 Give **two** reasons why large areas of Scotland are sparsely populated. [2 marks]

1.3 Identify **two** UK areas of high population density. [2 marks]

> **EXAM TIP** ⊚
>
> *Identify* as a command word requires you to name an example.

1.4 Which of the following is the proportion of the UK population living in urban areas? Shade **one** circle only. [1 mark]

A	21%	○	**C**	68%	○
B	45%	○	**D**	84%	○

1.5 Using the evidence shown in **Figure 1**, describe the distribution of major cities in the UK. [2 marks]

Questions referring to previous content

2.1 State **two** pull factors that attract people to move to cities. [2 marks]

2.2 Explain the consequences of uncontrolled rural–urban migration. [4 marks]

25 Urban change in the UK: a case study

📖 Case study: A major city in the UK: Bristol

What makes Bristol a major UK city?

Bristol is the largest city in the south-west of England.

> **SPECIFICATION TIP**
>
> You need a named example of one major UK city. A case study you may have studied is given here.

- **Education:** two large universities
- **Tourism:** the UK's eighth most popular city for foreign visitors
- **Industry:** largest concentration of silicon chip manufacturers outside California

The importance of Bristol

- **Regional importance:** largest city in south-west England
- **Culture and entertainment:** several theatres, music venues, and home to the creators of Wallace and Gromit
- **Religion:** a mix, including mosques, synagogues, and two Christian cathedrals

Why is Bristol an important international city?

Education
- Attracts international students

Transport
- Good road and rail links
- Ferry services to Europe
- Two major docks, including Avonmouth
- Bristol airport links to Europe and the USA

Industry
- Global industries, including aerospace, finance, high-tech businesses, and media
- Inward investment from abroad

What is the impact of migration on Bristol?

Until 2015, migration from abroad accounted for about half of Bristol's population growth, including large numbers from EU countries. Migration has brought both opportunities and challenges.

Opportunities
- A growing workforce
- Enriching the city's cultural life
- Mainly young migrants help to balance the ageing population

Challenges
- Pressures on housing and employment
- Teaching children whose first language might not be English
- Integration into the wider community

> **WATCH OUT**
>
> Make sure you understand the distinction between *opportunities* and *challenges*. Understand that opportunities inevitably bring challenges, as this will help you structure an argument on longer, high-mark questions.

What urban changes are affecting Bristol?

Bristol's population is growing rapidly. The high levels of migration have resulted in an ethnically diverse and youthful population. Good transport links (including motorways and a second River Severn crossing) have increased the city's **connectivity**, making it good for commuters. Over 2 million people live within 50 km of the city (**Figure 1**).

Urban changes clearly create opportunities, such as employment, cultural mixing, and **urban greening**. But they also create challenges, such as inequalities in employment, **social deprivation**, and dereliction. Note how these opportunities and challenges come under social, economic, and environmental headings.

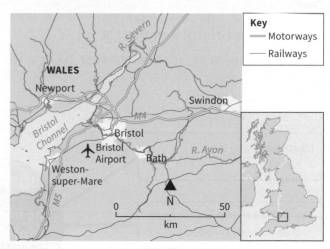

▲ *Figure 1 The location of Bristol*

Urban changes in Bristol creating social (cultural) opportunities

The growth of Bristol has created demand for a wide variety of recreation and entertainment.

Shopping

In the city centre, Cabot Circus, constructed in 2008 at a cost of £500 million, provides shops and entertainment facilities, including a cinema.

Sport

Sports include Bristol City and Bristol Rovers football teams, Bristol Bears rugby union, and the headquarters for Gloucestershire County Cricket. Stadium **redevelopment** has given opportunities to provide a range of leisure and conference facilities, such as the redeveloped stadium at Ashton Gate.

Entertainment

Bristol's Harbourside has seen workshops and warehouses converted into bars and nightclubs. Theatres include the Bristol Hippodrome and the Tobacco Factory.

Urban changes in Bristol creating economic opportunities

The growth of Bristol has created many economic opportunities for development and employment.

Following closure of Bristol's city centre port, deindustrialisation (traditional manufacturing moving out of an area) has given way to major developments in tertiary services and quaternary (high-tech) sectors. High-tech industries have been attracted by:

- superfast broadband connectivity
- collaboration with local universities
- a clean and non-polluted environment.

Major industries now include financial services employing 35 000 people, and Aardman Animations – famous for the stop-motion clay animation characters Wallace and Gromit.

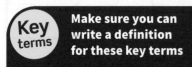

Key terms
Make sure you can write a definition for these key terms

brownfield site   connectivity   green belt   greenfield site   integrated transport system   redevelopment   social deprivation   urban greening   urban sprawl

Urban changes in Bristol creating environmental opportunities

In 2015, Bristol became the UK's first ever European Green Capital and the city plans to be carbon neutral by 2030. The city has:

- developed an **integrated transport system** (including MetroBus, cycle routes, and electrified railway), connecting suburban housing areas with retail parks, motorway junctions, railway stations, and universities
- increased urban open space, for recreation and health, through urban greening. More than one third of Bristol is now open space, including eight nature reserves and 400 parks and gardens.

Urban changes in Bristol creating challenges

Urban change in Bristol has created a number of social, economic and environmental challenges.

Social challenges: deprivation

15% of Bristol's residents live in some of the most deprived areas in England. For example, Filwood in south Bristol has:

- many council-run estates and high-rise flats in urgent need of modernisation
- lower than average levels of good health and life expectancy
- high levels of obesity and smoking
- Bristol's lowest participation rates in active sport and creative activities.

Economic challenges

The employment rate for Bristol is one of the highest in UK cities, emphasising some marked social and economic inequalities. Affluent suburbs (such as Stoke Bishop to the north-west) contrast markedly with deprived wards, such as Filwood, where:

- there are high levels of unemployment – especially among young adults
- only 34% of students gain top grades at GCSE, so many lack the necessary skills to benefit from Bristol's developing employment opportunities in the tertiary and quaternary sectors.

Environmental challenges

Dereliction	Building on brownfield and greenfield land	Urban sprawl	Waste disposal
Deindustrialisation, including the decline of the city centre port and railway industry, has left many warehouses and other historic buildings derelict.	• **Brownfield sites** can be costly to clear and decontaminate. • **Greenfield sites** require less groundwork before developing, but building on them may be met with objections from local people and environmentalists.	**Urban sprawl**, extending Bristol to the north and south, has been controversial owing to: • loss of countryside • impacts on wildlife biodiversity • increased traffic congestion, noise, and air pollution. Strict **green belt** planning restrictions now cover extensive areas.	Waste reduction initiatives have reduced Bristol's rubbish to 140 000 tonnes annually. Of this, 61% is recycled, leaving only 39% for mechanical and biological treatment (including biogas electricity generation).

Learn the answers to the questions below, then cover the answers column with a piece of paper and write down as many as you can. Check and repeat.

Questions / Answers

	Questions	Answers
1	What are the positive impacts of migration on Bristol?	opportunities such as a growing workforce helping to balance the ageing population, and enriching the city's cultural life
2	What are the negative impacts of migration on Bristol?	challenges such as pressures on housing and employment, language barriers in schools, and integration into the wider community
3	What has attracted high-tech industries to Bristol?	superfast broadband connectivity, collaboration with local universities, and a clean and non-polluted environment
4	What is urban greening?	process of increasing and preserving open space in urban areas, i.e., public parks and gardens
5	What is dereliction?	abandoned buildings and wasteland
6	What are examples of deprivation?	living at a high density; high rates of crime and unemployment; poor-quality housing; low incomes or relying on benefits
7	What is a brownfield site?	land that has been used, abandoned, and now awaits reuse – often found in urban areas
8	What is a greenfield site?	a plot of land, often in a rural area or on the edge of an urban area, that has not been built on before
9	What is urban sprawl?	unplanned growth of urban areas into the surrounding rural or rural–urban fringe areas
10	What is green belt land?	land protected from new developments (such as housing and industry) by strict planning regulations

Put paper here

Previous questions / Answers

	Previous questions	Answers
1	What are low-income countries (LICs)?	poorer countries with mainly primary jobs such as farming and mining (e.g., Bangladesh and Mali)
2	What are newly emerging economies (NEEs)?	countries experiencing higher rates of economic development, with a rapid growth of industrialisation
3	What are high-income countries (HICs)?	richer countries with lots of industry and service jobs (e.g., the UK and Japan)

Put paper here

Exam-style questions

1.1 Complete the following facts about a major UK city you
have studied. **[2 marks]**

Name of major UK city	
Location in the UK	
Importance in the UK	

1.2 Give **one** example of a service industry in which a major city
in the UK is internationally important. **[1 mark]**

1.3 For a major city in the UK, outline **two** challenges associated with
migration into the city. **[2 marks]**

> **EXAM TIP**
>
> *Outline* as a command word requires you to summarise the key points.

1.4 For a major city in the UK, describe ways in which migration into
the city has affected its character, by creating both opportunities
and challenges. **[4 marks]**

1.5 For a major city in the UK, explain what makes it important. **[4 marks]**

> **EXAM TIP**
>
> *Explain* as a command word requires you to give reasons why something is the case.

Study **Figure 1**. Stoke Bishop and Filwood are two contrasting
wards in Bristol. Stoke Bishop is an affluent suburb to the
north-west of the city. Filwood is one of the most socially deprived
wards in south Bristol.

▼ *Figure 1*

Housing tenure	Stoke Bishop (%)	Filwood (%)
Owner occupied	75	46
Social rented	12	41
Private and other rented	13	13

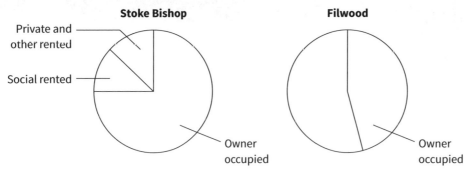

▲ *Figure 2*

2.1 Complete the pie chart for Filwood to compare the data in **Figure 1**. **[2 marks]**

LINK

To understand the skill of constructing and reading a pie chart, see the Geographical Skills section, page 229.

2.2 Compare the pie charts in **Figure 2**, suggesting reasons for your observations. **[3 marks]**

EXAM TIP

Compare as a command word requires you to identify similarities and differences (in the proportions shown).

EXAM TIP

Remember, while quoting percentages may have value on occasion, manipulating the data by highlighting proportional differences will show better understanding.

2.3 Describe **two** benefits of urban greening. **[2 marks]**

2.4 Outline what a brownfield site is. **[2 marks]**

2.5 For a major city in the UK, describe the environmental challenges of urban change. **[6 marks]**

EXAM TIP

Describe as a command word requires you to say what something is like. (No explanation is needed.)

EXAM TIP

To what extent as a command word requires you to judge the importance of something.

2.6 To what extent has urban change created social, economic, and environmental opportunities in a major UK city you have studied? **[9 marks]** **[+3 SPaG marks]**

Questions referring to previous content

3.1 Outline how the UK's population distribution is changing. **[3 marks]**

Study **Figure 3**, photographs of the eastern Scottish Highlands, near Glenshee, and Sheffield, West Yorkshire.

Population density: 8 per km²

Population density: 1500 per km²

▲ *Figure 3*

3.2 Explain how the distribution of population in the UK reflects both physical geography and human factors. **[6 marks]**

26 UK urban regeneration and sustainable development

Case study: Urban regeneration in Bristol

Urban regeneration is an attempt to reverse the decline and decay of an urban area by improving its physical structure. In Bristol, the deindustrialised Temple Quarter area, close to the railway station became an **Enterprise Zone** (EZ) in 2012, qualifying for government money to support its regeneration. An industrial legacy of abandoned factories and railway sidings, and dereliction and contamination, is now:

- an attractive, accessible, and clean environment

- creating new economic opportunities in almost 400 firms from the creative, digital, and green industries

- supporting the local community with housing, employment, and services.

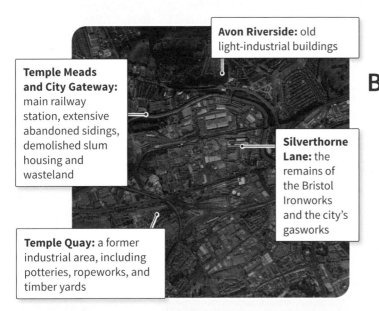

Avon Riverside: old light-industrial buildings

Temple Meads and City Gateway: main railway station, extensive abandoned sidings, demolished slum housing and wasteland

Silverthorne Lane: the remains of the Bristol Ironworks and the city's gasworks

Temple Quay: a former industrial area, including potteries, ropeworks, and timber yards

▲ **Figure 1** Aerial view of Bristol's Temple Quarter in the 1990s

> **SPECIFICATION TIP**
>
> You need a named example of an urban regeneration project in the UK. A case study you may have studied is given here.

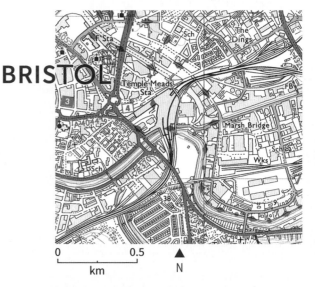

▲ **Figure 2** OS map of Bristol's Temple Quarter (showing the same area as **Figure 1**)

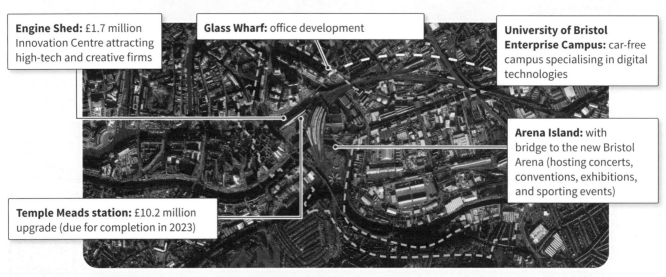

Engine Shed: £1.7 million Innovation Centre attracting high-tech and creative firms

Glass Wharf: office development

University of Bristol Enterprise Campus: car-free campus specialising in digital technologies

Arena Island: with bridge to the new Bristol Arena (hosting concerts, conventions, exhibitions, and sporting events)

Temple Meads station: £10.2 million upgrade (due for completion in 2023)

▲ **Figure 3** Aerial photo of Bristol's Temple Quarter regeneration

Sustainable urban development

What is urban sustainability?

Urban sustainability involves creating an environment that meets the social, economic, and environmental needs of existing residents without compromising those needs for future generations. This involves:

- water and energy conservation
- waste recycling
- creating green spaces
- reducing traffic congestion.

Water and energy conservation

Water conservation involves:

- using **green roofs** to collect (harvest) rainwater to use indoors
- pervious pavements that allow rainwater to soak through.

Energy conservation involves:

- using renewable energy sources, such as solar panels on roofs or burning biomass
- adopting combined heating and power systems
- increasing the efficiency of domestic services and appliances
- energy saving through building insulation and double-glazing.

Reducing traffic congestion

Traffic congestion is a major issue:

- causing air pollution, affecting people's health
- reducing economic efficiency, wasting people's time and money while they are stuck in traffic jams.

It can be reduced using the following measures:

- developing an integrated transport system (e.g., Bristol's MetroWest railway, MetroBus and **park and ride** schemes)
- making public transport more widespread and attractive (e.g., Beijing's rapid bus transit system)
- reducing car parking spaces or charging cars to enter city centres (e.g., London's Congestion Charge)
- encouraging people to cycle (e.g., Bristol's network of cycle routes).

Waste recycling

Waste recycling involves recovering and reprocessing urban waste. For example:

- reduced packaging using recyclable materials
- using organic (food) waste to create energy (biogas)
- enabling local authorities, homes, and businesses to collect recyclable waste.

Key terms

Make sure you can write a definition for these key terms

Enterprise Zone
green roofs   park and ride
urban regeneration
urban sustainability

Creating green spaces

Parks and gardens act as the 'lungs' of a city. They help to keep the air clean, and provide natural habitats for wildlife, as well as much-needed recreational and social space (**Figure 4**).

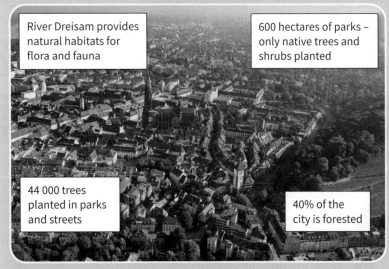

River Dreisam provides natural habitats for flora and fauna

600 hectares of parks – only native trees and shrubs planted

44 000 trees planted in parks and streets

40% of the city is forested

▲ **Figure 4** *Freiburg, south-west Germany – the 'green city'*

 Retrieval

Learn the answers to the questions below, then cover the answers column with a piece of paper and write down as many as you can. Check and repeat.

Questions / Answers

	Questions	Answers
1	What is urban regeneration?	an attempt to reverse the decline and decay of an urban area by improving its physical structure
2	What is an Enterprise Zone?	designated areas across England which provide tax breaks and government support for businesses
3	Name four areas of Bristol's Temple Quarter that required urban regeneration.	Avon Riverside; Silverthorne Lane; Temple Meads City Gateway; Temple Quay
4	What were the reasons for Bristol's Temple Quarter requiring regeneration?	an industrial legacy of abandoned factories and railway sidings, dereliction, and contamination
5	Name five key regeneration projects in Bristol's Temple Quarter.	Engine Shed; Glass Wharf; Arena Island; Temple Meads station; University of Bristol Enterprise Campus
6	What are the key features of business regeneration projects in Bristol's Temple Quarter?	office developments and the attraction of nearly 400 creative, digital, and green industries
7	What are the key features of leisure, recreation, and sporting projects in Bristol's Temple Quarter?	the Bristol Arena complex hosts concerts, conventions, exhibitions, and sporting events
8	What are the major infrastructure projects in Bristol's Temple Quarter?	railway station redevelopment, and a new car-free university campus specialising in digital technologies
9	What is urban sustainability?	creating an environment that meets the needs of existing residents without compromising those needs for future generations
10	What are the key features of sustainable cities?	water and energy conservation; waste recycling; creating green spaces; and reducing traffic congestion
11	What are green roofs?	a layer of vegetation planted over a waterproofing system installed on top of a flat or slightly sloped roof to collect (harvest) rainwater to use indoors
12	What is meant by a park and ride scheme?	a form of integrated transport that allows private transport users to park their vehicles at a large car park and travel into the city centre using public transport

Put paper here

Previous questions / Answers

	Previous questions	Answers
1	What is dereliction?	abandoned buildings and wasteland
2	What are examples of deprivation?	living at a high density; high rates of crime and unemployment; poor-quality housing; low incomes or relying on benefits
3	What is a brownfield site?	land that has been used, abandoned, and now awaits reuse – often found in urban areas

Put paper here

Exam-style questions

Study **Figure 1**, a 1: 25 000 Ordnance Survey map showing part of Bristol, a city in the UK.

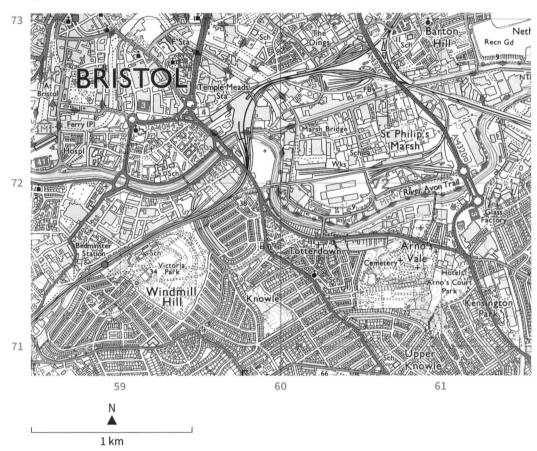

▲ *Figure 1*

1.1 What is the approximate area covered by the map extract?
Shade **one** circle only. **[1 mark]**

A   2 km²   ○   C   6 km²   ○

B   4 km²   ○   D   8 km²   ○

LINK

To understand the skill of interpreting an Ordnance Survey map, see the Geographical Skills section, pages 225–226.

1.2 Using **Figure 1**, state the four-figure grid reference for Victoria Park. **[1 mark]**

1.3 Using **Figure 1**, what is the name of the river that flows roughly from east to west across the OS map? **[1 mark]**

1.4 Using **Figure 1**, state the six-figure grid reference of Marsh Bridge. **[1 mark]**

1.5 Using **Figure 1**, describe the location of Temple Meads station. **[2 marks]**

1.6 Explain how the sustainability of urban areas can be improved through creating urban green space. **[3 marks]**

1.7 For an urban regeneration project in a major city in the UK, describe the features of the project. **[6 marks]**

EXAM TIP

Describe as a command word requires you to say what something is like. (No explanation is needed.)

Exam-style questions

Study **Figures 2**, **3** and **4**.

▲ **Figure 2** *Broadway in Filwood – one of the most socially deprived wards in south Bristol*

▲ **Figure 3** *The centre of Stoke Bishop – an affluent suburb to the north-west of Bristol*

Measure	Filwood	Stoke Bishop	Bristol (average)
Health (% with health conditions)	31	25	26
Free school meals (%)	40	16	23
School absence rate (%)	10	7	7

▲ **Figure 4** *Measures of health and education in Filwood and Stoke Bishop (2020)*

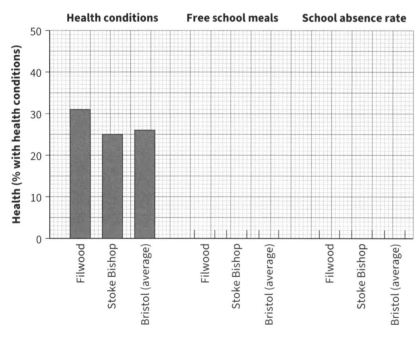

▲ **Figure 5**

2.1 Complete the bar graph **(Figure 5)** to compare the data in **Figure 4**. **[2 marks]**

2.2 In which of the two wards do people tend to be healthier? **[1 mark]**

2.3 Explain your answer to **2.2** above. **[3 marks]**

2.4 Suggest how 'school absence rate' may contribute to Filwood's relatively low GCSE attainment score (34%) compared with Stoke Bishop (48.8%) and the Bristol average (44.2%). **[2 marks]**

2.5 In addition to **Figures 2**, **3** and **4**, what other data would enable you to make a more accurate comparison of social inequalities between Filwood and Stoke Bishop? **[2 marks]**

LINK

To understand the skill of constructing and reading a bar graph, see the Geographical Skills section, page 227.

3.1 What is meant by urban regeneration? **[2 marks]**

3.2 Study **Figure 6**, which shows Bristol's Temple Quarter area after regeneration.

▲ *Figure 6*

Using **Figure 6**, describe **two** features of the regeneration project. **[2 marks]**

3.3 For an urban regeneration project in a major city in the UK, explain why the area needed regeneration. **[6 marks]**

3.4 For an urban regeneration project in a major city in the UK, explain how the area has been improved. **[6 marks]**

3.5 Explain how the sustainability of urban areas can be improved through traffic management strategies. **[4 marks]**

3.6 Explain how the sustainability of urban areas can be improved through water and energy conservation schemes. **[6 marks]**

3.7 'Urban change creates more opportunities than challenges.' Using a case study of a major city in the UK, discuss to what extent you agree with this statement. **[9 marks]**
[+3 SPaG marks]

EXAM TIP

Explain as a command word requires you to give reasons why something is the case.

EXAM TIP

Discuss as a command word requires you to give the points on both sides of an argument and come to a conclusion. *To what extent* requires you to judge the importance of something. So, for any stated opportunities and challenges, you need to gauge their relative importance before concluding whether there are more opportunities than challenges.

3.8 Evaluate the contribution of water and energy conservation, waste recycling, and reducing traffic congestion to sustainable urban living. **[9 marks]**
[+3 SPaG marks]

EXAM TIP

Evaluate as a command word requires you to make judgements about which are most or least effective.

Questions referring to previous content

4.1 For a major city in the UK, outline its international importance. **[3 marks]**

4.2 For a major city in the UK, explain how urban changes have created economic opportunities. **[4 marks]**

⚙ Knowledge

27 Our unequal world and measuring development

Development and the development gap

Development is the progress a country has made in terms of economic growth, use of technology, and human welfare. It usually improves living standards and **quality of life**. But there are wide-ranging differences in these standards between the world's richest and poorest countries. This is the **development gap**.

Economic and social measures of development

Gross National Income (GNI) is the total income of a country, including earnings abroad, divided by its population total (per capita). There are huge global variations in GNI between HICs, NEEs, and LICs.

The **Human Development Index (HDI)** is the most widely used measure of development. This UN 'composite' social measure considers income, life expectancy, and years in education. Values range from 0–1 (**Figure 1**).

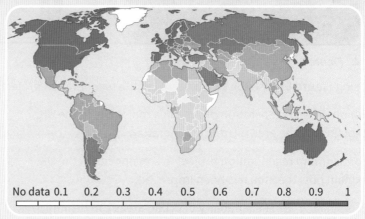

No data 0.1 0.2 0.3 0.4 0.5 0.6 0.7 0.8 0.9 1

▲ **Figure 1** The Human Development Index (2019)

Other measures of development

Birth rate: Poorer LICs often have a high birth rate as large families ensure a decent family income and support for ageing relatives. The birth rate drops as countries become more developed, as women usually receive more education and have fewer children.

Other measures of development

Infant mortality: A good measure of development, reflecting a country's healthcare system.

Death rate: Often low in LICs and NEEs as their healthcare improves. But it is usually high in HICs with ageing populations, and in the poorest LICs too (with high infant mortality), so it is a poor measure of development.

Literacy rate: A good indicator of development, but only easy to measure in HICs.

Access to clean water: High in HICs, but lower in LICs where modern infrastructure (e.g., dams, reservoirs, and treatment plants) may be less widespread.

WATCH OUT ❗

Take care! Measures such as birth, death, infant mortality, and literacy rates – not least GNI per capita – can give a false picture of development because they:

- average everyone throughout the whole country
- include hard-to-measure, unreliable, and out-of-date data.

How are levels of development related to population change and structure?

The Demographic Transition Model

As a country develops, its population characteristics change. The Demographic Transition Model (DTM) shows these changes over time, as birth and death rates change (natural change), though it does not account for migration (**Figure 2**).

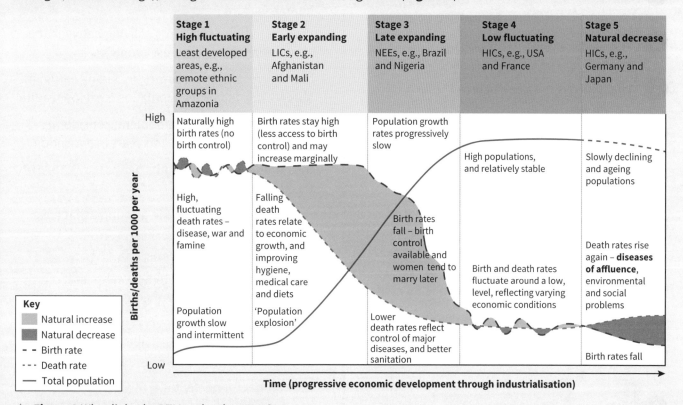

▲ *Figure 2 What links the DTM to development?*

Population structure

Countries at different stages of the DTM have different **population structures**, shown by population pyramids (**Figure 3**). We can also calculate **dependency ratios** (the proportion of people below and above working age). The lower the ratio, the more workers there are, and so less dependency, such as in HICs.

$$Dependency\ ratio = \frac{dependent\ population}{working\ population} \times 100$$

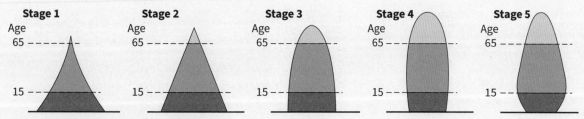

▲ *Figure 3 Population pyramids for the stages of the DTM*

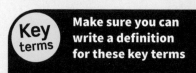

Key terms — **Make sure you can write a definition for these key terms**

dependency ratios   development   development gap
diseases of affluence   GNI   HDI   population structure
quality of life

Retrieval

Learn the answers to the questions below, then cover the answers column with a piece of paper and write down as many as you can. Check and repeat.

Questions

Answers

	Put paper here	
1 What is meant by development?		the progress a country has made in terms of economic growth, use of technology, and human welfare
2 What is the development gap?		the difference in standards of living between the world's richest and poorest countries
3 What is Gross National Income (GNI)?		the total income of a country, including earnings abroad, divided by its population total (per capita)
4 What is the Human Development Index (HDI)?		a social measure of development, considering income, life expectancy, and years in education
5 What are birth and death rates?		the number of births/deaths per year, per 1000 of the total population
6 What is the literacy rate?		the percentage of people in a country that have basic reading and writing skills
7 Name three things that indicate quality of life.		all the variables contributing to human welfare, including happiness, material wealth and possessions, safety, security, freedom, voting rights, good health, and so on
8 What are diseases of affluence?		degenerative diseases such as cancer, heart disease, and dementia – most associated with HICs
9 What is population structure?		the number (or percentage) of males and females in a population by age – shown on population pyramids
10 What is the dependency ratio?		the proportion of people below and above normal working age; the lower the ratio, the more workers there are (and so less dependency)

Previous questions

Answers

	Put paper here	
1 What is urban regeneration?		an attempt to reverse the decline and decay of an urban area by improving its physical structure
2 What is urban sustainability?		creating an environment that meets the needs of existing residents without compromising these needs for future generations

Exam-style questions

Study **Figure 1**, which shows selected measures of development in contrasting countries.

Figure 1

Country (2020)	GNI (US$ per person per year)	Birth rate (per 1000 per year)	HDI
Japan	41 690	7.32	0.919
China	10 410	11.62	0.761
Bangladesh	1940	18.13	0.632

1.1 In **Figure 1**, which country would be best described as a newly emerging economy (NEE)? **[1 mark]**

1.2 Outline any relationships in the data in **Figure 1**. **[2 marks]**

1.3 State **two** reasons for the differences in birth rates shown in **Figure 1**. **[2 marks]**

1.4 Explain why the birth rate is a better measure of development than the death rate. **[4 marks]**

1.5 What is meant by 'quality of life'? **[2 marks]**

1.6 Why is the Human Development Index (HDI) the most widely used measure of development? **[2 marks]**

> **EXAM TIP**
>
> *Explain* as a command word requires you to give reasons why something is the case.

Study **Figure 2** and **Figure 3**, which show population percentages, by gender, for Nigeria.

Figure 2

Age	Male	Female
20–24	4.5	4.3
25–29	3.7	3.6
30–34	3.2	3.1
35–39	2.8	2.7
40–44	2.3	2.3
45–49	1.9	1.9
50–54	1.4	1.5

2.1 Complete the population pyramid in **Figure 3**. **[2 marks]**

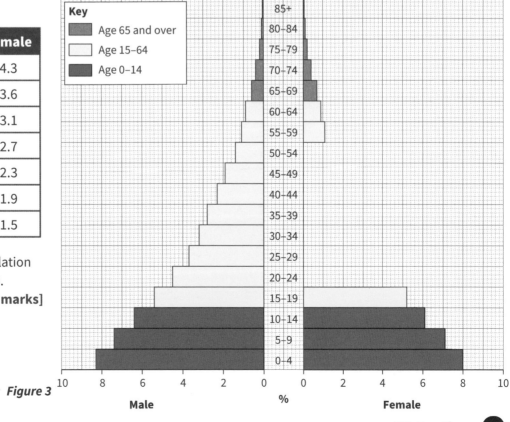

▶ *Figure 3*

Exam-style questions

2.2 Suggest why the data in **Figure 3** has been colour-coded into age-range groupings. **[1 mark]**

2.3 Using **Figure 3**, in which age range do males outnumber females? **[1 mark]**

2.4 Suggest reasons for your answer to **2.3** above. **[3 marks]**

2.5 What does the overall shape of the population pyramid suggest about Nigeria's level of development? **[1 mark]**

2.6 How might the shape of the population pyramid change over the next 50 years? **[2 marks]**

2.7 Suggest reasons for your answer to **2.6** above. **[2 marks]**

2.8 Look again at **Figure 3**. Explain how effective this technique is in comparing different levels of development. **[4 marks]**

> **EXAM TIP**
>
> *Suggest* as a command word requires you to present a possible case, idea, solution, or answer.

> **LINK**
>
> To understand the skill of constructing and reading a population pyramid, see the Geographical Skills section, page 229.

Study **Figures 4** and **5**, which show annotated population pyramids of countries at two different stages of development.

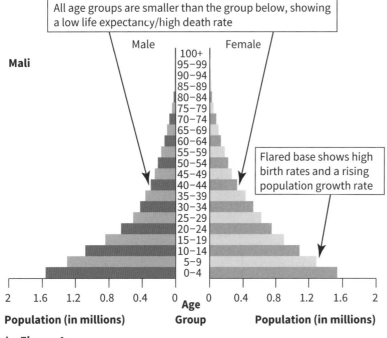

▲ *Figure 4*

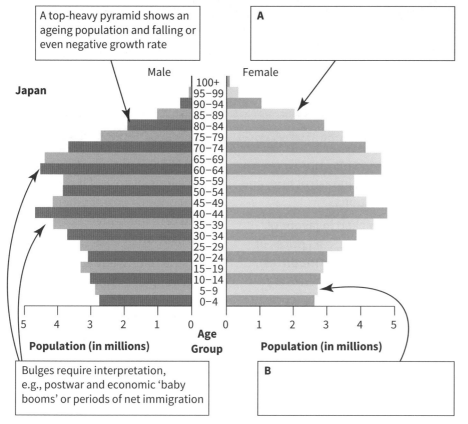

A top-heavy pyramid shows an ageing population and falling or even negative growth rate

A

Male   Female

Japan

Bulges require interpretation, e.g., postwar and economic 'baby booms' or periods of net immigration

B

▲ *Figure 5*

3.1 Using **Figure 5**, complete the annotations for boxes **A** and **B**. [4 marks]

EXAM TIP

Labels simply identify or name features, whereas *annotations* give details such as explanations. Treat each annotation box as a 2-mark question.

3.2 Evaluate the extent to which the Demographic Transition Model (DTM) represents a reliable indication of relative levels of economic and social development. [9 marks]
[+3 SPaG marks]

4.1 Define the term 'infant mortality rate'. [2 marks]

4.2 What are 'diseases of affluence'? [2 marks]

4.3 In which stage or stages of the Demographic Transition Model (DTM) would you expect to find most newly emerging economies (NEEs), and why? [3 marks]

4.4 Explain how a falling birth rate can reflect economic and social development. [3 marks]

4.5 Explain the economic impacts of, and potential responses to, a country being in Stage 5 of the Demographic Transition Model (DTM). [4 marks]

EXAM TIP

Evaluate as a command word requires you to make judgements about how effective something is. Likewise, *the extent to which* requires you to judge the importance of something. Making judgements based upon sound evidence from your understanding of the DTM is the key to successfully answering this question.

28 The causes and consequences of unequal development

Physical, economic, and historical causes of unequal development

Physical	Economic	Historical
Extreme climatic and weather conditions create hostile environments to live and work in, e.g., climate-related pests and diseases, clean water shortages, and tropical storms, floods, and droughts. **Landlocked** countries are cut off from sea trade, which is important for economic development. Harsh relief, e.g., remote mountainous regions, is difficult to develop infrastructure in.	Poverty prevents improvements to education, infrastructure, and living conditions. **Trade** is stacked in favour of richer countries, e.g., prices of raw materials (**commodities**), which LICs rely on, fluctuate widely and are always worth far less than the products made from them.	Many HICs, especially in Europe, have a long history of industrial and economic development based on exploitative **colonisation** of LICs. From the mid-twentieth century, the gaining of LIC independence has often been difficult, resulting in ethnic rivalries, power struggles, civil wars, and corruption, all of which continue to hold back development.

Consequences of unequal development: disparities in wealth

Imbalances in development exist both between countries and within them.

- The highest levels of wealth are found in the most developed regions, e.g., 34% of global wealth is found in North America (**Figure 1**).

- Of the NEEs, growth since 2000 has been highest in China, and personal wealth in India and China has quadrupled.

- Africa's share of global wealth remains very small (about 1%), despite having over 12% of the world's population.

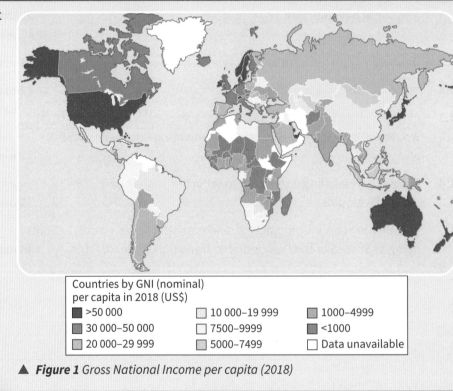

Countries by GNI (nominal) per capita in 2018 (US$)
■ >50 000	□ 10 000–19 999	▨ 1000–4999
▨ 30 000–50 000	□ 7500–9999	■ <1000
▨ 20 000–29 999	▨ 5000–7499	□ Data unavailable

▲ *Figure 1 Gross National Income per capita (2018)*

Key terms | Make sure you can write a definition for these key terms

colonisation   commodities   displaced persons   economic migrants
landlocked   multicultural   refugees   trade

Consequences of unequal development: disparities in health

Countries with a low level of development tend to experience poorer health care, with uneven access to doctors, clinics, and hospitals. Infectious diseases dominate, in contrast to degenerative diseases in HICs.

	LICs	HICs
Infants	High infant mortality	Low infant mortality
Children	4 in every 10 deaths	Only 1 in every 100 deaths
Elderly	2 in every 10 deaths	7 in every 10 deaths
Main causes of death	Infectious diseases (e.g., HIV/AIDS, diarrhoea, tuberculosis)	Chronic, degenerative diseases of affluence (e.g., cancer, heart disease, diabetes, and dementia)

Consequences of unequal development: international migration

Migration is the movement of people from place to place – whether by choice (voluntary) or forced (e.g., **displaced persons** fleeing their homes, but staying in their country of origin).

International migration (immigration and emigration) is one of the main consequences of uneven development, as people seek to improve their quality of life.

International migration

Voluntary

Economic migrants
moving voluntarily to seek a better life, such as a better-paid job

Forced

Refugees
forced from their countries of origin, due to conflict or natural disaster

▶ **Figure 2** *Diagram of international migration*

Economic migration to the UK

The (**multicultural**) UK has a long history of accepting migrants from all over the world:

- Until 2020, most **economic migrants** came from EU countries such as Poland.

- Many economic sectors, such as agriculture, hospitality, and health care, relied on these migrants.

- Following Brexit in 2020, many migrants returned home, creating worker shortages in these sectors, and reducing taxation revenue to the UK government.

Syrian refugee crisis

Since 2011, an estimated 6.6 million people have fled Syria due to an ongoing civil war, representing 25% of the world's **refugees**.

Retrieval

Learn the answers to the questions below, then cover the answers column with a piece of paper and write down as many as you can. Check and repeat.

Questions

		Answers
1	What are the physical causes of uneven development?	extreme climatic and weather conditions; lack of clean water sources; landlocked countries cut off from sea trade; harsh relief
2	What are the economic causes of uneven development?	poverty preventing improvements to education, infrastructure, and living conditions; trade stacked in favour of richer countries
3	What are the historical causes of uneven development?	many European HICs have a long history of development based on exploitative colonisation of LICs, many of which since gaining independence have suffered from ethnic rivalries, power struggles, civil wars, and corruption
4	What are the main causes of death in LICs?	infectious diseases (e.g., HIV/AIDS, diarrhoea, tuberculosis)
5	What are the main causes of death in HICs?	chronic, degenerative diseases of affluence (e.g., cancer, heart disease, diabetes, and dementia)
6	What is a displaced person?	a person forced to flee their home, but staying in their country of origin
7	What is immigration?	coming into a foreign country to live there permanently
8	What is emigration?	leaving your own country to settle permanently in another
9	What is an economic migrant?	a migrant moving voluntarily to seek a better life, such as a better-paid job
10	What is a refugee?	a person forced from their country of origin, often because of conflict or a natural disaster

Put paper here (repeated in centre column)

Previous questions

		Answers
1	What is meant by development?	the progress a country has made in terms of economic growth, use of technology, and human welfare
2	What is the Human Development Index (HDI)?	a social measure of development, considering income, life expectancy, and years in education
3	Name three things that indicate quality of life.	all the variables contributing to human welfare, including happiness, material wealth and possessions, safety, security, freedom, voting rights, good health, and so on
4	What is the dependency ratio?	the proportion of people below and above normal working age; the lower the ratio, the more workers there are (and so less dependency)

Put paper here (repeated in centre column)

Exam-style questions

Study **Figure 1**, a scattergraph showing Gross National Income (GNI) and the Human Development Index (HDI) for selected countries in 2020.

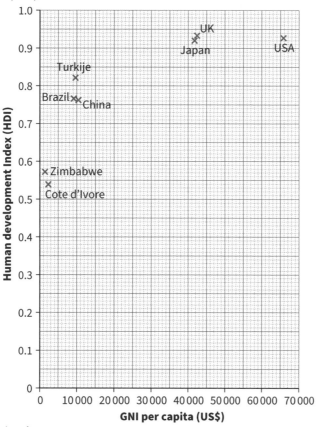

▲ *Figure 1*

1.1 Plot the following data onto **Figure 1**.   **[1 mark]**

Country	GNI (US$ per person per year)	Human Development Index
Bangladesh	1940	0.632

1.2 Draw a best-fit line on **Figure 1**.   **[1 mark]**

1.3 Outline any relationships in the data in **Figure 1**.   **[2 marks]**

1.4 Compare the main causes of death in LICs with those in HICs.   **[3 marks]**

1.5 Outline physical causes of uneven development.   **[4 marks]**

1.6 State **two** ways in which climate and weather can affect economic development.   **[2 marks]**

1.7 What is the difference between an economic migrant and a refugee? **[2 marks]**

1.8 Explain how physical and historical factors can cause uneven development.   **[6 marks]**

Questions referring to previous content

2.1 Suggest how the shape of a country's population pyramid might change between Stages 2 and 4 of the Demographic Transition Model (DTM).   **[2 marks]**

2.2 Explain the reasons for your answer to **2.1**.   **[4 marks]**

> **LINK**
>
> To understand the skill of constructing and reading a scattergraph, see the Geographical Skills section, page 229.

> **EXAM TIP**
>
> *Compare* as a command word requires you to identify similarities and differences. Use data in support of your answer.

29 Reducing the development gap

Eight strategies to reduce the development gap

1 Investment

Both countries and **transnational corporations (TNCs)** invest money and expertise in LICs to increase their profits. This supports LIC development by providing work, training, new industries, and infrastructure. For example, 10 000 Chinese companies now operate in Africa – many are involved in massive infrastructure projects, including railways, port developments, and communications.

2 Industrial development

Industrial development can generate a **multiplier effect**, bringing employment, higher incomes, and opportunities to invest in housing, education, and infrastructure (**Figure 1**).

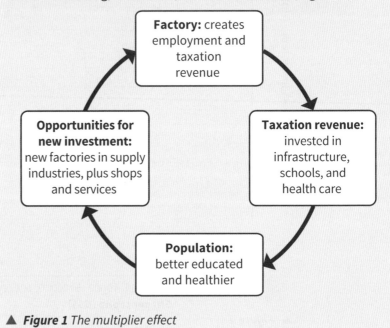

▲ **Figure 1** The multiplier effect

3 Fair trade

Richer countries benefit more from world trade than poorer countries, which explains why in some cases the development gap is widening. Rich countries protect their trade using:

- **tariffs** (taxes) paid on imports, making imported goods more expensive and less attractive than home-produced goods

- **quotas** limiting the quantity of goods that can be imported

- **subsidies:** government grants to less competitive sectors, such as agriculture, making their products cheaper than those produced by poorer countries.

Free trade refers to trade without tariffs or quotas, which has the potential to help poorer countries and reduce the development gap.

Trading groups (e.g., the EU) are countries which have grouped together to increase trade between them by cutting tariffs and discouraging trade with non-members (**Figure 2**).

Fairtrade is an international movement that sets standards for trade and environmentally friendly production. It helps to invest in local development projects and encourages participation in community cooperatives to ensure that farmers in LICs get a fair price for their produce.

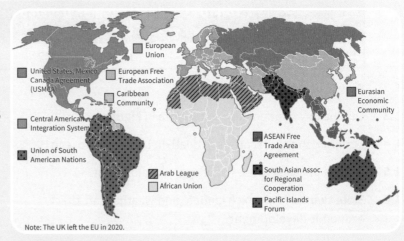

Note: The UK left the EU in 2020.

▲ **Figure 2** Global trading groups in 2019

WATCH OUT

Take care not to confuse *fair trade*, as in making trade fairer, with the *Fairtrade* movement that is helping producers in LICs and NEEs achieve sustainable and equitable trade relationships.

4 Tourism

For some countries (e.g., those with tropical beaches, spectacular landscapes, or abundant wildlife) tourism has led to investment and increased income from abroad, which can be used for improving education, infrastructure, and housing.

Case study: Tourism in Jamaica

Jamaica is one of the largest islands in the Caribbean, boasting an all-year-round tropical climate, stunning sandy beaches, a rich cultural heritage, excellent air and sea communications, and wonderful flora and fauna (**Figure 3**). Tourism, along with bauxite and oil, is one of the few growth sectors in its struggling economy, helping to raise the level of development and reducing the development gap. Income from tourism raises over US$2 billion every year – 35% of Jamaica's **Gross Domestic Product (GDP)** in 2019 – and this is expected to rise in the future.

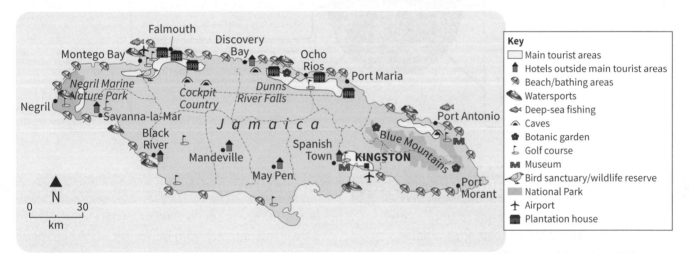

▲ *Figure 3* Tourist attractions in Jamaica

Other impacts of tourism on Jamaica's development include:

- employment: jobs for 200 000 people in hotels, shops, transport, agriculture, etc.
- infrastructure: improved to support the tourism sector, such as the new port and cruise-liner facilities at Trelawney
- quality of life: the main tourist areas, such as Montego Bay (**Figure 3**), still demonstrate marked contrasts in wealth and poverty
- the environment: improved by conservation, landscaping, designated nature parks, water treatment projects, and sustainable **ecotourism**; degraded by footpath erosion, excessive waste, and harmful cruise-liner emissions.

 Key terms Make sure you can write a definition for these key terms

debt crisis   ecotourism   GDP   intermediate technology
microfinance   multiplier effect   quotas
subsidies   tariffs   TNCs

SPECIFICATION TIP

You need a named example of how the growth of tourism in an LIC or NEE has helped to reduce the development gap. A case study you may have studied is given here.

WATCH OUT

Always think about whether impacts are positive or negative. For example, most of the impacts here are positive, but marked contrasts in wealth and poverty, and environmental degradation are definite negatives.

REVISION TIP

Learning key 'standout' case study facts, statistics, locations, etc., will help you access the highest marks in level-marked exam questions.

29 Reducing the development gap

5 Aid

Aid is money, goods, or services given by governments or non-governmental organisations (NGOs) to help improve the quality of life and the economy of another country. For example, Pakistan receives more aid from the UK than from any other country. It is spent mainly in education, and to reduce hunger and poverty.

Short-term: emergency aid following a disaster, e.g., tents and medicines

Tied: aid coming with conditions, e.g., trade deals with the donor country

Multilateral: rich countries giving money to international organisations (e.g., the World Bank) to redistribute

Types of aid

Long-term: sustainable aid to improve resilience, e.g., improvements to agriculture

Voluntary: money donated by the public, and distributed by NGOs (e.g., Oxfam)

Bilateral: aid from one country to another (often tied)

6 Intermediate technology

Intermediate technology refers to small-scale, sustainable technology projects appropriate to the needs, skills, knowledge, and wealth of local communities. Such projects create employment opportunities well-suited to the local environment.

7 Microfinance

Microfinance is small-scale financial support that is available directly from banks, set up to help poor people start businesses and become self-sufficient. For example, the Grameen Bank (a microfinance provider in Bangladesh) now has over 9 million members, 96% of which are women.

8 Debt relief

Many of the world's poorest countries are in a **debt crisis**, where they are unable to repay loans that were taken out in the 1970s and 1980s. These are highly indebted poor countries (HIPCs) with the highest levels of poverty and debt (**Figure 4**). In 2005, the world's richest countries (the G7) agreed to cancel the debts of HIPCs (debt relief), if they could demonstrate:

- they could manage their own finances
- no corruption
- a willingness to spend the saved money on education, health care, and reducing poverty.

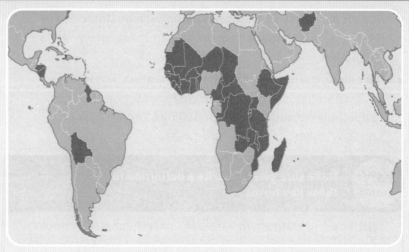

▲ **Figure 4** The world's highly indebted poor countries (HIPCs) in 2020

Learn the answers to the questions below, then cover the answers column with
a piece of paper and write down as many as you can. Check and repeat.

Questions | Answers

	Questions		Answers
1	What are transnational corporations (TNCs)?	Put paper here	large companies that have operations (e.g., factories, offices, research and development) in more than one country
2	What are the positive impacts of developing tourism in LICs and NEEs?		wealth generation by creating taxation revenue and employment; developing infrastructure to benefit both locals and visitors; improving the environment
3	Give three negative impacts of developing tourism in LICs and NEEs.	Put paper here	tourist areas attracting the most investment and generating the most wealth, leaving poorer areas relatively worse off; environmental degradation by footpath erosion, excessive waste, and harmful emissions
4	What is ecotourism?		nature tourism, usually involving small groups with minimal impact on the environment
5	What is intermediate technology?	Put paper here	small-scale, sustainable technology projects appropriate to the needs, skills, knowledge, and wealth of local communities
6	What is free trade?		trade without tariffs (import taxes) or quotas (limits on the quantity of goods that can be imported) – with the potential to help poorer countries and reduce the development gap
7	What is Fairtrade?	Put paper here	an international movement setting standards for trade and environmentally friendly production
8	What is microfinance?		small-scale financial support that is available directly from banks, set up to help poor people start businesses and become self-sufficient

Previous questions | Answers

	Previous questions		Answers
1	What are the physical causes of uneven development?	Put paper here	extreme climatic and weather conditions; lack of clean water sources; landlocked countries cut off from sea trade; harsh relief
2	What are the economic causes of uneven development?		poverty preventing improvements to education, infrastructure, and living conditions; trade stacked in favour of richer countries
3	What are the historical causes of uneven development?	Put paper here	many European HICs have a long history of development based on exploitative colonisation of LICs, many of which since gaining independence have suffered from ethnic rivalries, power struggles, civil wars, and corruption

Practice

1.1 Which statement best describes a benefit of transnational corporation (TNC) investment into LICs and NEEs? Shade **one** circle only. **[1 mark]**

    A   TNCs have been known to create poor working conditions. ◯

    B   TNCs provide work, training, and infrastructure. ◯

    C   TNC profits are often returned to their country of origin. ◯

    D   TNCs may bring in managers from other countries. ◯

1.2 What is the meaning of 'the multiplier effect'? **[3 marks]**

1.3 Outline **two** negative impacts of tourism in an LIC or NEE. **[2 marks]**

1.4 Explain the role of fair trade in reducing the development gap. **[4 marks]**

1.5 Suggest reasons why microfinance and intermediate technology are important for reducing the development gap. **[4 marks]**

1.6 Explain the role of aid in reducing the development gap. **[6 marks]**

> **EXAM TIP** ◎
>
> You will need to consider different forms of aid in your answer. Use examples if they help you to illustrate or clarify any point.

> **EXAM TIP** ◎
>
> *To what extent* as a command requires you to judge the importance of something. Make sure you present evidence in support of your judgements, and refer to both positive and negative impacts.

1.7 To what extent can industrial development and tourism reduce the development gap? **[9 marks]**
[+3 SPaG marks]

Study **Figure 1**, an article about an aid project in Ethiopia.

An aid project in Ethiopia

Adis Nifas is a village in northern Ethiopia, North Africa. A small dam has been built using local stones to create a reservoir close to the village's fields. Each family has been given an area of irrigated land with fruit trees. Treadle pumps (human-powered suction pumps) have been provided to lift water to the fields. Elephant grass is grown to divide the fields and help prevent soil erosion. The irrigated land is now providing a permanent food supply for the villagers.

▲ *Figure 1*

2.1 Which one of the statements below best describes this aid project? Shade **one** circle only. **[1 mark]**

    A   Large-scale aid raising levels of development ◯

    B   Small-scale aid raising levels of development ◯

    C   Short-term sustainable aid using intermediate technology ◯

    D   Long-term sustainable aid using intermediate technology ◯

2.2   Explain how tourism can reduce the development gap.   **[6 marks]**

2.3   Explain the role of debt relief in reducing the development gap.   **[4 marks]**

Look at **Figure 2**, the Fairtrade logo.

▲ *Figure 2*

2.4   Outline the role of the international Fairtrade movement.   **[3 marks]**

Questions referring to previous content

3.1   Explain how economic factors can cause uneven development.   **[3 marks]**

3.2   Compare the disparities in health between HICs and LICs.   **[4 marks]**

Knowledge

30 The changing economic world: a case study (1)

📖 Case study: A newly emerging economy: Nigeria

What is Nigeria's location and importance?

Nigeria is a **newly emerging economy** (**NEE**) in West Africa (**Figure 1**). It has global importance:

- Ranked the world's 27th largest economy (2020)
- Supplying 2.2% of the world's oil (the 15th largest producer)
- A diverse economy
- A major contributor to UN peacekeeping missions

Nigeria also has regional importance:

- One of the fastest-growing economies in Africa
- Africa's highest Gross Domestic Product (GDP) and third largest manufacturing sector (2020)
- The largest population of any African country
- Africa's highest farm output and number of cattle

Nigeria retains some characteristics of LICs: a lack of infrastructure, with poor roads and frequent power cuts, and 35% of the population (2020) still employed in agriculture (mostly **subsistence farming**). But the country has developed over recent decades.

SPECIFICATION TIP

You need a named example of economic development in an LIC or NEE. A case study you may have studied is given here.

▲ **Figure 1** The location of Nigeria

REVISION TIP

Think about which statistics have the most impact. Which two of the bullet points would you highlight and learn?

Political, social, cultural, and environmental aspects of Nigeria

Political context
• Former UK colony that gained independence in 1960
• Political instability and civil war followed independence
• Stable government since 1999, encouraging overseas investment

Social context
• Multi-ethnic and multi-faith country
• More recent religious and ethnic tensions (e.g., the Islamic fundamentalist group Boko Haram) have destabilised the economy

Cultural context
• Music (e.g., Fela Kuti)
• A large film industry (known as 'Nollywood')
• Literature (e.g., Wole Soyinka)
• Sport: won the African Cup of Nations (football) three times

Environmental context
• Natural environment ranges from tropical rainforest in the south to semi-desert in the north
• Pests and diseases (e.g., Tsetse fly – lethal to livestock)
• 14% of rainforest lost between 2005 and 2020

Nigeria's economy

Industrial structure shows the proportion of the workforce employed in different sectors: primary (agriculture), secondary (manufacturing industry) and tertiary (services) **(Figure 2)**.

Nigeria's industrial structure is changing:

- Employment in agriculture is declining due to increased mechanisation and rural–urban migration.
- Manufacturing is growing rapidly.
- There is rapid growth of communications, retail, and finance (all expanding the service sector).

Oil and gas account for 90% of Nigeria's export earnings. Nigeria may have a diverse and largely developed economy, but it is not a balanced one.

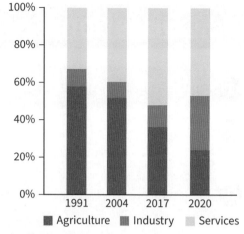

▲ **Figure 2** Nigeria's employment structure, 1991–2020

Manufacturing in Nigeria

In 2020, manufacturing accounted for about 13% of Nigeria's GDP. The sector's growth stimulates further economic development through:

- multiplier effects
- providing regular, secure incomes and therefore tax revenues
- using oil for chemical industries, including plastics and detergents.

Transnational corporations (TNCs) in Nigeria

Around 40 TNCs operate in Nigeria, with the majority headquartered in the UK, USA, and Europe. They bring advantages and disadvantages:

Advantages of TNCs in Nigeria	Disadvantages of TNCs in Nigeria
They provide employment, training, and the development of new skills.	Working conditions may be poor and badly regulated.
They invest in local infrastructure, services, and education.	Wages may be low with management jobs often held by foreign employees.
They stimulate the multiplier effect (supply industries, etc.).	Environmental damage may be caused.
Their revenues earn the government income from export taxes.	Most of the profits go abroad.

Shell in the Niger Delta

Shell's investment in Nigeria has been controversial. It employs thousands, pays taxes, awards contracts to Nigerian companies, and has built natural gas plants and invested in health care, education, and renewable energy projects (e.g., solar power). But most of its oil is exported unrefined, production is lost through sabotage and theft, and environmental degradation contaminates soils and pollutes the Niger Delta, impacting agriculture and fishing.

Key terms **Make sure you can write a definition for these key terms**

industrial structure
NEE   subsistence farming

Retrieval

Learn the answers to the questions below, then cover the answers column with a piece of paper and write down as many as you can. Check and repeat.

Questions | Answers

#	Questions	Answers
1	What is a newly emerging economy (NEE)?	countries experiencing higher rates of economic development, with a rapid growth of industrialisation
2	What is subsistence farming?	agriculture that produces only enough food and materials for the benefit of a farmer and their family
3	What indicates Nigeria's global importance?	it is ranked the world's 27th largest economy (2020) and 15th largest producer of oil. It is also a diverse economy and is a major contributor to UN peacekeeping missions around the world
4	What indicates Nigeria's regional importance?	it is one of the fastest-growing economies in Africa, with Africa's highest GDP and third largest manufacturing sector (2020)
5	What is a country's industrial structure?	the proportion of the workforce employed in different industrial sectors – primary (agriculture and mining), secondary (manufacturing), and tertiary (services)
6	How does the growth of manufacturing stimulate economic development in Nigeria?	through multiplier effects (encouraging further growth); by providing regular, secure incomes and therefore tax revenues; by using Nigerian oil for chemical industries, including plastics and detergents
7	What are the advantages of transnational corporations (TNCs) operating in LICs and NEEs?	they provide employment, training, and the development of new skills; they invest in local infrastructure, services, and education; they stimulate multiplier effects; their revenues earn government income from export taxes
8	What are the disadvantages of TNCs operating in LICs and NEEs?	working conditions may be poor and badly regulated, with low wages and higher-paid management jobs often held by foreign employees; environmental damage may be caused; most of the profits go abroad
9	What are the advantages of Shell operating in Nigeria?	they employ thousands; pay taxes; award contracts to Nigerian companies; invest into health care, education, and renewable energy projects
10	What are the disadvantages of Shell operating in Nigeria?	most of its oil is exported unrefined; production is lost through sabotage and theft; it contaminates soils and pollutes the Niger Delta

Put paper here

Previous questions | Answers

#	Previous questions	Answers
1	What are the main causes of death in LICs?	infectious diseases (e.g., HIV/AIDS, diarrhoea, tuberculosis)
2	What are the main causes of death in HICs?	chronic, degenerative diseases of affluence (e.g., cancer, heart disease, diabetes, and dementia)

Put paper here

Exam-style questions

Study **Figure 1**, a map of West Africa.

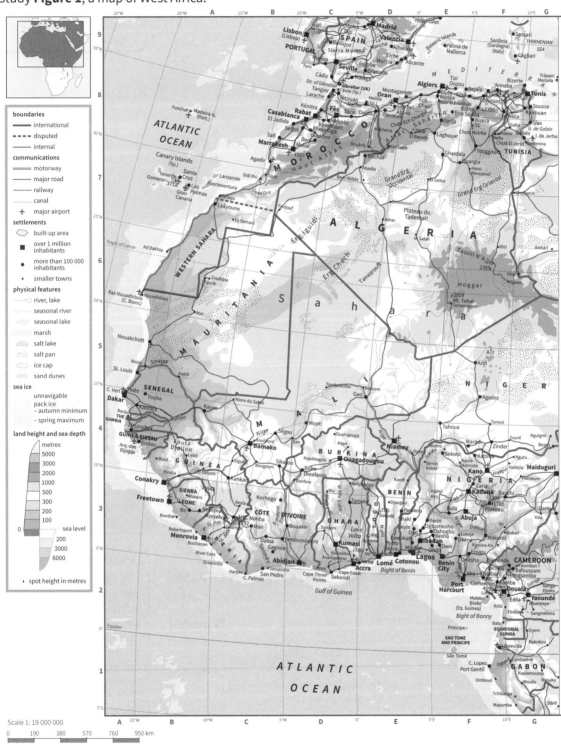

▲ *Figure 1*

1.1 Using **Figure 1**, name the major city found at 6° 27' N 3° 28' E. **[1 mark]**

1.2 Using **Figure 1**, name the upland area found around 9° 54' N 8° 53' E. **[1 mark]**

1.3 Using **Figure 1**, state how physical relief is shown on the map. **[1 mark]**

LINK

To understand the skill of reading an atlas map, see the Geographical Skills section, page 224.

Exam-style questions

1.4 Using **Figure 1**, state the scale of this map. **[1 mark]**

2.1 Use the data in **Figure 2**, which shows urban population in Nigeria, West Africa, to complete the graph. **[1 mark]**

LINK

To understand the skill of constructing and reading a line graph, see the Geographical Skills section, page 228.

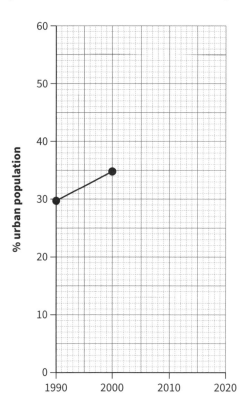

▼ *Figure 2*

Year	% urban population
2020	52.0
2010	43.6

2.2 Using **Figure 2**, outline how the trend on this graph might relate to Nigeria's changing industrial structure. **[3 marks]**

2.3 For a named LIC or NEE you have studied, describe its global importance. **[3 marks]**

2.4 Explain how the manufacturing industry can stimulate economic development in a named NEE or LIC. **[4 marks]**

2.5 To what extent do transnational corporations (TNCs) operating in LICs or NEEs bring both advantages and disadvantages? **[9 marks]**
[+3 SPaG marks]

3.1 What is a transnational corporation (TNC)? **[2 marks]**

3.2 Outline the advantages of transnational corporations (TNCs) operating in LICs or NEEs. **[4 marks]**

3.3 Outline the main characteristics of the natural environmental regions of a named NEE or LIC. **[3 marks]**

3.4 Describe the regional importance of a named LIC or NEE. **[4 marks]**

3.5 Assess the importance of Nigeria globally and its significance to the rest of Africa. **[6 marks]**

Questions referring to previous content

4.1 Outline the difference between fair trade and Fairtrade. **[3 marks]**

4.2 Explain how HICs protect their trade. **[4 marks]**

EXAM TIP

Explain as a command word requires you to give reasons why something is the case.

EXAM TIP

While general points are useful (weighing up how TNCs bring both advantages and disadvantages), specific evidence (facts, figures, and named examples) based upon TNC operations in a named LIC or NEE is essential to access the highest levels of the mark scheme.

31 The changing economic world: a case study (2)

 Case study: A newly emerging economy: Nigeria

Nigeria's changing political links

Until 1960, Nigeria was part of the British Empire. Now it is a member of the British **Commonwealth** and a leading member of other political and economic groups:

- UN (United Nations) – peacekeeping role
- WTO (World Trade Organisation) – promoting free trade
- OPEC (Organisation of the Petroleum Exporting Countries)
- African Union – economic and peacekeeping role
- ECOWAS (Economic Community of West African States) – trade group
- CEN–SAD (Community of Sahel–Saharan States) – trade and sporting links.

Nigeria's global trading relationships

Nigeria is a major global trading nation. Its main **imports** include refined oil from the EU and the USA, cars from Brazil and the USA, and telephones from China. Its main **exports** include crude oil, natural gas, rubber, cocoa, and cotton. However, high-quality (low sulphur) crude oil (petroleum) dominates Nigeria's exports, reducing the importance of Nigeria's agricultural products.

Why does Nigeria still receive international aid?

Despite rapid economic growth, poverty remains common in Nigeria. Over 60% of the population lives on less than US$1 (£0.63) a day. Birth rates and infant mortality rates are high, and life expectancy is low. This is particularly true in rural areas (with limited access to services such as safe water, sanitation, and a reliable electricity supply) and in the sprawling squatter settlements of large cities like Lagos.

Consequently, Nigeria receives aid. But official aid has been less successful than long-term sustainable aid delivered direct to communities, owing to:

- high levels of corruption
- previous and current governments using aid money for other purposes (e.g., defence)
- donors having political influence over what happens to aid
- money often being used to promote the commercial self-interest of the donor.

> **SPECIFICATION TIP**
>
> You need a named example of economic development in an LIC or NEE. A case study you may have studied is given here.

> **REVISION TIP**
>
> The 5Ws – What, Where, When, Why, and Who? – can help you structure your revision. Make sure you keep them at the front of your mind.

31 The changing economic world: a case study (2)

Nigeria's environmental problems

- Economic growth: this can bring many benefits. But it can also have a negative impact on the environment.
- Urban growth: leads to squatter settlements in most urban areas. Traffic congestion and waste disposal add to the challenges.

- Commercial farming and deforestation: lead to land degradation and a reduction in biodiversity.
- Mining and oil extraction: tin mining leads to soil erosion and water pollution by toxic chemicals. The oil industry is associated with oil spills, fires increasing CO_2 emissions, and **acid rain** damaging ecosystems.

Air pollution: excessive air pollution causes respiratory and heart problems

Chemical waste: when dumped on land, this pollutes groundwater

Desertification: a major problem, made worse by irrigation and large-scale dam schemes

Negative impacts of economic growth on the environment

Harmful industrial pollutants: these go directly into open drains and water channels, damaging ecosystems

Deforestation: 96% of Nigeria's forests have been destroyed through logging, agriculture, urban expansion, and industrial development

Quality of life in Nigeria

Quality of life is commonly measured by the Human Development Index (HDI) (see **Figure 1**, page 154). Nigeria's HDI has been increasing steadily since 2005, but poverty is still endemic. Thirty years ago, Nigeria was at a similar stage of development to Malaysia and Singapore. But since then, these two countries have developed economically far ahead of Nigeria, despite Nigeria's huge oil revenues. Corruption has been a major problem and oil wealth has not been used to diversify the economy as much as it could have been.

Will quality of life continue to improve?

Continuing improvements to Nigerians' quality of life will depend on:

- political will: a stable government will encourage inward investment
- environmental awareness: investment to tackle pollution, pests (such as the Tsetse fly), and desertification
- social tolerance: efforts to resolve tribal and religious differences.

Key terms Make sure you can write a definition for these key terms

acid rain   Commonwealth
exports   imports

Learn the answers to the questions below, then cover the answers column with
a piece of paper and write down as many as you can. Check and repeat.

Questions | Answers

	Questions		Answers
1	What is the Commonwealth?		a voluntary association of 53 independent and equal sovereign states (most being former UK colonies)
2	What are exports?	Put paper here	goods or services sent to another country for sale
3	What are imports?		goods or services brought into a country from abroad for sale
4	Why does Nigeria still receive international aid?	Put paper here	despite rapid economic growth, poverty remains endemic in Nigeria; birth rates and infant mortality rates are high, and life expectancy is low (in rural areas and in urban squatter settlements)
5	What prevents international aid to Nigeria being used effectively?		corruption; aid money being used for other purposes; donors having political influence over what happens to aid
6	What environmental problems are caused by Nigeria's rapid economic growth?	Put paper here	excessive air pollution; industrial pollutants damaging ecosystems; chemical waste polluting groundwater; extensive deforestation; desertification made worse by irrigation and large-scale dam schemes
7	What environmental problems are associated with Nigeria's urban growth?		sprawling squatter settlements in most urban areas; traffic congestion; waste disposal
8	What environmental problems are associated with Nigeria's commercial farming?	Put paper here	land degradation; reduction in biodiversity; soil erosion
9	What environmental problems are associated with Nigeria's mineral and oil extraction?		water pollution by toxic chemicals; oil spills; fires increasing CO_2 emissions; acid rain damaging ecosystems

Previous questions | Answers

	Previous questions		Answers
1	What is a country's industrial structure?	Put paper here	the proportion of the workforce employed in different industrial sectors – primary (agriculture and mining), secondary (manufacturing), and tertiary (services)
2	What are the advantages of TNCs operating in LICs and NEEs?		they provide employment, training, and the development of new skills; they invest in local infrastructure, services, and education; they stimulate multiplier effects; their revenues earn government income from export taxes
3	What are the disadvantages of TNCs operating in LICs and NEEs?	Put paper here	working conditions may be poor and badly regulated, with low wages and higher-paid management jobs often held by foreign employees; environmental damage may be caused; most of the profits go abroad

Practice

Look at **Figure 1**, a photograph of rubbish dumped along a Nigerian roadside, West Africa.

▲ *Figure 1*

1.1 Describe the waste that has been dumped in **Figure 1**. **[2 marks]**

1.2 Outline the environmental problems that might result from the waste dump shown in **Figure 1**. **[3 marks]**

1.3 Describe the causes of environmental problems in a named LIC or NEE. **[4 marks]**

1.4 For a named LIC or NEE you have studied, identify the purpose of **three** political and/or economic groups of which it is a member. **[3 marks]**

1.5 Outline the global trading relationships of a named LIC or NEE. **[3 marks]**

1.6 How has international aid benefitted poor people in a named LIC or NEE? **[4 marks]**

1.7 Assess the extent to which economic development has improved the quality of people's lives in a named LIC or NEE. **[9 marks] [+3 SPaG marks]**

> **EXAM TIP** ◎
>
> *Identify* as a command word requires you to name an example.

> **EXAM TIP** ◎
>
> In some 9-mark questions there are 3 extra marks available for SPaG (spelling, punctuation, grammar, and use of specialist terminology). The full 3 marks will be awarded if your spelling and punctuation are accurate, your meaning is clear, and you have used a wide range of specialist terms.

Study **Figures 2** and **3**, which show Gross National Income (per capita) and employment in agriculture for selected African countries (2019).

▼ *Figure 2*

Country	GNI per capita (US$)	Employment in agriculture (%)
Nigeria	5710	37
Ghana	4650	41
Sierra Leone	1490	61
Cameroon	3700	62
Togo	1780	38
South Africa	3250	6
Kenya	3440	38
Uganda	1970	69
Niger	1300	75
Tanzania	3160	67

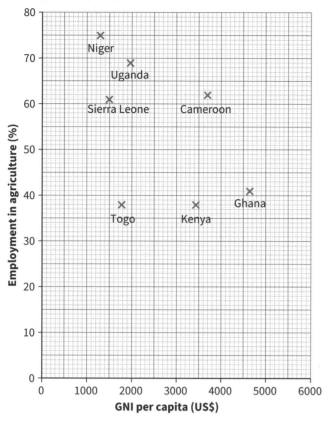

▲ *Figure 3*

2.1 Use the data in **Figure 2** to plot Nigeria, South Africa, and Tanzania onto the scattergraph. **[1 mark]**

2.2 Draw a trend line on the scattergraph. **[1 mark]**

2.3 Draw a circle around each of the residuals on the scattergraph. **[1 mark]**

2.4 Describe the relationship between Gross National Income (GNI) and employment in agriculture. **[2 marks]**

2.5 Is the answer to **2.4** what you expected to find? Why? **[2 marks]**

2.6 Suggest reasons for the anomalies (residuals). **[3 marks]**

2.7 For a named LIC or NEE you have studied, describe the changes in the country's industrial structure. **[3 marks]**

2.8 What are the different types of international aid? **[4 marks]**

2.9 Explain the harmful environmental impacts of economic development in a named LIC or NEE. **[6 marks]**

Questions referring to previous content

3.1 Outline the disadvantages of transnational corporations (TNCs) operating in LICs or NEEs. **[4 marks]**

3.2 Discuss the advantages and disadvantages of transnational corporations (TNCs) operating in LICs or NEEs. **[9 marks]**
[+3 SPaG marks]

> **LINK**
>
> To understand the skill of constructing and reading scattergraphs, see the Geographical Skills section, page 229.

> **EXAM TIP**
>
> *Discuss* as a command word requires you to give points on both sides of an argument. So, examine both the advantages and disadvantages in some detail before coming to a conclusion as to whether TNC involvement in LICs or NEEs is, overall, good, bad, or a mixed blessing.

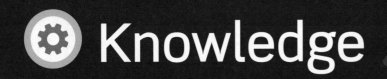

⚙ Knowledge

32 The changing UK economy: how and why has it changed?

How and why has the UK economy changed?

The UK has a **post-industrial economy**, where declining manufacturing industry has been replaced largely by tertiary and quaternary jobs (**Figure 1**). There are three main reasons for this change.

Deindustrialisation

The decline in the UK's traditional heavy industries is due to:

- machines and technology replacing people
- lack of investment, outdated machinery, and high labour costs
- competition from other countries (e.g., China) producing cheaper goods.

Globalisation

Globalisation is the growth and spread of ideas around the world, which is made possible by developments in transport, communications, and the internet.

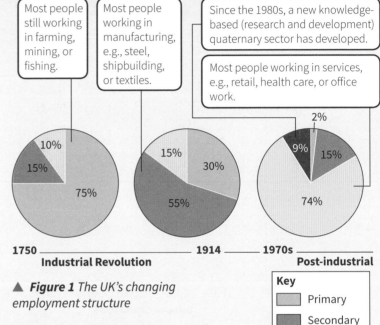

Most people still working in farming, mining, or fishing.

Most people working in manufacturing, e.g., steel, shipbuilding, or textiles.

Since the 1980s, a new knowledge-based (research and development) quaternary sector has developed.

Most people working in services, e.g., retail, health care, or office work.

▲ **Figure 1** The UK's changing employment structure

Key
- Primary
- Secondary
- Tertiary
- Quaternary

Government policies

1945–1979	State-run industries created to support outdated, unprofitable, declining sectors
1979–2010	**Privatisation** of these sectors to encourage competition, innovation, and change
2010 onwards	'Rebalancing' the economy by promoting high-tech industries and 'levelling up' to improve opportunities in less prosperous parts of the UK

The UK's post-industrial economy

Science and business parks

Science parks are where a group of scientific, technical knowledge-based businesses and support services locate on a single site, often associated with a university, enabling them to use the university's research facilities and employ their skilled graduates. **Business parks** are purpose-built areas occupied by a cluster of businesses, usually at the edge of an urban area, with good transport links.

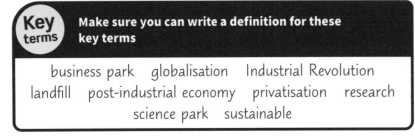

Key terms — Make sure you can write a definition for these key terms

business park   globalisation   Industrial Revolution
landfill   post-industrial economy   privatisation   research
science park   sustainable

The development of information technology

The UK is one of the world's leading digital economies and the UK government is committed to making the UK the world's best place to start a technology business. IT developments stimulate the growth of research, and specialist manufacturing and servicing jobs.

Research

Research in the UK (part of the quaternary sector) employs around 250 000 people. It is a major growth area in universities, private companies, charities, and government bodies.

Service industries and finance

The service sector (including finance) now contributes over 80% of the UK's GDP, and the UK is the world's leading centre for financial services.

WATCH OUT (!)

Don't think of science and business parks as completely separate things: they are similar and often overlap. For example, there are benefits to businesses having a close association with each other and sharing key infrastructure.

Environmental impacts of industry

Negative environmental impacts of industry are not solely a relic of the **Industrial Revolution**. Modern manufacturing industries and large-scale extraction industries (such as quarrying) can affect both the landscape and the environment:

- as unsightly eyesores
- by causing air and water pollution
- by adding waste products to **landfill**, introducing toxins into groundwater and soil.

But today there is a greater expectation for industries to be environmentally **sustainable**. This is achieved by:

- strict environmental targets on water quality, air pollution, and landscape damage
- technology to reduce harmful emissions (e.g., desulphurisation of heavy industry and power-station smoke)
- monitoring and regulation of industrial operations and quarrying
- strict planning guidelines on quarry blasting, removal of dust from roads, and restorative landscaping.

Torr quarry

Planned restoration

Torr Quarry, Mendip Hills, Somerset

- A nationally important limestone quarry, producing aggregate for construction and roads
- Monitored to control noise, dust, and water quality
- Being restored and landscaped to create wildlife lakes

Retrieval

Learn the answers to the questions below, then cover the answers column with
a piece of paper and write down as many as you can. Check and repeat.

Questions / Answers

#	Questions	Answers
1	How did the UK's employment structure change from the 18th century to 1914?	from a pre-industrial economy dominated by the primary sector, to a much larger secondary sector (manufacturing) due to the Industrial Revolution
2	How did the UK's employment structure change from 1914 to the 1980s?	increasing domination of tertiary (service) employment
3	How did the UK's employment structure change from the 1980s onwards?	development of today's post-industrial economy (with a strong quaternary sector)
4	What term is used for the growth and spread of ideas around the world, which is made possible by developments in transport, communications, and the internet?	globalisation
5	What is privatisation?	state-run industries are sold to private shareholders to create a more competitive business environment
6	What is a post-industrial economy?	where the manufacturing industry declines, to be replaced largely by growth in tertiary and quaternary jobs
7	What is a science park?	a group of scientific, technical knowledge-based businesses and support services on a single site
8	What is a business park?	an area of land occupied by a cluster of businesses that benefit from working together
9	What was the Industrial Revolution?	the period around 1750–1914 where an agriculturally based economy changed to mainly manufacturing
10	What is landfill?	the dumping of any waste (not recycled or reused) directly on the ground or in a disused quarry
11	How can industry adapt to become more sustainable?	adopt technology to reduce harmful emissions (e.g., desulphurisation of heavy industry and power-station smoke)
12	How does government force industry to become more sustainable?	setting strict environmental targets on water quality, air pollution, and landscape damage; monitoring and regulation of industrial operations and quarrying

Put paper here

Previous questions / Answers

#	Previous questions	Answers
1	What are exports?	goods or services sent to another country for sale
2	What are imports?	goods or services brought into a country from abroad for sale
3	What is subsistence farming?	agriculture that produces only enough food and materials for the benefit of a farmer and their family

Put paper here

Exam-style questions

Study **Figure 1**, line graphs showing changing industrial (employment) structure in England and Wales.

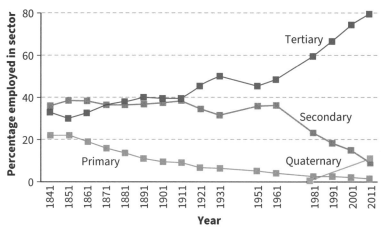

▲ *Figure 1*

1.1 Describe the trend for the primary sector shown in **Figure 1**. **[2 marks]**

1.2 Describe the trend for the tertiary sector shown in **Figure 1**. **[2 marks]**

1.3 Suggest connections and reasons for all four trends shown in **Figure 1**. **[4 marks]**

1.4 Define the term 'deindustrialisation'. **[2 marks]**

1.5 Discuss the causes of deindustrialisation in the UK. **[6 marks]**

1.6 Suggest how the UK might now best be described as a post-industrial economy. **[6 marks]**

2.1 Define the term 'quaternary sector'. **[2 marks]**

2.2 What is a post-industrial economy? **[2 marks]**

LINK

Line graphs are explained in the Geographical Skills section, page 228.

EXAM TIP

Describing graphs

When describing graphs, trends, examples, and anomalies (TEA) should be identified:

- **T**rends cover the general direction – use adjectives like rising, falling, steady, accelerating, etc.
- **E**xamples illustrate the general trend and should include the highest and lowest values.
- **A**nomalies should cover any exceptions to the general trend – examples that stand out as different, radical changes in gradient in line or bar graphs, etc.

You might even want to stretch the mnemonic further, to TEAM. **M** is for manipulation (making comparisons, calculating percentage increase or decrease, etc.).

EXAM TIP

Suggest as a command word requires you to give a well-reasoned guess to explain something where you can't be sure of the answer.

2.3 Compare science parks and business parks. **[3 marks]**

2.4 Explain how the development of information technology (IT) has contributed to the development of a post-industrial economy in the UK. **[4 marks]**

Study **Figure 2**, an aerial photograph of Cambridge Science Park, and **Figure 3**, selected key features of Cambridge Science Park.

▲ *Figure 2*

Selected key features of Cambridge Science Park

- Over 100 businesses
- Most are in biomedical research, IT, and telecommunications (high-tech, quaternary industries)
- New firms are attracted to this collection of similar firms by the prospect of networking and sharing ideas
- Cambridge University provides a steady supply of highly trained graduates to work at these firms
- 3 km from Cambridge city centre – with ready access to the A14 and M11
- 62 hectares of the park have been carefully landscaped to maintain a peaceful and serene environment
- 8 hectares of open, public space with benches and footpaths

▲ *Figure 3*

3.1 Describe **two** characteristics of the site of Cambridge Science Park. Use **Figure 2**, **Figure 3**, and your own understanding. **[2 marks]**

3.2 Suggest how science parks provide opportunities for regional economic growth. Use **Figure 2**, **Figure 3**, and your own understanding. **[4 marks]**

3.3 Why do science parks such as Cambridge Science Park form an important part of the UK post-industrial economy? **[6 marks]**

3.4 Describe how modern industrial development can be environmentally sustainable. **[4 marks]**

Questions referring to previous content

In 2020, the UK government spent £14.5 billion on overseas aid.

4.1 Which of the statements below is an example of international aid? Shade **one** circle only. **[1 mark]**

A	Tied	○	**C**	Multilateral	○
B	Bilateral	○	**D**	All of the above	○

4.2 Describe the problems often associated with international aid. (Refer to a named LIC or NEE you have studied if it clarifies your answer.) **[3 marks]**

33 The changing UK economy: social and economic change and transport

Social and economic changes in the UK's rural landscape

Rural landscapes are changing:
- Some, close to thriving towns and cities, are growing in population.
- Others are declining, as younger people move away to seek employment elsewhere.

South Cambridgeshire: an area of population growth

People migrate here from Cambridge, other parts of the UK, and Eastern Europe, including many highly skilled and well-educated people, mainly employed in high-tech industries, but the proportion of people over 65 is also growing.

Economic effects	Social effects
• Reduction in agricultural employment as farmers sell land for construction • Lack of affordable housing • Growing population puts pressure on services	• Commuters still use Cambridge services, negatively impacting the local rural economy • 80% car ownership reduces demand for (and so provision of) public transport • Modern developments and **gentrification** in villages breaks down community spirit

The Outer Hebrides: an area of population decline

Despite a small population increase in recent years, outward migration from the Outer Hebrides has more than halved the population since 1901.

Economic effects	Social effects
• Sheep farming is declining • Local deep-sea fishing has declined, but shell fishing has increased. Environmentally controversial fish farming is limited • Tourism is restricted by insufficient infrastructure, including poor ferry services	• School closures as pupil numbers fall • Fewer people of working age • An increasingly ageing population

Road and rail improvements

Government strategies aim to increase capacity and improve the condition of the UK's roads, including:
- new motorway and A-road links
- adding lanes and improving 'smart' motorways
- **levelling-up** strategies to improve access to the north.

The government's levelling-up agenda also involves rail improvements:
- TransPennine Route upgrade between Manchester and York
- HS2 (High Speed 2) – a planned high-speed rail line between London and Manchester
- completing Crossrail, improving cross-London journey times.

 Key terms Make sure you can write a definition for these key terms

container trade   gentrification
levelling-up   north—south divide

 # Knowledge

33 The changing UK economy: social and economic change and transport

Developing the UK's ports

The UK ports industry is the largest in Europe, due to the length of the coastline and the UK's long trading history. The ports handle both freight (e.g., **container trade**) and passengers. Major ports include:

- Felixstowe: the UK's busiest port, dealing with 48% of all container trade
- Southampton: dealing with freight, cars, and cruise-line passengers
- Grimsby (Immingham): operating Ro-Ro (roll-on, roll-off) cargo and passenger ferries
- Liverpool 2: a new container terminal doubling the port's capacity.

Developing the UK's airports

UK aviation (both passenger and freight) is crucial for:

- linking the UK with 114 countries worldwide
- contributing £22 billion to the UK's Gross Domestic Product (GDP)
- supporting about one million jobs.

Heathrow is the UK's busiest airport, with two runways, four terminals, and a capacity of 80 million passengers a year. But further expansion is needed and a report in 2015 recommended building a third runway (costing £18.6 billion), creating up to 77 000 local jobs. However, the recommendation is controversial given concerns over the necessary demolishing of homes, tunnelling of the M25, and additional long-term noise pollution.

The north–south divide

Look at **Figure 1**. The **north–south divide** refers to real or imagined cultural and economic differences between:

- the south of England (including Greater London, the south-east, the south-west, and parts of eastern England)
- the north of England and the rest of the UK.

The divide's origins lie in Industrial Revolution growth being centred on coalmining and associated heavy industry in the north, which has since declined due to deindustrialisation. Meanwhile, the south rapidly developed its service sector (and especially its financial centre in London).

Strategies to address the divide include government encouragement of business development in the north through:

- Enterprise Zones with simpler planning, business rate discounts, and allowances for plant and machinery
- financial support for foreign investors (e.g., Nissan in Tyne and Wear)
- local enterprise partnerships (e.g., Lancashire LEP)
- the levelling-up agenda.

▲ *Figure 1 The UK's north–south divide*

Learn the answers to the questions below, then cover the answers column with a piece of paper and write down as many as you can. Check and repeat.

Questions | Answers

#	Question	Answer
1	What is gentrification?	the improvement of built-up areas by individual property owners
2	What is the UK government's levelling-up agenda?	a programme aiming to spread opportunity more equally across the UK
3	What are the aims of the UK government's investment in roads?	increase traffic capacity; improve the condition of the UK's roads; boost local and regional economies; create thousands of jobs
4	What are the aims of the UK government's plans to improve the rail network?	TransPennine route between Manchester and York upgraded; a new high-speed rail line between London and Manchester (HS2); the completion of Crossrail, improving journey times across London
5	What are the functions of the UK's ports?	supporting trade with Europe and beyond, including container freight, Ro-Ro cargo, cars, and cruise-line passengers
6	What is the significance of UK aviation?	crucial to regional and national growth of the UK economy – linking the UK with 114 countries worldwide; contributing £22 billion to the UK's GDP; and supporting about one million jobs
7	What is the north–south divide?	real or imagined cultural and economic differences between the south of England, and the north of England and the rest of the UK
8	Give three strategies that address the north–south divide.	government encouragement of business development in the north, through Enterprise Zones with simpler planning, business rate discounts, and allowances for plant and machinery; financial support for foreign investors; local enterprise partnerships; the levelling-up agenda

Put paper here

Previous questions | Answers

#	Question	Answer
1	What is a post-industrial economy?	where the manufacturing industry declines, to be replaced largely by growth in tertiary and quaternary jobs
2	How can industry adapt to become more sustainable?	adopt technology to reduce harmful emissions (e.g., desulphurisation of harmful heavy industry and power-station smoke)
3	What is a transnational corporation (TNC)?	a large company that has operations (e.g., factories, offices, research and development) in more than one country

Put paper here

Practice

1.1 Outline **two** reasons why the UK port industry is the largest in Europe. **[2 marks]**

1.2 Outline the significance of aviation to the UK economy. **[3 marks]**

Study **Figure 1**, showing the M25 (London's orbital motorway), some sections of which are now 'smart' motorways.

> **EXAM TIP**
>
> *Outline* as a command word requires you to summarise the key points, so keep your answers 'punchy', and remember to support your answers with examples.

▲ *Figure 1*

1.3 Using **Figure 1** and your own understanding, suggest what road improvements can improve the UK's economy, and why. **[4 marks]**

1.4 Suggest reasons for the economic and social changes in the rural landscape in an area of population decline. **[6 marks]**

2.1 What is meant by the UK's north–south divide? **[3 marks]**

2.2 Outline **two** strategies that can be used to resolve regional differences. **[4 marks]**

2.3 Explain how developments in transport infrastructure can improve the UK's economy. **[6 marks]**

2.4 Explain the economic and social impacts on the rural landscape in an area of population growth. **[6 marks]**

3.1 Outline **three** examples of improving the UK rail network. **[3 marks]**

3.2 Suggest reasons why the UK's ports are so important to the UK economy. **[4 marks]**

> **EXAM TIP**
>
> *Suggest* as a command word requires you to give a well-reasoned guess to explain something where you can't be sure of the answer.

Questions referring to previous content

4.1 State **two** negative environmental impacts of large-scale industry. **[2 marks]**

4.2 Explain how governments can force large-scale industries to minimise their negative environmental impacts. **[4 marks]**

34 The changing UK economy: the UK and the wider world

What is the UK's place in the wider world?

The UK has significant global influence through its membership of the UN Security Council and the **G7**.

Trade: post-**Brexit**, the main trading partners are within the EU, although already strong links with the USA and China are likely to develop further.

Culture: including art, music, fashion, television, and film. The English language is globally important and so strengthens UK cultural links.

The UK's worldwide links

Transport: Heathrow is one of the biggest airports in the world, and mainland Europe is accessed by both ferries and the Channel Tunnel.

Electronic communication: around half of the world's population have internet access, and over 90% in the UK. 99% of all internet traffic passes along a network of submarine high-power cables, which are notably focused on the UK.

Economic and political links

The UK was a member of the **European Union** from 1973 to 2020. Goods, services, workers, and finance can move freely between EU member states, encouraging trade. The EU also financially supports agriculture, fisheries, and disadvantaged regions in member states.

In a June 2016 referendum, UK voters voted (narrowly) to leave the EU. It will take many years for the UK to determine its new relationship with the EU, and for the consequences to be fully established. Since Brexit, a free trade agreement between the UK and EU has been reached, but freedom of movement no longer exists. The UK is no longer subject to EU rules and regulations, but many working practices and standards remain mutually beneficial, so are likely to continue.

Links with the Commonwealth

The UK is a key country within the Commonwealth because most members were once British **colonies**. All members are represented by the Commonwealth Secretariat, which advises on all items of common interest, such as:

- trading, cultural, and sporting links
- economic and social development.

Key terms Make sure you can write a definition for these key terms

Brexit colonies European Union G7

Retrieval

Learn the answers to the questions below, then cover the answers column with
a piece of paper and write down as many as you can. Check and repeat.

Questions	Answers
1 Who is in the G7?	Canada, France, Germany, Italy, Japan, the UK, and the USA (these countries dominate the international financial system)
2 What is the G7?	an intergovernmental political forum
3 What percentage of the UK's population have access to the internet?	90%
4 What are colonies?	distant territories belonging to or under the control of another nation; UK colonies, before their independence, were part of the British Empire
5 What is the European Union (EU)?	an economic and political union of 27 European countries designed to establish peace, common agreements, and laws – to promote trade, and remove economic and social barriers
6 What is meant by the term Brexit?	an abbreviation of 'Britain' and 'exit', referring to the withdrawal process of the UK from the European Union (EU)

Put paper here

Previous questions

Previous questions	Answers
1 What is the UK government's levelling-up agenda?	a programme aiming to spread opportunity more equally across the UK
2 What are the functions of the UK's ports?	supporting trade with Europe and beyond, including container freight, Ro-Ro cargo, cars, and cruise-line passengers
3 What is the north–south divide?	real or imagined cultural and economic differences between the south of England, and the north of England and the rest of the UK
4 Give three strategies that address the north–south divide.	government encouragement of business development in the north, through Enterprise Zones with simpler planning, business rate discounts, and allowances for plant and machinery; financial support for foreign investors; local enterprise partnerships; and the levelling-up agenda
5 What is landfill?	the dumping of any waste (not recycled or reused) directly on the ground or in a disused quarry

Put paper here

Exam-style questions

Study **Figure 1**, the UK's major export destinations (2018).

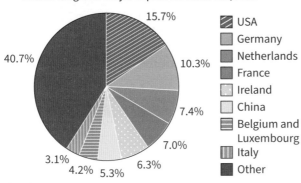

United Kingdom major export destinations, 2018

15.7%
40.7%
10.3%
7.4%
7.0%
3.1%
4.2%   5.3%   6.3%

- USA
- Germany
- Netherlands
- France
- Ireland
- China
- Belgium and Luxembourg
- Italy
- Other

▲ *Figure 1*

1.1   Using **Figure 1**, name the UK's top **three** export countries.   [1 mark]

1.2   Using **Figure 1**, calculate the total percentage of export trade going to the named European countries. Shade **one** circle only.   [1 mark]

A	17.7%	◯	**C**	27.8%	◯
B	24.7%	◯	**D**	38.3%	◯

1.3   Outline **two** cultural links between the UK and the wider world.   [2 marks]

1.4   Outline the UK's main trade links.   [2 marks]

1.5   Describe the UK's transport links with the rest of the world.   [4 marks]

1.6   Describe how the UK benefits from links with the European Union and the Commonwealth.   [6 marks]

1.7   'UK links with the rest of the world maintain the UK's place as a significant global economy.' Discuss.   [9 marks]
[+3 SPaG marks]

2.1   What is the European Union (EU)?   [2 marks]

2.2   Describe the UK's role in the wider world.   [6 marks]

Questions referring to previous content

3.1   Outline strategies that have been adopted to reduce the UK's north–south divide.   [4 marks]

3.2   Compare the economic impacts of population growth and decline in two rural areas in the UK.   [6 marks]

> **EXAM TIP**
>
> *Outline* as a command word requires you to summarise the key points, not give one-word answers.

> **EXAM TIP**
>
> This is a demanding question.
>
> - You should think about what form these 'links' take.
> - The word 'maintain' suggests you should think about the past as well as current issues.
> - 'Significant global economy' could mean several things, so you should be clear about what you are focusing on.
>
> Planning your answer and organising your thoughts will help you address all aspects of the question. And remember that for 9-mark questions you will need to support the points you make with specific examples – make sure you have key facts at your fingertips.

Knowledge

35 The global distribution of resources and resource provision in the UK

The world's key resources

The three most important resources are food, water, and energy, but these are distributed unevenly across the world. Most HICs have plentiful resources and use far more than poorer countries.

	Food	Water	Energy
Global significance	• We need 2000–2400 calories per day for growth, health, and productivity.	• Vital for drinking, and producing crops and energy.	• Required for economic development. • Powers machinery, factories, and transport. • Traded worldwide.
Global inequalities	• Over a billion people are undernourished (not eating enough to remain healthy). • A further two billion are **malnourished** (suffering undernutrition or overnutrition). • Obesity (overnutrition) is an increasing problem in HICs.	• Climate and rainfall variations affect water supply. • Rainwater capture, storage (e.g., reservoirs) and extraction (e.g., pumping underground aquifers) is expensive, so easier in HICs. • Many of the world's poorest LICs suffer water scarcity.	• The world's richest countries use far more energy than poorer countries. • As NEEs become more industrialised, the demand for energy will increase, and patterns of energy trading will change.

Provision of food in the UK

Around half of the UK's food is produced here, and the rest is imported. This is because the UK's demands have changed significantly in recent years, as people seek:

- greater variety (e.g., exotic high-value foods from abroad)
- year-round availability (out-of-season produce)
- healthier options (e.g., **organic produce**).

But importing food has environmental costs in terms of the distances covered (**food miles**) and its **carbon footprint**. Two contrasting trends result from this:

- modern, technological, highly specialised, mechanised, intensive, commercial agribusinesses maximise production using agrochemicals and **economies of scale**
- locally sourced food goes directly to the public through farm shops, farmers' markets and 'pick your own' – cutting food miles and carbon footprints.

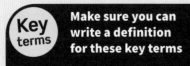

Key terms	Make sure you can write a definition for these key terms	carbon footprint economies of scale energy mix energy security food miles fracking malnourished organic produce water stress

Provision of water in the UK

Demand for water in the UK is already high, growing, and may exceed supply by 2034. This is due to:

- population increase
- more houses and domestic appliances
- agricultural irrigation.

Look at **Figure 1**. As the climate changes, matching the UK's water supply and demand is a growing challenge:

- demand exceeds supply (so-called **water stress**) in the south and east – a *water deficit*
- supply exceeds demand in the north and west – a *water surplus*
- expensive reservoir and pipeline water transfer schemes aim to resolve the mismatches.

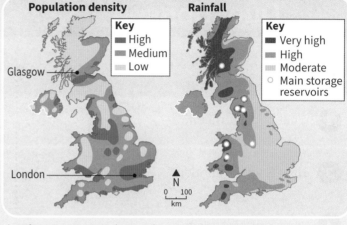

▲ *Figure 1* UK population density and water supply

Managing water quality

UK water sources – whether rivers, reservoirs, or groundwater aquifers – are vulnerable to pollution from:

- agriculture: agrochemical residues and farm waste (slurry)
- housing: leaking sewers and detergents
- industry: toxic effluent from manufacturing and chemical processes.

The Environment Agency is responsible for managing these impacts through practical initiatives (e.g., water treatment) and the implementation of strict government regulation and legislation (e.g., controlling pollution).

Provision of energy in the UK

The UK's **energy mix** has changed significantly since the 1990s. Electricity generation remains the UK's main use of energy, but non-renewable 'fossil fuel' domination has declined markedly in favour of renewables and nuclear. Energy consumption has also fallen due to increased energy efficiency.

But the UK is no longer self-sufficient in energy: 75% of its known oil and gas reserves have been exhausted and over one third of its energy is now imported. **Energy security** is not guaranteed, leading to difficult future decisions on:

- **fracking** – controversial owing to concerns about earthquakes, groundwater pollution, and climate change
- nuclear – carbon-neutral, but expensive to build and decommission, and producing radioactive waste that needs safe storage
- coal – cheap, abundant, but contrary to all greenhouse gas emission targets
- wind farms – visually controversial and with variable output (**Figure 2**).

▲ *Figure 2* By 2020, UK electricity generated by renewables (such as offshore wind turbines) had quadrupled

Retrieval

Learn the answers to the questions below, then cover the answers column with a piece of paper and write down as many as you can. Check and repeat.

	Questions	Answers
1	What are the world's three most important resources?	food, water, and energy
2	What is malnutrition?	an inadequately balanced diet, whether through undernutrition or overnutrition (obesity)
3	What is undernutrition?	when people do not eat enough nutrients to cover their needs for energy and growth, or to maintain a healthy immune system
4	What is water scarcity?	severe water stress – when water supplies fall below 1000 m³ per person
5	What is organic produce?	food produced without the use of agrochemicals such as fertilisers and pesticides
6	What are food miles?	the distances covered supplying food to consumers (e.g., foods imported into the UK)
7	What is the carbon footprint?	measurement of the greenhouse gases individuals or organisations produce through burning fossil fuels (e.g., cultivating and transporting food)
8	What are agribusinesses?	large commercial farms, with high levels of investment, that produce, package, and transport food
9	What are agrochemicals?	chemicals used in commercial farming such as pesticides, herbicides, or fertilisers
10	What are economies of scale?	proportionate saving in costs gained by increased levels of production, mechanisation, and bulk buying
11	What is water stress?	where demand for water exceeds supply in a certain period or when poor quality restricts its use
12	What is the role of the Environment Agency in managing UK water quality?	carrying out practical initiatives (e.g., water treatment) and the implementation of strict government regulation and legislation (e.g., controlling pollution)
13	What is meant by the term 'energy mix'?	the range and proportions of a country's different energy sources – both non-renewable and renewable
14	What is meant by the term 'energy security'?	uninterrupted availability of energy sources at an affordable price
15	What are renewable energy sources?	resources that cannot be exhausted, i.e., HEP, wind, solar, tidal, and biomass
16	What is fracking?	hydraulic fracturing of oil- and gas-bearing shale by drilling, then high-pressure injection of water, sand, and toxic chemicals

Put paper here

35 The global distribution of resources and resource provision in the UK

Exam-style questions

1.1 Which **one** of the energy sources below would best be described as a fossil fuel? Shade **one** circle only.   [1 mark]

A   Biomass   ◯   **C**   Natural gas   ◯

B   Solar   ◯   **D**   Nuclear   ◯

Study **Figure 1**, projected areas of water scarcity by 2025.

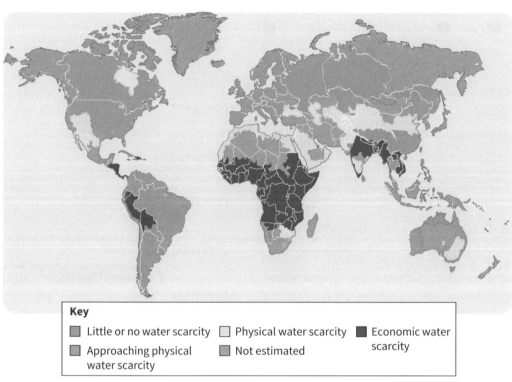

Key

◼ Little or no water scarcity   ◻ Physical water scarcity   ◼ Economic water scarcity

◼ Approaching physical water scarcity   ◼ Not estimated

▲ *Figure 1*

1.2 Define the term 'water scarcity'.   [2 marks]

1.3 Using **Figure 1**, describe the distribution of the areas experiencing physical water scarcity.   [2 marks]

1.4 What is meant by 'seasonal produce'?   [2 marks]

1.5 Explain why UK food miles have increased over recent decades.   [4 marks]

1.6 Outline the environmental consequences of your answer to **1.5**.   [2 marks]

1.7 Explain how water quality in the UK is managed.   [6 marks]

1.8 Outline global inequalities in the availability of food and water.   [6 marks]

> **EXAM TIP** ⊚
>
> *Describe* as a command word requires you to say what something is like. (No explanation is needed.) Remember, distribution refers to the way something is spread out or arranged over a geographic area.

Study **Figure 2**, the UK's sources of energy, 1990–2020

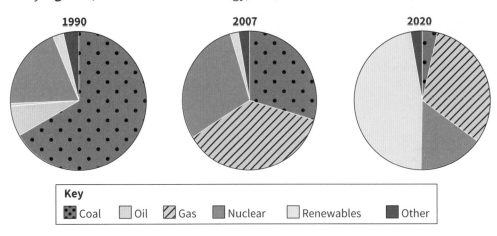

▲ *Figure 2*

2.1 Using **Figure 2**, describe the changes in UK energy sources between 1990 and 2020. **[3 marks]**

2.2 Outline **two** economic issues caused by exploiting renewable energy resources. **[2 marks]**

2.3 Identify **one** environmental and **one** economic issue associated with the production of nuclear energy. **[2 marks]**

2.4 Explain why renewables are so important to the UK's changing energy mix. **[4 marks]**

2.5 'Future UK energy security cannot be assured unless controversial decisions on exploiting new energy sources are made.' Discuss. **[9 marks]**
[+3 SPaG marks]

Study **Figure 3**, maps showing UK population density and water supply.

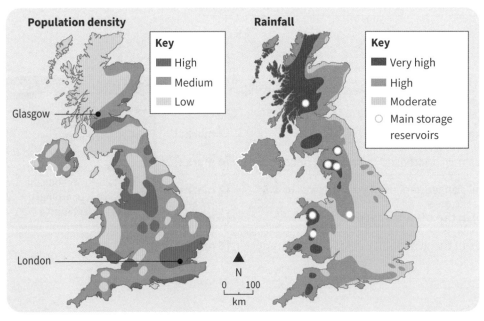

▲ *Figure 3*

EXAM TIP

Discuss as a command word requires you to give the points on both sides of an argument. Showing understanding of the word 'controversial' is important, so revisiting it as a theme throughout will help you in your answer.

EXAM TIP

In some 9-mark questions there are 3 extra marks available for SPaG (spelling, punctuation, grammar, and use of specialist terminology). The most credit is given to clear and accurate answers which use a wide range of specialist terms.

3.1 Using **Figure 3**, state whether Glasgow is likely to have a water surplus or a deficit. [1 mark]

3.2 Using **Figure 3**, state whether London is likely to have a water surplus or a deficit. [1 mark]

3.3 Explain the need for water transfers in the UK. [4 marks]

3.4 Explain how locally sourced food reduces carbon emissions. [4 marks]

3.5 Describe global inequality in the availability of energy. [4 marks]

Knowledge

36 Food management: global food supply

Global patterns of food supply

- There is currently enough food produced to supply everyone on the planet, but it is not distributed evenly.
- Many people in HICs exceed their daily food needs (calorie intake).
- Average food consumption in poorer areas does not reach the recommended daily intake of 2000–2400 calories.
- Cereals (e.g., rice and wheat) form a **staple crop** for most of the world's population, with climatic conditions dictating which crops grow best.

Furthermore, global food demand is expected to increase by over 60% by 2050 due to:

- population growth – by 2050 the global population is expected to reach 9.3 billion
- economic development and higher standards of living
- greater availability of food
- dietary changes (especially an increasing demand for meat and proteins).

> **SPECIFICATION TIP**
>
> You will have studied any two of food, water, or energy management. So, check carefully if you need to revise this topic.

Food security

Food security means having access to enough safe, affordable, and nutritious food to maintain a healthy and active life. Some countries have a food *surplus*. Most, however, do not produce enough to feed their people, and rely on imported food. Some of these (food *deficit*) countries also experience food insecurity (**Figure 1**).

▶ **Figure 1** Global food security (2018)

Key
- High
- Moderate
- Low
- Insecure
- No data

Factors affecting food supply

Climate: regions experiencing extreme temperatures and rainfall struggle to produce food

Pests and diseases: rising global temperatures are causing these to spread from the Tropics

Poverty: the world's poorest people cannot afford technology, irrigation, or agrochemicals

Factors affecting food supply

Technology: in HICs, mechanisation and agribusiness give high levels of productivity

Water stress: lack of water affects many areas that suffer food scarcity

Conflict: can lead to the destruction of crops and livestock

> **WATCH OUT** !
>
> Most times you use the term 'agrochemicals' you'll have to specify which ones you mean – fertilisers, pesticides, and/or herbicides (weedkillers).

The impacts of food insecurity

Food insecurity occurs when a country can't supply enough food (home grown and imported) to feed its population. This can have significant economic, social, and environmental impacts.

Famine

Famine is the most severe impact of food insecurity, causing malnutrition, undernutrition, weakened immune systems, starvation, and death.

Soil erosion

Soil erosion involves the removal of fertile topsoil by wind and water. It is caused by:

- overgrazing destroying (protective) vegetation
- over-cultivation exhausting soils
- cultivation of marginal land (such as steep slopes)
- deforestation.

Rising prices

Food prices are rising across the world. This is mainly due to higher prices for agrochemicals, animal feed, food storage, processing, and transportation. Furthermore, both the Covid-19 global **pandemic** and conflict in Ukraine impacted food supply chains, causing significant food price rises.

LICs and the poorest people in NEEs are hit hardest by higher food costs because food represents a larger share of their spending.

Social unrest

Incidents of social unrest ('food riots') in Africa and the Middle East have been linked to large food price rises (e.g., Algeria in 2011).

Increasing food supply

Irrigation: the artificial watering of land using water extracted from rivers and aquifers. Large-scale irrigation projects involve the construction of expensive dams and reservoirs (e.g., the Indus Basin Irrigation System in Pakistan)

Biotechnology: modification of products or processes, including the development of genetically modified (GM) crops

How food supply can be increased

Appropriate technology: often set up by NGOs and charities, these are small-scale, low-tech projects using local skills and materials to maximum effect (e.g., water harvesting, irrigation, or crop processing, such as dehusking coffee beans using bicycle power)

Aeroponics and hydroponics: use modern scientific techniques to grow crops without soil in artificially lit and heated greenhouses

The green revolution: modern farming techniques – adopting mechanisation, irrigation, agrochemicals, and new strains of crops – introduced into poorer countries in the 1950s and 1960s
Today's 'new' green revolution involves a more sustainable and environmentally friendly approach – adopting water harvesting (collecting and storing water), soil conservation, and improved seeds and livestock

REVISION TIP

When thinking about how food supply can be increased, make sure you can strengthen your argument by learning examples whenever relevant.

Knowledge

36 Food management: global food supply

 ## Case study: Large-scale agricultural development in Almeria, Spain

Almeria – an arid region in southern Spain – has developed the largest concentration of greenhouses (31 000 hectares) in the world.

Advantages	Disadvantages
All-year round production of fresh fruit and vegetables.	Health concerns over use of agrochemicals (especially pesticides).
Drip irrigation and hydroponics reduce water use.	Some natural water sources under stress.
Jobs created in production, packaging, and transportation.	Immigrant labour is low paid, and can lead to clashes with local people.

SPECIFICATION TIP

You need a named example of the advantages and disadvantages of one large-scale agricultural development. A case study you may have studied is given here.

Sustainable food production

Sustainable food supplies would ensure that fertile soil, water, and environmental resources are available for future generations.

Organic farming: does not use agrochemicals. Produce is more expensive because production and labour costs are higher.

Urban farming: the cultivation, processing, and distribution of food in and around settlements. Benefits include job creation and bringing communities together.

Reducing food waste and loss: currently one third of all food produced is wasted or lost. This can be addressed by:

- refrigerated food storage and distribution
- clear and sensible 'use by' food labelling
- using sealed plastic bags for fresh produce.

Permaculture: follows the patterns and features of natural ecosystems, involving harvesting rainwater, organic gardening, crop rotation and managing woodland.

 ## Case study: The Makueni County Food and Water Security Programme

This eastern Kenyan sustainable food supply programme has successfully improved both crop yields and local health by:

- harvesting rainwater and building sand dams for two small villages to increase food and water security
- introducing a training programme to support local farmers producing maize, beans, cassava, and sweet potatoes
- growing trees to reduce soil erosion, increase biodiversity, and provide medicinal products.

SPECIFICATION TIP

You need a named example of one local, sustainable food production scheme in an LIC or NEE. A case study you may have studied is given here.

 Key terms Make sure you can write a definition for these key terms

appropriate technology   biotechnology   famine
food security   irrigation   pandemic   permaculture
soil erosion   staple crop   urban farming

Learn the answers to the questions below, then cover the answers column with
a piece of paper and write down as many as you can. Check and repeat.

Questions

Answers

1 What is a staple crop?

the major part of a diet, supplying the main proportion of energy and nutrient needs

2 Why is global food demand expected to increase by over 60% by 2050?

population growth; economic development and higher standards of living; greater availability of food; dietary changes

3 What is meant by 'food security'?

having access to enough safe, affordable, and nutritious food to maintain a healthy and active life

4 What is meant by 'food insecurity'?

when a country can't supply enough food (home grown and imported) to feed its population

5 What factors negatively affect food supply?

extreme climates; lack of technology; pests and diseases; poverty (restricting use of irrigation or agrochemicals); water stress; conflict

6 What is soil erosion?

the removal of fertile topsoil by wind and water

7 Why are food prices rising across the world?

higher prices for agrochemicals, animal feed, food storage, processing, and transportation, as well as the Covid-19 pandemic and conflict in Ukraine impacting food supply chains

8 How can food supply be increased?

widespread adoption of appropriate technology and irrigation in LICs and NEEs, plus 'new' green revolution initiatives; aeroponics, hydroponics, and biotechnology in HICs

9 What is appropriate (or intermediate) technology?

technology suited to the needs, skills, knowledge, and wealth of local communities and their environment

10 What is biotechnology?

the modification of products or processes, including the development of genetically modified (GM) crops

11 What are the advantages of large-scale greenhouse production in Almeria, Spain?

all-year round production of fresh fruit and vegetables; drip irrigation and hydroponics reducing water use; jobs created in production, packaging, and transportation

12 What are the disadvantages of large-scale greenhouse production in Almeria, Spain?

health concerns over the use of agrochemicals (especially pesticides); some natural water sources under stress; low-paid immigrant labour can lead to clashes with local people

13 How has the eastern Kenyan Makueni County Food and Water Security Programme successfully improved both crop yields and local health?

by harvesting rainwater and building sand dams to increase food and water security; introducing a training programme to support local farmers; and growing trees to reduce soil erosion, increase biodiversity, and provide medicinal products

Put paper here

Practice

Exam-style questions

Study **Figure 1**, global food consumption (in calories).

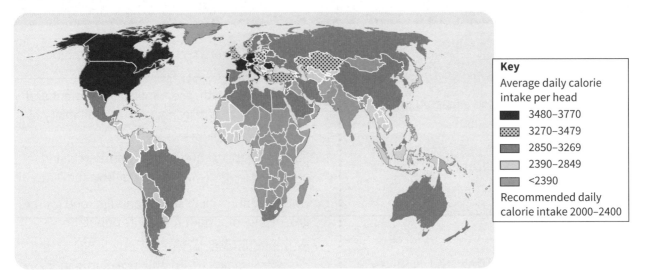

Key
Average daily calorie intake per head
■ 3480–3770
▨ 3270–3479
▨ 2850–3269
□ 2390–2849
□ <2390
Recommended daily calorie intake 2000–2400

▲ *Figure 1*

1.1 Using **Figure 1**, which one of statements below is correct?
Shade **one** circle only. **[1 mark]**

    A   Daily calorie intake is lower in North America than in South America. ○

    B   Daily calorie intake in Australia is 2850–3269 calories. ○

    C   Daily calorie intake in sub-Saharan Africa averages
          2850–3269 calories. ○

    D   Daily calorie intake is higher in Asia than in Europe. ○

1.2 Using **Figure 1**, describe the global pattern of food consumption
(in calories). **[3 marks]**

1.3 Outline the factors responsible for increasing global food demand. **[3 marks]**

1.4 Define the term 'food security'. **[2 marks]**

1.5 Explain the impacts of food insecurity. **[6 marks]**

1.6 Briefly discuss the significance of biotechnology to increasing
food supply. **[4 marks]**

1.7 Outline how reducing food waste and losses can increase
sustainable food supplies. **[4 marks]**

1.8 Outline the benefits of urban farming initiatives. **[4 marks]**

1.9 'Future global food supply can be increased to meet increasing
demands due to population growth, economic development,
higher standards of living, and dietary changes.' To what extent
do you agree with this optimistic forecast? **[9 marks] [+3 SPaG marks]**

> **EXAM TIP** ◎
>
> *Describe* as a command word requires you to say what something is like. (No explanation is needed.)

> **EXAM TIP** ◎
>
> *Discuss* as a command word requires you to give the points on both sides of an argument.

> **EXAM TIP** ◎
>
> *To what extent* as a command requires you to judge the importance of something. Make sure that you consider all factors covered in the quotation before coming to a clear, reasoned conclusion. Remember, there is no 'correct' conclusion – just the strength of your argument and evidence.

Study **Figure 2**, changes in the Food Security Index (FSI) 2019–2020 for selected countries.

Figure 2

Change 2019–2020 (%)	+4.7	+2.7	+2.6	−3.1	−4.3
Country	Haiti	Ukraine	Romania	Guinea	Egypt

Of the 113 countries assessed, Finland records the highest FSI score (85.3) and Yemen the lowest (35.7).

2.1 Using **Figure 2**, calculate the range between the highest FSI score (Finland) and the lowest (Yemen). **[1 mark]**

2.2 Use the data in **Figure 2** to complete the bar graph showing the positive and negative trends in FSI scores. **[2 marks]**

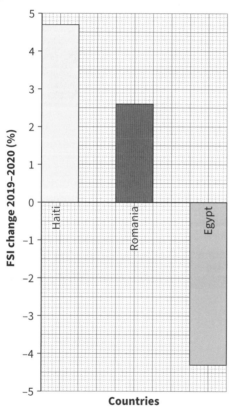

2.3 Describe **three** factors affecting food supply. **[6 marks]**

2.4 What is meant by the term 'food insecurity'? **[2 marks]**

2.5 What is meant by a sustainable food supply? **[2 marks]**

2.6 Outline how aeroponics and hydroponics can be used to increase food supply. **[4 marks]**

2.7 Explain how 'new' green revolution technology can be used to increase food supply. **[4 marks]**

2.8 To what extent has a local, sustainable food production scheme in an LIC or NEE you have studied been successful? **[6 marks]**

2.9 Evaluate various methods of sustainable food production. **[9 marks]**
[+3 SPaG marks]

EXAM TIP
Calculate means work out.

LINK
To understand the skill of constructing and reading a bar graph, see the Geographical Skills section, page 227.

EXAM TIP
In some 9-mark questions there are 3 extra marks available for SPaG (spelling, punctuation, grammar, and use of specialist terminology).

Knowledge

37 Water management: global water supply

Global patterns of water supply and demand

Water security means having access to enough safe, clean water. Regions with water surpluses have plentiful supplies. But water scarcity or **water insecurity** exists on every continent except Antarctica (**Figure 1**).

Global water consumption is expected to increase by 20–30% by 2050 due to:

- population growth – by 2050 the global population is expected to reach 9.3 billion

- economic development and higher standards of living

- increased demands for food

- increased urbanisation (increasing demand for drinking water, sanitation, and industry).

▶ **Figure 1** *Global physical and economic water scarcity*

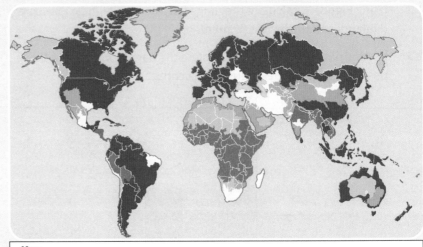

Key
- ■ Little or no water scarcity
- □ Approaching physical water scarcity
- ■ Physical water scarcity
- ■ Not estimated
- ■ Economic water scarcity

Factors affecting water availability

Limited infrastructure: e.g., limited pipelines and pumping stations may result in *economic* water scarcity. Provision and maintenance of water infrastructure is expensive.

Pollution of supply: agrochemical residues and industrial effluent pollute rivers and groundwater. In ome LICs and NEEs, open sewers spread waterborne diseases.

Climate: regions with high and reliable rainfall rarely experience *physical* water scarcity. Areas of low rainfall may experience **water stress** (with >80% of available water used each year).

Factors affecting water availability

Poverty: 2.2 billion people in poorer communities in LICs and NEEs do not have access to safe water.

Geology: aquifers are extremely important sources of water globally. Unsustainable demand threatens these sources, especially 'fossil' aquifers in the Middle East, created thousands of years ago when the climate was wetter.

Over-abstraction: occurs when water is pumped out of the ground faster than it is replaced by rainfall. This is unsustainable, and caused by excessive commercial irrigation and industrial processing demands.

The impacts of water insecurity

Water insecurity occurs when a country can't supply enough safe water to support the needs of its population.

Waterborne diseases and water pollution

Open sewers and high levels of pollution in rivers contaminate drinking water supplies, causing life-threatening diseases such as cholera and dysentery.

Food production

Agriculture is by far the major consumer of water, accounting for about 70% of the global supply. Countries experiencing water insecurity cannot irrigate crops, so suffer low food productivity. Droughts can also lead to crop failures.

Industrial output

Industry is the second largest consumer of water, accounting for about 19% of the global supply.

Water is used in processing, cleaning, cooling, and electricity generation. Future demands are likely to rise rapidly, particularly in NEEs.

Water conflict

Water sources, such as rivers and aquifers, cross national borders. As pressures on demand increase, so does the potential for 'water wars'.

Increasing water supply

Desalinisation	This involves extracting salt from seawater to produce freshwater. It is an extremely expensive and energy-consuming process, so currently only an option in wealthy HICs.
Water transfers	These schemes redistribute water from areas of surplus to areas of deficit using pipelines and canals.
Dams and reservoirs	Dams control river water flow by creating reservoirs. Multi-purpose schemes provide domestic and industrial water, HEP, and flood control – but are expensive to build, displace landowners, and lose capacity through evaporation and silting.
Water diversion and storage	Where evaporation rates are high, it is possible to divert surface water and pump it underground into aquifers for storage.

Case study: China's south-north water transfer scheme

China's rainfall is unevenly distributed (**Figure 2**), so this ambitious scheme will transfer water from the Yangtze River in the south to the Yellow River Basin in the arid north by 2050.

Advantages	Disadvantages
Arid northern regions will be able to be used for food production. Will address increased water demands due to urbanisation.	Reduced discharge of the Yangtze River is already negatively impacting its ecosystem. Minority Chinese groups forced to relocate. Expected cost is huge: US$80 billion.

SPECIFICATION TIP

You need a named example of one large-scale water transfer scheme. A case study you may have studied is given here.

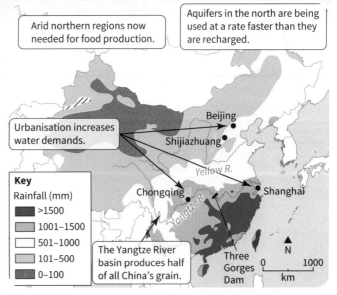

▲ *Figure 2 China's rainfall is unevenly distributed*

37 Knowledge   (205)

Knowledge

37 Water management: global water supply

Sustainable water supplies

Water conservation through:
- reducing leakages
- water meters and water charges
- improving public awareness of the need to save water
- preventing pollution

Groundwater management: abstraction (loss) must be balanced by recharge (gain). Letting aquifer volumes reduce too far increases contamination risks (requiring costly water treatment)

Sustainable approaches to water supply

Using 'grey' water: domestic wastewater used to water gardens and irrigate crops

Water recycling: reusing treated domestic or industrial wastewater for crop production or industrial processes

 ## Case study: The Wakel River Basin Project

In Southern Rajasthan, India, over-abstraction of irrigation water led to salinisation, waterlogging, and falling **water tables** in aquifers. This successful project used rainwater-harvesting techniques:

- *taankas* – collecting (and storing underground) water from roofs
- *johed* – small earth dams capturing rainfall
- *pats* – irrigation channels transferring water to the fields.

SPECIFICATION TIP

You need a named example of one local, sustainable water supply scheme in an LIC or NEE. A case study you may have studied is given here.

 Key terms Make sure you can write a definition for these key terms

'grey' water   over-abstraction   water conservation   water insecurity   water security   water stress   water table

Learn the answers to the questions below, then cover the answers column with a piece of paper and write down as many as you can. Check and repeat.

Questions / Answers

#	Questions	Answers
1	What is meant by 'water security'?	having access to enough clean water to sustain well-being, good health, and economic development
2	What is meant by 'water insecurity'?	not having access to sufficient safe water supplies – also known as 'water scarcity'
3	Why is global water consumption expected to increase by 20–30% by 2050?	population growth; economic development and higher standards of living; increased demands for food; and increased urbanisation (increasing demand for drinking water, sanitation, and water for industry use)
4	What is meant by 'water stress'?	where demand for water exceeds supply in a certain period or when poor quality restricts its use
5	What factors affect water availability?	climate (e.g., reliable rainfall); geology (e.g., aquifer potential); over-abstraction; pollution of supply; poverty; limited infrastructure
6	What is water over-abstraction?	when water is used more quickly than it is being replaced
7	What are the advantages of China's south–north water transfer scheme?	water demands due to increased urbanisation and industrialisation will be met; arid northern farming regions can be irrigated
8	What are the disadvantages of China's south–north water transfer scheme?	reduced discharge of the Yangtze River is already negatively impacting its ecosystem; minority Chinese groups will be forced to relocate; the expected cost is huge (US$80 billion)
9	What are sustainable approaches to water supplies?	water conservation; groundwater management; water recycling; and using 'grey' water
10	What is 'grey' water?	dirty water from sinks, baths, showers, and washing machines
11	How has the Wakel River Basin Project successfully improved water security, and so crop yields?	by using appropriate technology rainwater-harvesting techniques – namely *taankas*, *johed*, and *pats*

Put paper here

Practice

Exam-style questions

Study **Figure 1**, a map showing global water stress.

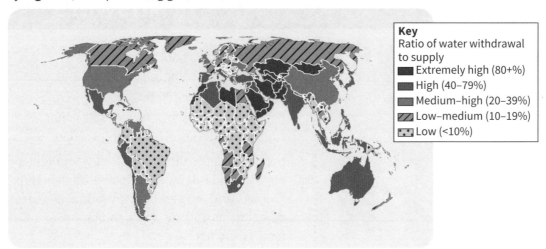

Key
Ratio of water withdrawal to supply
- ■ Extremely high (80+%)
- ■ High (40–79%)
- ■ Medium–high (20–39%)
- ▨ Low–medium (10–19%)
- ⦂ Low (<10%)

▲ *Figure 1*

1.1 Using **Figure 1**, which **one** of the statements below is correct?
Shade **one** circle only. **[1 mark]**

  A The ratio of water withdrawal to supply is lower in North America ○
  than in South America.

  B The ratio of water withdrawal to supply in Australia is ○
  extremely high (80+%).

  C The ratio of water withdrawal to supply in sub-Saharan Africa ○
  is mostly low, or low–medium.

  D The ratio of water withdrawal to supply in India is ○
  medium–high (20–39%).

> **EXAM TIP** ⊚
> *Describe* as a command word requires you to say what something is like. (No explanation is needed.)

1.2 Describe the global pattern of water stress. **[3 marks]**

1.3 Outline the factors affecting water availability. **[3 marks]**

> **EXAM TIP** ⊚
> *Suggest* as a command word requires you to give a well-reasoned guess to explain something where you can't be sure of the answer.

1.4 Suggest why economic development will lead to increasing
water consumption. **[4 marks]**

1.5 Outline **two** impacts of water insecurity on agricultural production. **[4 marks]**

1.6 Outline what is meant by a sustainable water supply. **[2 marks]**

1.7 Explain how water conservation and water recycling can increase
sustainable supplies of water. **[6 marks]**

> **EXAM TIP** ⊚
> *Justify* as a command word means give evidence to support your ideas. Do you agree with the statement? For such a high-mark question, referencing case-study evidence throughout your answer is essential if you are to access the highest levels of the mark scheme.

1.8 'Large-scale water transfer schemes have significant potential
to solve water shortages.' Justify the validity of this statement. **[9 marks]**
[+3 SPaG marks]

Study **Figure 2**, predicted trends in water use to 2030 and 2050.

Figure 2

Water use	2030 (% change)	2050 (% change)
Agricultural	−3.6	−6.9
Industrial	+53.3	+119.8
Domestic	+36.5	+65.1

2.1 Using **Figure 2**, calculate the range in percentage change for 2030. **[1 mark]**

EXAM TIP

Calculate means work out.

2.2 Use the data in **Figure 2** to complete the bar graph showing the positive and negative trends. **[2 marks]**

LINK

To understand the skill of constructing and reading a bar graph, see the Geographical Skills section, page 227.

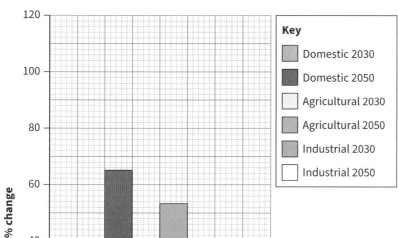

Key
- Domestic 2030
- Domestic 2050
- Agricultural 2030
- Agricultural 2050
- Industrial 2030
- Industrial 2050

2.3 Suggest reasons why water use is expected to increase at a high rate in the industrial and domestic sectors. **[4 marks]**

2.4 Define the term 'water insecurity'. **[2 marks]**

2.5 Outline the reasons for increasing global water insecurity. **[4 marks]**

2.6 Define the term 'water stress'. **[2 marks]**

2.7 Explain how water supply can be increased. **[6 marks]**

2.8 Evaluate sustainable approaches to water supply. **[9 marks]**
[+3 SPaG marks]

EXAM TIP

Evaluate as a command word requires you to make judgements about which approaches are most or least effective.

Knowledge

38 Energy management: global energy supply

Global patterns of energy consumption and supply

- Energy consumption per person is very high in HICs and low in LICs.

- When supply (production) exceeds demand, a region has an energy *surplus* and therefore **energy security**.

- When demand exceeds production there is an energy *deficit* and energy insecurity.

Global energy consumption is increasing (**Figure 1**). This is due to:

- population growth expected to reach 9.3 billion by 2050

- economic development – urbanisation, industrialisation, and greater wealth

- increased technology – e.g., computers, electric cars, air conditioners, and air conditioners.

> **SPECIFICATION TIP**
>
> You will have studied any two of food, water, or energy management. So check carefully if you need to revise this topic.

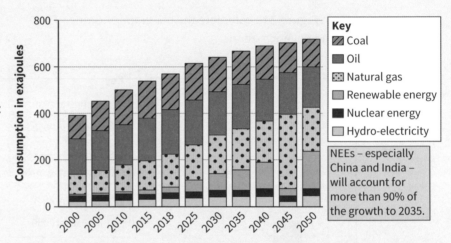

> NEEs – especially China and India – will account for more than 90% of the growth to 2035.

▲ **Figure 1** *Global energy consumption, 2000–2018, with a forecast to 2050*

Factors affecting energy supply

Technology:
- Technological developments allow exploitation of energy in remote or hostile environments.
- New fracking technology allows the extraction of shale gas.
- Renewable energy exploitation is becoming increasingly efficient.

Cost of exploitation and production:
- Determines whether energy reserves can be exploited.
- Most energy sources are expensive to develop, especially nuclear.
- Costs fluctuate according to demand and supply.

Factors affecting energy supply

Political factors:
- Energy insecurity has contributed to global conflicts.
- Conflicts can disrupt energy supplies.
- There are fears that Iran might hide non-peaceful motivations in developing nuclear power.

Physical factors:
- Geology determines the location of fossil fuels.
- Mountainous areas with high rainfall have hydro-electric power (HEP) potential.
- **Geothermal energy** is produced in areas of tectonic activity.

The impacts of energy insecurity

Energy insecurity occurs when a country does not have access to sufficient, reliable, and affordable energy supplies. This means it is unable to supply enough energy to meet the demands of its people.

Exploration of difficult and environmentally sensitive areas

Countries look for new sources of energy often in challenging or environmentally-sensitive environments.

Economic and environmental costs

Energy exploitation is costly and can lead to environmental catastrophes such as oil spills.

Food production

Modern large-scale agriculture requires a large amount of energy.

Industrial output

Energy is required for power and as a raw material (e.g., oil used in manufacturing chemicals and plastics). Shortages and fluctuating prices impact production.

Potential for energy conflict

Energy insecurity may lead to:

- difficult government decisions regarding prioritising agricultural, industrial, or domestic consumers; threats of sabotage on energy pipelines and transport
- wars in fear of oil shortages and rising prices.

Increasing energy supply

There are two main options for increasing energy supplies:

- Continue to develop non-renewable fossil fuels and nuclear power.
- Develop and increase the use of sustainable, renewable alternatives.

Fossil fuels – non-renewable, but global reserves remain.
- Important for electricity generation.
- Carbon capture technology could help offset high CO_2 emissions.

Nuclear power – controversial.
- A safe, efficient, low-carbon technology.
- Very expensive to develop, and concerns persist over radioactive waste disposal and the fear of further accidents.

How can energy supplies be increased?

Biomass and geothermal – renewable, but have 'issues':
- Biomass can be burned (polluting) or processed into biofuel.
- Geothermal is expensive to install and restricted to tectonically active areas.

HEP, tidal, and waves – renewable, but expensive and controversial:
- HEP dams and reservoirs flood valuable farmland, and displace landowners.
- Tidal barrages have environmental impacts (on intertidal ecosystems).
- Wave power farms are wind and weather dependent.

Wind and solar – increasingly dominant renewable choices:
- Wind turbines are now a proven technology, but visually (aesthetically) controversial and weather dependent.
- Solar photovoltaic cells are improving in efficiency, but expensive and need land and sunlight.

Knowledge

 ## Case study: Fossil fuel extraction – natural gas

Advantages	Disadvantages
Lower CO_2 emissions than coal or oil. Lower risk of environmental accidents. Easy to transport by pipeline or tankers.	Some reserves are in politically unstable countries. Contributes to global warming by producing CO_2 and methane. Fracking is highly controversial.

SPECIFICATION TIP

You need a named example of one non-renewable fossil fuel to show how its extraction has both advantages and disadvantages. A case study you may have studied is given here.

Sustainable approaches to energy supply

Energy conservation:

- Reducing individual energy use and carbon footprint
- Designing new homes and workplaces for sustainability.

Transport:

- electric trams and 'green' buses
- car-sharing or buying a hybrid or electric car.

Reducing energy demand:

- government incentives or grants for energy-efficient home improvements
- use of 'smart' electricity meters and raising public energy awareness.

Technology to increase fossil fuel efficiency:

- energy-efficient home appliances and cars
- carbon capture and storage.

Case study: The Chambamontera micro-hydro scheme, Peru

The scheme helped this isolated community harness the high rainfall and steep slopes to generate renewable, low-maintenance electricity, which:

- heats homes without soil-erosion-inducing deforestation
- improves cooking, education, and health care
- is used to process locally grown coffee beans
- slows depopulation from rural–urban migration.

SPECIFICATION TIP

You need a named example of one local sustainable energy scheme in an LIC or NEE. A case study you may have studied is given here.

 Key terms Make sure you can write a definition for these key terms

biomass   energy exploitation   energy security
geothermal energy   micro-hydro scheme

Learn the answers to the questions below, then cover the answers column with
a piece of paper and write down as many as you can. Check and repeat.

Questions

Answers

	Questions	Answers
1	What is meant by 'energy security'?	uninterrupted availability of energy sources at an affordable price
2	What is meant by 'energy insecurity'?	not having access to sufficient, reliable, and affordable energy supplies
3	Why is the trend of currently increasing global energy consumption expected to continue to 2050?	population growth; economic development; urbanisation; industrialisation; greater wealth; increased technology (e.g., computers, electric cars, air conditioners, and other electrical equipment)
4	Give three factors that affect energy supply.	technological developments allowing alternatives (e.g., fracking) and exploitation in remote or hostile environments; fluctuating costs of exploitation and production; political factors such as conflicts; physical factors such as geology, relief, climate, and geothermal potential
5	What is biomass?	renewable organic materials (such as wood, agricultural crops, and waste), especially when used as a source of fuel or energy
6	What is geothermal energy?	energy generated by heat stored deep in the Earth. Water, heated underground in contact with hot rocks, creates steam that drives turbines to generate electricity
7	How is natural gas formed?	from the decomposition of organisms deposited on the seabed, buried, and trapped millions of years ago
8	What are the advantages of natural gas extraction?	lower CO_2 emissions than coal or oil; lower risk of environmental accidents; easy to transport by pipeline or tankers
9	What are the disadvantages of natural gas extraction?	some reserves are in politically unstable countries; its use contributes to global warming by producing CO_2 and methane; fracking is highly controversial
10	What is energy (or fuel) poverty?	a household spending more than 10% of its income on fuel to maintain an adequate level of warmth
11	What are sustainable energy supplies?	energy that can potentially be used well into the future without harming future generations
12	What is a micro-hydro scheme?	a renewable, sustainable, small-scale hydro-electric power (HEP) scheme
13	What are the environmental benefits of the Chambamontera micro-hydro scheme?	the non-polluting, renewable HEP generation has little environmental impact; has reduced deforestation (for fuelwood) and so soil erosion

Put paper here

Exam-style questions

Study **Figure 1**, a map showing global energy consumption.

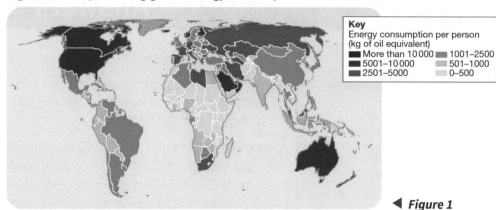

Key
Energy consumption per person
(kg of oil equivalent)
■ More than 10 000 ■ 1001–2500
■ 5001–10 000   ■ 501–1000
■ 2501–5000   ■ 0–500

◀ *Figure 1*

1.1 Using **Figure 1**, which one of the statements below is correct?
Shade **one** circle only.   **[1 mark]**

    A   Energy consumption per person in Australia is 5001–10 000   ◯
        (kg of oil equivalent).

    B   Energy consumption per person is lower in North America   ◯
        than in South America.

    C   Energy consumption per person in India is 2501–5000   ◯
        (kg of oil equivalent).

    D   Energy consumption per person in sub-Saharan Africa is   ◯
        mostly above 2501 (kg of oil equivalent).

1.2 Describe the global pattern of global energy consumption.   **[3 marks]**◀

1.3 Complete the pie chart (**Figure 3**) to compare the data in **Figure 2**.   **[1 mark]**

Figure 2

Type of energy	%
Oil	30
Natural gas	24
Coal	26
Biomass	10
Electricity (other renewables and nuclear)	10

▲ *Figure 3 Global use of energy*

> **EXAM TIP**
>
> *Describe* as a command word requires you to say what something is like. (No explanation is needed.)

> **LINK**
>
> To understand the skill of constructing and reading a pie chart, see the Geographical Skills section, page 229.

1.4 Describe the global use of energy.   **[2 marks]**

1.5 Outline **one** advantage and **one** disadvantage of using wind turbines to increase energy supply.   **[2 marks]**

1.6 Explain how physical and political factors influence energy supply.   **[4 marks]**

1.7 Outline the economic, political, and environmental impacts of energy insecurity.   **[6 marks]**

1.8 Evaluate the issues affecting global energy supply.   **[9 marks] [+3 SPaG marks]**

Study **Figure 4**, change in carbon content of electricity for selected countries, 2008–2017 (g/kWh).

▼ *Figure 4*

Country	Change in carbon content of electricity 2008–2017 (g/kWh)
Japan	+55
Norway	+3
Canada	−50
China	−125
UK	−260

2.1 Using **Figure 4**, calculate the range in the changing carbon content of electricity (2008–2017) between Japan and the UK. [1 mark]

EXAM TIP
Calculate means work out.

2.2 Use the data in **Figure 4** to complete the bar graph showing positive and negative trends in the changing carbon content of electricity (2008–2017). [2 marks]

LINK
To understand the skill of constructing and reading a bar graph, see the Geographical Skills section, page 227.

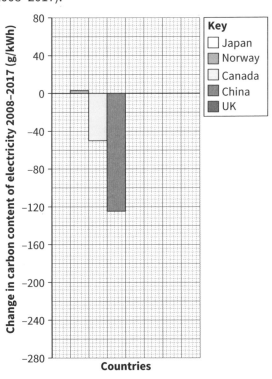

2.3 Using **Figure 4**, suggest reasons why the UK recorded the highest decrease in the carbon content of electricity. [3 marks]

EXAM TIP
Suggest as a command requires you to give a well-reasoned guess to explain something where you can't be sure of the answer.

2.4 Define the term 'energy security'. [2 marks]

2.5 Outline the factors responsible for increasing global energy consumption. [3 marks]

2.6 Using a named example of a fossil fuel, explain how its extraction has both advantages and disadvantages. [6 marks]

2.7 Outline **one** advantage and **one** disadvantage of using solar photovoltaic panels to increase energy supply. [2 marks]

EXAM TIP
Evaluate as a command word requires you to make judgements about which approaches are most or least effective.

2.8 Evaluate sustainable approaches to energy supply. [9 marks] [+3 SPaG marks]

 **Knowledge**

Geographical applications and skills are assessed by **Paper 3** in two sections:

- **Section A:** Issue evaluation
- **Section B:** Fieldwork

Section A: Issue evaluation

This section tests your critical-thinking and problem-solving skills. You will become very familiar with the Pre-release resources booklet (studied thoroughly with your teacher in class time). Note that the issue evaluation exercise is *synoptic* – covering knowledge and understanding from both **Papers 1** and **2**.

How to be successful in the exam

Remember:

- You are not allowed to take your annotated (classroom) booklet into the exam, but you *will* be given a new copy.
- You'll be asked throughout to make decisions and judgements based on the Pre-release booklet, so you must focus on the evidence to support your choices.
- Do not ignore any of the resources – the examiner included all of them for a reason.
- Early questions will require you to interpret and **analyse** the resources.
- The final *decision-making* question requires an **evaluative** judgement – applying your knowledge and understanding of all the resources to develop a critical perspective of the issue or issues (**Figure 1**).
- All this classroom preparation is for a reason – a confident and anxiety-free exam (**Figure 2**).

> **EXAM TIP**
>
> There are few if any wrong answers in the *Issue evaluation* section of the exam, but always the danger of poor answers not supported by evidence.

1 Read the question carefully – make sure you fully understand the issue.

↓

2 Study *all* the evidence, considering *all* points of view, then make your final decision(s).

↓

3 Always quote evidence from the resources to support your decision(s).

↓

4 Read through and check that you have backed up your decision(s) with relevant facts.

↓

5 Evaluate throughout your answer.

↓

6 Write a conclusion, referring to the original question.

▲ *Figure 1* How to approach a decision-making question

---

1 Read through the questions:
- *before* you start writing any answers
- *before* you apply any more of these top tips!

→

2 Maps and diagrams:
- Quickly review them again, checking headings, keys, and scales.

→

3 Graphs:
- Quickly review them again, checking headings, axes, trends, and patterns.

↓

6 Text extracts:
- Quickly review them again, especially their sources and quotations from different stakeholders.
- Again, remember your class discussion, and don't be afraid to (quickly) repeat any annotations you made on your Pre-release booklet.

←

5 Statistics:
- Quickly review them again, but think about how you'll manipulate them rather than just quote them.
- Manipulation means making comparisons, calculating percentage increase or decrease, etc.

←

4 Photos and satellite images:
- Quickly review them again, checking headings.
- Remember your class discussion, and any annotations you made on your Pre-release booklet.

↓

7 Links:
- Think again about the links and connections between the resources.

→

8 Opposing points of view:
- Consider again the arguments *for* and *against* the issue(s).
- Consider the *advantages* and *disadvantages*.

→

9 Timing:
- You have about 37 minutes for this section – around a mark a minute.
- Be concise (to the point) in your writing – you don't have time to waffle.
- Allow time to check your answers.

▲ *Figure 2* Top tips for successfully completing the Issue evaluation *section*

Section B: Fieldwork

You will have completed two geographical enquiries, one physical and one human. Both enquiries will have involved the collection of **primary data** (on field trips, **Figure 3**) and the use of **secondary data** in support. One of your enquiries will have involved you considering both physical and human geography and their interactions.

How to be successful in the exam

Remember:

- Literacy skills are important for clearly communicating information in all three of your exam papers. But for this section of Paper 3, you must remember that the examiner was not present for your fieldwork enquiries. Consequently, ensuring you communicate well about your fieldwork experiences is particularly important.

- Revise *all* your geographical skills (pages 224–233).

- You will be expected to apply, use, adapt, and **justify** a variety of skills and techniques relating to geographical enquiries in general, as well as to your own fieldwork experiences.

▲ **Figure 3** *Primary (fieldwork) data collection*

Titles:
- Learn the titles of your fieldwork enquiries – you *will* be required to write them in the exam.

Aims and objectives:
Make sure that you understand the reasons behind each enquiry:
- what you were seeking to investigate and the choice of location(s)
- the potential risks in the fieldwork, and how they were minimised **(Figure 5)**
- justifying *why* you did things – your data collection/sampling methods, how you avoided **bias**, presentation techniques, etc.

Command words:
- Make sure you understand the higher-level command words: 'assess', 'evaluate', 'justify', 'discuss', and 'to what extent'.

Top tips to prepare for a successful Fieldwork section of your exam

Revision:
Summarise each enquiry into factual notes – focusing on *why* you did things, not *what* you did – including:
- an assessment of the appropriateness of your data collection and **sampling methods**
- an assessment of the appropriateness of your presentation methods
- an evaluation of the accuracy and reliability of your results and conclusion.

Timing:
- You have about 38 minutes for this section – around a mark a minute.
- Be concise (to the point) in your writing – you don't have time to waffle.
- Allow time to check your answers.

Enquiry stages:
- Make sure you understand the different stages (or strands) of each enquiry, and how they fit together **(Figure 6)**.

▲ **Figure 4** *Top tips for preparing for the Fieldwork section of Paper 3*

- You will be expected to apply knowledge and understanding to interpret, analyse, justify, evaluate, and reach conclusions about geographical enquiries in general, as well as to your own fieldwork experiences.

- The early exam questions will be based on the use of fieldwork data from an unfamiliar context. They'll mostly be short-answer questions, and based on skills (including statistics).

- The later exam questions will be based specifically on your own individual enquiries, using high-level command words such as 'assess' and 'evaluate'.

- Summarising and revising your fieldwork enquiries will help you ensure a confident and anxiety-free exam (**Figure 4**).

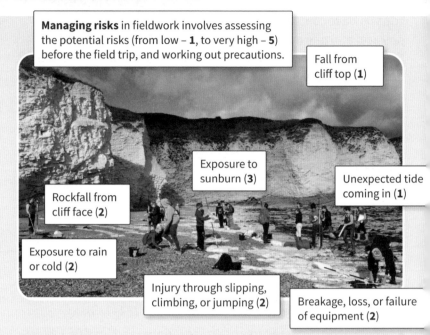

Managing risks in fieldwork involves assessing the potential risks (from low – **1**, to very high – **5**) before the field trip, and working out precautions.

Fall from cliff top (**1**)

Exposure to sunburn (**3**)

Unexpected tide coming in (**1**)

Rockfall from cliff face (**2**)

Exposure to rain or cold (**2**)

Injury through slipping, climbing, or jumping (**2**)

Breakage, loss, or failure of equipment (**2**)

▲ **Figure 5** *Would you agree with these risk assessments? If not, why?*

▼ **Figure 6** *The six stages of geographical enquiry*

Stage (or strand)	You will have followed this clear, logical six-stage sequence when planning and preparing for – and completing and writing up – your two fieldwork investigations. The exam will test these strands and your understanding of how they fit together
1 The question	Deciding on a suitable question for investigation (or hypothesis to test)
2 Data collection	Selecting, measuring, and recording **quantitative** and **qualitative** fieldwork (and secondary) data appropriate to the enquiry
3 Processing and presentation of the data	Selecting appropriate ways of processing and presenting the primary and secondary data collected (e.g., visual, cartographic, and graphical methods)
4 Description, analysis, and explanation of the data	Describing, analysing, and explaining the results (including use of statistical methods)
5 Conclusions	Reaching evidenced conclusions supported by the data (referring to the original aims of the enquiry)
6 Evaluation	Evaluating the enquiry. (What went well? What didn't go well? To what extent are the conclusions reliable? How might the **limitations** be addressed, and the enquiry improved?)

EXAM TIP

In Paper 3 you are very likely to be asked to make a calculation or complete a diagram, so remember to include a calculator with your exam stationery.

WATCH OUT

Be careful with the restrictions that often apply to *Fieldwork* questions (e.g., asking you to discuss your '**human**' enquiry or describe '**one**' technique). These will usually be emphasised in bold.

 Key terms Make sure you can write a definition for these key terms

analyse   bias
evaluative   justify
limitations   primary data
qualitative
quantitative
sampling methods
secondary data

Learn the answers to the questions below, then cover the answers column with
a piece of paper and write down as many as you can. Check and repeat.

Questions

Answers

1 What is the meaning of 'analyse'?

to examine something methodically and in detail;
to explain and interpret it

2 What is meant by the term 'evaluative'?

an assessment to form an idea of the quality,
importance, or value of something

3 Who or what are stakeholders?

an individual or group that has an interest in any
issue, activity, or decision

4 What is primary data?

data collected first-hand – real-time data specific
to the needs of the enquiry

5 What is secondary data?

data collected by others – to support the primary
data, or to allow studies of changes through time
(e.g., census data)

6 What is quantitative data?

measurable data – numerical and so verifiable and
transformable into useful statistics

7 What is qualitative data?

descriptive data – exploratory in nature, involving
research and analysis (e.g., interviews)

8 What is meant by bias?

a tendency to prefer one thing over another.
In geographical enquiry, bias usually involves
subconsciously selecting samples to fit the
expected outcome (e.g., interviewing elderly
women in a study investigating fear of crime)

9 What is random sampling?

every item, person, or place has an equal chance
of being selected

10 What is stratified sampling?

a proportionate number of observations is
taken from each part of the 'population'
(e.g., rock types in geology)

11 What is systematic sampling?

a sample taken at regular intervals (e.g., every 25 m
along a footpath, or interviewing every 20th person
in the street)

12 What are limitations in geographical fieldwork?

'forced' errors or weaknesses in data collection
preventing the production of fair and reliable
data (e.g., insufficient time to interview sufficient
pedestrians)

13 What does 'assess' mean?

to judge and decide the value of something – and
to weigh up which is the most/least important

14 What is meant by the command word 'discuss'?

To give the points on both sides of an argument,
and come to a conclusion

15 What is meant by the command word 'justify'?

to give evidence to support your ideas

16 What is meant by the command phrase
'to what extent'?

to judge the importance of something

Put paper here

Exam-style Fieldwork questions

Study **Figure 1**, a line graph showing a beach profile of slope angle up a beach.

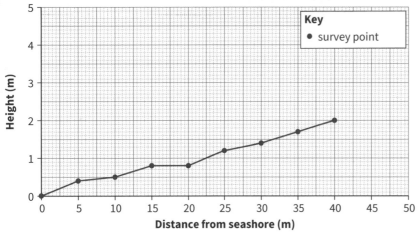

Height (m)	Distance from seashore (m)
3	45
4	50

▲ **Figure 2** Beach survey values

▲ *Figure 1*

1.1 Use the data in **Figure 2** to plot beach heights on **Figure 1**, at 45 m and 50 m from the seashore. **[1 mark]**

1.2 Using **Figure 1**, what is the height of the beach 20 m from the seashore? **[1 mark]**

1.3 Explain **one** advantage of using a line graph to show a beach gradient cross-section. **[2 marks]**

1.4 Outline **one** potential risk of collecting data in a coastal environment. **[2 marks]**

> **LINK**
>
> To understand the skill of constructing and reading a line graph, see the Geographical Skills section, page 228.

Study **Figure 3**, types of vehicles recorded at a road intersection.

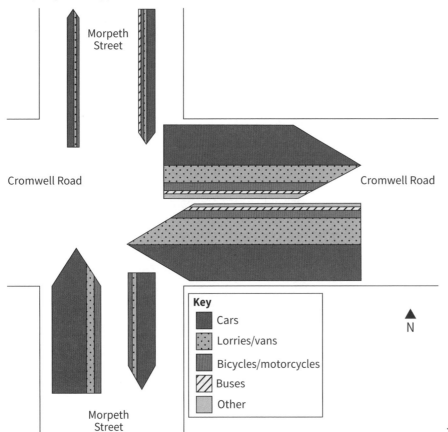

Key
- Cars
- Lorries/vans
- Bicycles/motorcycles
- Buses
- Other

◀ *Figure 3*

Figure 4

	Cars	Lorries/vans	Bicycles/motorcycles	Buses	Other
Cromwell Rd (travelling west)	105	77	22	10	10
Cromwell Rd (travelling east)	125	54	25	10	15

1.5 What is the presentation method used in **Figure 3**? **[1 mark]**

1.6 Suggest **one** way in which the data presentation in **Figure 3** could be adapted. **[2 marks]**

1.7 Describe the vehicle flows recorded in **Figure 3**. **[3 marks]**

1.8 Complete **Figure 5**, the graph for Cromwell Road (travelling west). **[2 marks]**

> **LINK**
>
> To understand the skill of constructing and reading a bar graph, see the Geographical Skills section, page 227.

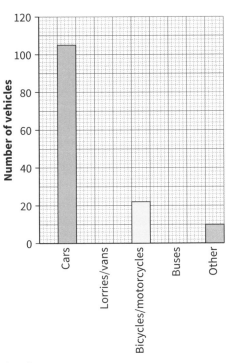

▲ *Figure 5*

1.9 What is secondary data? **[1 mark]**

2.1 For your **physical** fieldwork enquiry, explain **one** way in which you attempted to make your data collection reliable. **[2 marks]**

2.2 For your **human** fieldwork enquiry, outline how you analysed your primary data. **[3 marks]**

2.3 For your **physical** fieldwork enquiry, explain how the data presentation techniques you used helped you reach conclusions. **[6 marks]**

2.4 For **one** of your fieldwork enquiries, to what extent did your results allow you to reach a valid conclusion to your original question or hypothesis? **[9 marks] [+3 SPaG marks]**

> **EXAM TIP**
>
> *To what extent* as a command requires you to judge the importance of something. Which results, if any, led you to reach valid conclusions? There is no penalty for stating that your results did not lead to valid conclusions. The marks are awarded for explaining your interpretation and reasoning, not for what you recorded in the field.

Study **Figure 6**, a questionnaire page for a village tourism study in Castleton (the Peak District).

Date .... Time ....

Could you help us? We are GCSE Geography students conducting a survey into aspects of tourism in the village and wondered if you would mind answering a few questions. We won't take up much of your time.

1. Do you visit Castleton – more than once a month? ☐
    – once a month? ☐
    – two or three times a year? ☐
    – less than once a year? ☐

2. Are you – staying in Castleton? ☐
    – staying within 1 mile of Castleton? ☐
    – staying between 1 and 5 miles from Castleton? ☐
    – staying between 5 and 15 miles from Castleton? ☐
    – staying more than 15 miles from Castleton? ☐

3. Could you tell us what kind of work you do? ....

4. Are you visiting Castleton now to – shop for groceries? ☐
    – shop for gifts or souvenirs? ☐
    – visit a café? ☐
    – look round the village? ☐
    – visit a friend? ☐
    – for other reasons? ☐

5. Do you find this village – very attractive? ☐
    – quite attractive? ☐
    – average? ☐
    – unattractive? ☐
    – very unattractive? ☐

6. Could you put the following features of Castleton in order of their attractiveness? – the buildings ☐
    – the surroundings ☐
    – the shops ☐
    – the peace and quiet ☐
    – the amenities provided ☐
    – others ☐

That was the last question. Thank you for your help. Is there anything you would like to ask us before we go?

▲ *Figure 6*

3.1 What is the data collection method used in **Figure 6**? **[1 mark]**

3.2 Question 1 could present a problem in that locals trying to be helpful might engage in the survey without the interviewer realising it until later questions are asked. Suggest and explain a better opening question to the survey. **[2 marks]**

3.3 Explain why the students have adopted mostly closed questions in this survey. **[2 marks]**

3.4 Explain why sample size is an important consideration in surveys such as these. **[2 marks]**

3.5 Outline the relevance of question 3. **[2 marks]**

3.6 Explain the teacher's insistence on 'interviewing in a pair, but not in a group'. **[2 marks]**

3.7 Explain how bias might be introduced into surveys such as these. **[3 marks]**

Study **Figure 7**, an inner city area in Lincoln.

▲ *Figure 7*

3.8 Suggest **one** question that could form the basis of a human geographical enquiry in the environment shown in **Figure 7**. **[1 mark]**

3.9 Suggest how fieldwork risks might be reduced in urban environments. **[4 marks]**

4.1 For your **human** geographical enquiry, explain **one** factor about your own primary data which could have affected your results. **[2 marks]**

4.2 For your **physical** geographical enquiry, outline the limitations of a data collection technique(s) used. **[3 marks]**

4.3 For your **human** geographical enquiry, assess the extent to which your conclusion(s) matched your aims at the start of the enquiry. **[6 marks]**

4.4 For **one** of your fieldwork enquiries, assess the extent to which additional sources of data could have improved the reliability of your conclusions. **[9 marks]**
[+3 SPaG marks]

Additional questions based on **your** fieldwork experiences:

5.1 For your **human** geographical enquiry, outline **one** limitation of a data collection technique used in this enquiry. **[2 marks]**

5.2 Outline ways in which you analysed your **human** fieldwork data. **[3 marks]**

5.3 For your **physical** geographical enquiry, assess the appropriateness of the sites selected for your primary data collection. **[6 marks]**

5.4 For **one** of your fieldwork enquiries, evaluate the reliability of your fieldwork conclusions. **[9 marks]**
[+3 SPaG marks]

EXAM TIP

Assess as a command word requires you to weigh up which is the most important and which is the least important. So, state which data sources in the field proved to be very important in reaching your conclusions, before considering what additional sources of data would improve the reliability of your conclusions further. The marks are awarded for your appreciation of the enquiry data strengths, evaluation of limitations, and explanations for potential improvements.

EXAM TIP

Evaluate as a command word requires you to make judgements about which approaches are most or least effective. So, how confident are you about the reliability of your fieldwork conclusions? Which data sources proved to be most important in reaching your conclusions? Given another field trip, what additional sources of data would improve the reliability of your conclusions further? The marks are awarded for your appreciation of enquiry strengths, evaluation of limitations and errors, and explanations of potential improvements.

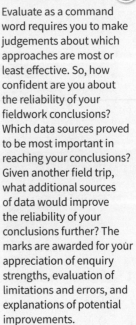

Knowledge

40 Geographical skills

Introduction

GCSE Geography requires you to demonstrate good literacy skills in communicating information, but also a variety of geographical skills, most of which fall into three broad categories:

- maps at different scales (cartographic)
- graphs, specialist maps, and diagrams (graphical)
- numbers and statistics (numerical and statistical).

All these skills (and associated ones) will have been integrated into your course content, although some might have been taught separately (e.g., when preparing for fieldwork). Don't be alarmed if you cannot recall specific lessons on the seemingly wide range of skills covered in the exam specification.

Also, don't forget that all geographical skills are primarily useful, supportive tools. So, revisiting and practising them (as you would your theory) will help you when they come up in exam questions.

> **EXAM TIP**
>
> Geographical skills will be tested in many exam questions. So, remember:
>
> - to maintain a 'can do' attitude
> - be careful in your approach
> - check any calculations as you progress
> - review again at the end of the exam.

Atlas maps

Small-scale atlas maps are useful sources of information for geographers. For example:

- basic maps showing physical relief, settlements, and political boundaries
- thematic maps showing factors such as climate or vegetation.

Any place on an atlas map can be located by lines of latitude and longitude:

- lines of **latitude** run parallel to the equator, reaching 90° at the north and south poles
- lines of **longitude** run between the north and south poles, east and west from the Prime Meridian (0° longitude, running through Greenwich in London) (**Figure 1**).

Both lines of latitude and longitude are measured in degrees (using the symbol °). Each degree is subdivided into 60 minutes (using the symbol ').

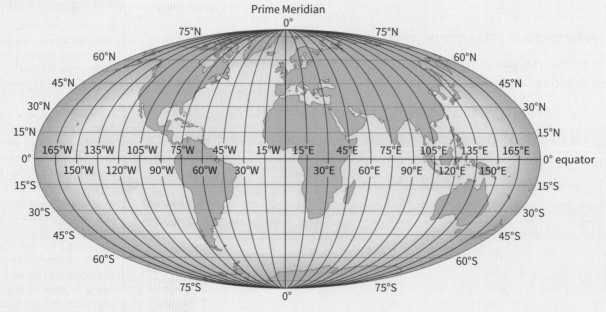

▲ **Figure 1** Latitude and longitude

Ordnance survey (OS) maps and photos

We use larger-scale OS maps to locate places; determine area, distance, and direction; and both visualise and understand land use, **communications**, relief, and drainage. Each map extract is a section of a national grid covering the whole of Great Britain.

Scales of 1:25 000 and 1:50 000 are most used. For example, a scale of 1:50 000 means that 1 unit on the map (e.g., 1 cm) represents 50 000 units on the ground (e.g., 50 000 cm or 500 m).

Four-figure and six-figure grid references

All OS maps are covered by a numbered grid made up of sequential numbers: *eastings* (identifying longitude) and *northings* (identifying latitude). They form the basis of the four- and six-figure references used to locate features on the map. Four-figure references identify the whole square, and six-figure references locate specific points (by estimating tenths of the whole square – **Figure 2**).

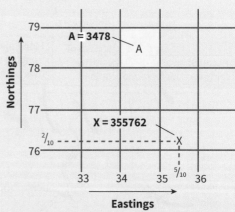

▲ **Figure 2** Using four- and six-figure references

Calculating distances and areas

Straight-line distances can be marked on the edge of scrap paper and read directly from the map's 'linear' scale line. Curving distances, such as along a road, river, or coastline, are best measured by dividing the route into straight sections (**Figure 3**).

Calculating areas requires judgement of the proportion of a grid square (or squares) an area feature occcupies. On 1:25 000 and 1:50 000 maps, 1 square on the map represents 1 km² in real life.

WATCH OUT

The number combinations work from the bottom left-hand corner, reading eastings first, then northings. (You 'crawl before you climb', so go 'along the corridor and up the stairs'!)

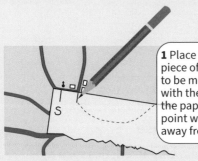

1 Place the straight edge of a piece of paper along the route to be measured. Mark the start with the letter S. Look along the paper and mark off the point where the route moves away from the straight edge.

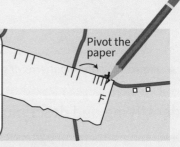

2 Pivot the paper and mark off the next straight section. Repeat this until you reach the end of the route. Mark this finishing point with the letter F. Convert the total length to kilometres using the map scale.

▲ **Figure 3** Measuring distance along a curved line

The eight-point compass

Always check the north point on a map; do not assume it is straight up (as on OS maps).

Look at **Figure 4**. In an eight-point compass, the four main *cardinal points* (north, east, south, and west) are divided by *intercardinal points* (north-east, south-east, south-west, and north-west).

▲ **Figure 4** The eight points of a compass

40 Geographical skills

Identifying and describing landscape features

Contour patterns can be used to identify basic physical features (**Figure 5**). Remember:

- relief refers to the height and shape of the land
- drainage refers to how water is drained from the land.

Drawing cross-sections

A cross-section is an imaginary 'slice' through a landscape, to help you visualise what a landscape actually looks like. Drawing a cross-section is not unlike drawing a line graph, although the x-axis intervals (determined by the contour spacing) are irregular (**Figure 6**).

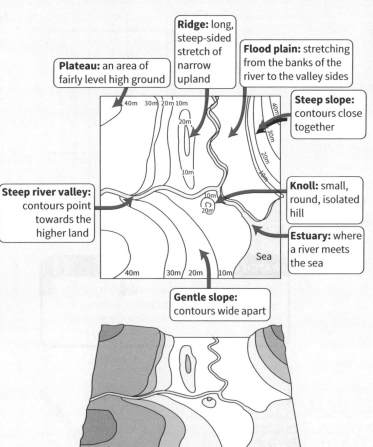

▲ *Figure 5 Contour patterns of selected landscape features*

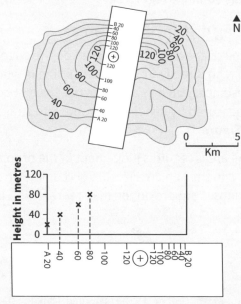

▲ *Figure 6 Drawing a map cross-section with only a strip of paper and a sharp pencil*

Identifying and describing settlements, communications, and land use

Describing settlement patterns involves terms such as:

- *linear* (the built-up area extending along a road or river)
- *nucleated* (dense and focused on a central point)
- *dispersed* (spread out at low density).

Function refers to main characteristics such as 'market town' or 'heavy industrial centre'.

Communications primarily refer to transport networks, such as roads and railways, and frequently reflect the relief of an area.

Finally, *land use* refers to human modification or management of the area.

Using photos

You are likely to come across aerial photos (taken from aeroplanes), satellite photos, and ground photos (**Figure 7**). When describing them, use directional language (e.g., 'foreground', 'background', 'right', 'left').

Geographical information systems (GIS)

A GIS is a computer database system capable of capturing, storing, analysing, and displaying geographical data from a vast variety of sources. All this data is identified according to location – hence a GIS is most often associated with maps and layered digital information such as satellite images, aerial photographs, statistical data, and written text.

Background: concrete sea wall deflects waves.

Middle right: wooden groynes maintain the beach by preventing longshore drift.

Foreground: rip-rap (rock armour) dissipates wave energy before it can hit the sea wall.

▲ **Figure 7** *Describing sea defences at Hornsea, East Yorkshire*

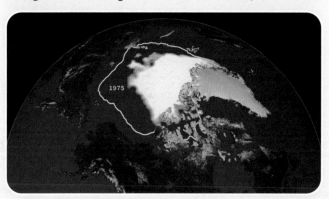

▶ **Figure 8** *GIS-enhanced satellite image showing the extent of the retreat of Arctic sea ice since 1979. Further GIS layering could be added to include further dates, and a scale to measure the exact rate of retreat*

Bar graphs, histograms, and divided bar graphs

Bar graphs

A bar graph is a way of comparing quantities or frequencies in different categories (**Figure 9**). The bars are drawn in different colours, with gaps between them because they are unconnected.

Histograms

A histogram also uses bars, but with no gaps because the data is continuous, or from a single sample (**Figure 10**).

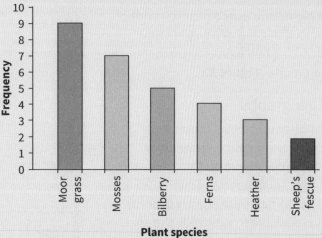

▲ **Figure 9** *A bar graph showing different types of vegetation at a fieldwork location*

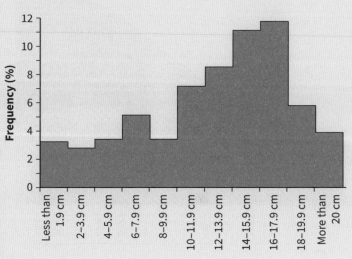

◀ **Figure 10** *A histogram showing daily rainfall values over a one-month period*

40 Geographical skills

Divided bar graphs

Divided bar graphs show multiple data by subdividing the individual bars. They are particularly useful when comparisons are required in place and/or time (**Figure 11**).

> **EXAM TIP** ◎
>
> When describing graphs, trends, examples, and anomalies (TEA) should be identified:
>
> - **T**rends cover the general direction – use adjectives like rising, falling, steady, accelerating, flared and so on.
> - **E**xamples illustrate the general trend and should include the highest and lowest values.
> - **A**nomalies should cover any exceptions to the general trend – examples that stand out as different, residuals/outliers in scattergraphs, radical changes in gradient in line or bar graphs, and so on.
>
> You might even want to stretch the mnemonic further, to TEAM. **M** is for manipulation (making comparisons, calculating percentage increase or decrease, etc.).

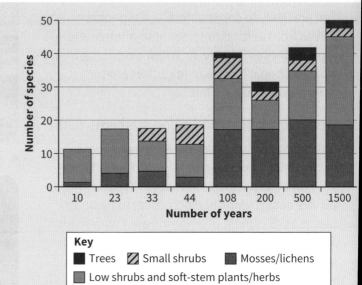

Key
- ■ Trees
- ▨ Small shrubs
- ▨ Mosses/lichens
- ▨ Low shrubs and soft-stem plants/herbs

▲ **Figure 11** A divided bar graph showing the number of species exposed by a retreating glacier

---

Pictograms, line graphs, pie charts, and scattergraphs

Pictograms

A pictogram uses a pictorial symbol or icon instead of a bar, but any resulting half icons can prove imprecise (**Figure 12**).

Line graphs

A line graph shows continuous changes over time. Remember that time, shown on the horizontal x-axis, must have an equal spacing (e.g., so dates are equally spaced). It is possible to subdivide the area below a line graph to show different proportions of the total. This creates a compound line graph (**Figure 13**).

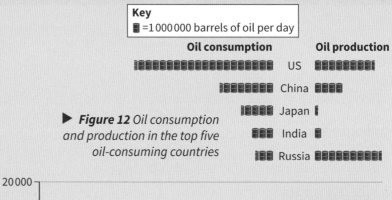

Key
🛢 = 1 000 000 barrels of oil per day

▶ **Figure 12** Oil consumption and production in the top five oil-consuming countries

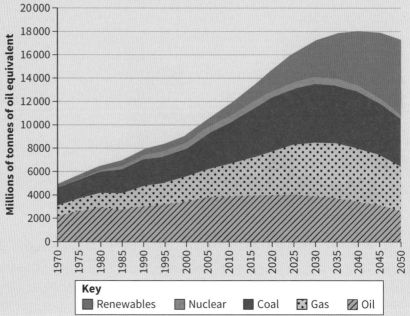

▶ **Figure 13** Long-term global energy demand predictions

Key
- ▨ Renewables
- ▨ Nuclear
- ■ Coal
- ▨ Gas
- ▨ Oil

Pie charts

Pie charts show proportions of a total as segments of a circle. They work best when kept simple – between four and six segments – and when using solid, contrasting colours (**Figure 14**). However, annotation using raw percentage figures can help interpretation.

Scattergraphs

If two sets of data (variables) are thought to be related, they can be plotted on a scattergraph. Once plotted, the 'scattered' points may allow you to visualise a trend (correlation) or pattern.

Whether smooth curves or straight lines, trend lines should be drawn approximately through the middle of the points, with roughly the same number of points on either side. Your trend line effectively becomes the line of best-fit.

Types of correlation

A relationship between two variables is called a **correlation**. Correlations can be shown on scattergraphs and/or tested statistically to see if the relationship is real or accidental. Occasionally a point may lie a long way from the line of best-fit. These points are called residuals (anomalies or outliers) and must be explained separately.

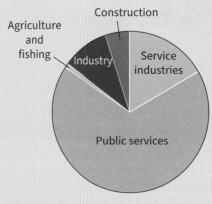

▲ *Figure 14* Types of employment in Rio de Janeiro, Brazil

EXAM TIP

Percentages are converted into degrees for the pie chart by multiplying the value by 3.6.

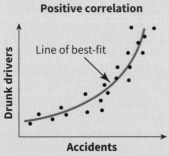

▲ *Figure 15* Types of correlation

Population pyramids, choropleth maps, and dot maps

Population pyramids

A population pyramid is a type of histogram showing the proportions of a population in different age and gender categories (**Figure 16**). The shape of the 'pyramid' shows the population structure at that moment in time. From this we can suggest likely levels of economic development, dependency ratios, impacts of migration, and probable immediate growth trends.

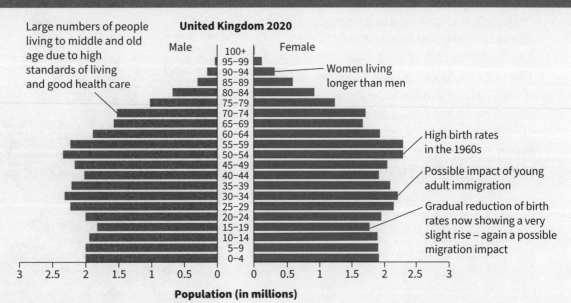

▲ *Figure 16* Population pyramid for the UK (2020)

40 Geographical skills

Choropleth maps

A choropleth map uses different colours and/or density shadings to show the distribution of data categories (**Figure 17**). Ideally, there should be between four and six categories, with eight as an absolute maximum. Category values should not overlap, and should preferably be equal (or, if not, be in a logical geometric sequence). A drawback, however, is that they imply uniformity – by averaging values across a wide area (e.g., county or country) – and therefore hide local variations. Furthermore, the sudden changes at boundaries are unlikely in reality.

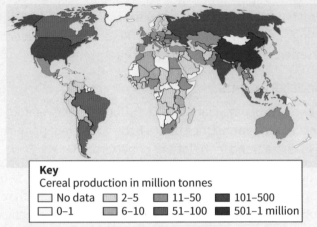

Key
Cereal production in million tonnes

☐ No data ☐ 2–5 ▨ 11–50 ▪ 101–500
☐ 0–1 ▨ 6–10 ▪ 51–100 ▪ 501–1 million

▲ *Figure 17 Global pattern of cereal production, 2018*

Dot maps

A dot map uses located dots to represent particular values or numbers, with their density (spread) creating the visual impact (**Figure 18**). Their greatest strength is their immediacy of impact, particularly if dots merge, but they are difficult to extract accurate information from.

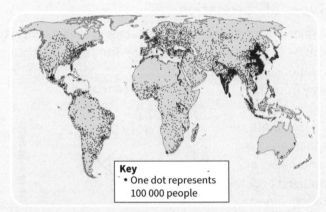

Key
• One dot represents 100 000 people

▲ *Figure 18 Dot map showing global population distribution*

Proportional symbols, isoline maps, desire line maps, and flow line maps

Proportional symbols

Proportional circles (and to a lesser degree proportional squares) are very useful for comparing located data (e.g., city populations). The size of each circle is proportional to the value it represents. Given thoughtful consideration of scale, and good design, proportional circles maps can be very informative (**Figure 19**).

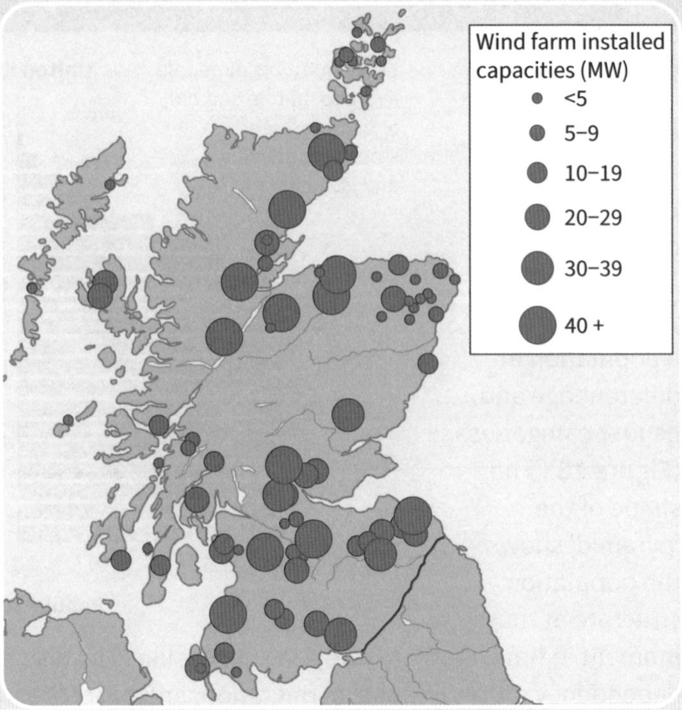

Wind farm installed capacities (MW)
• <5
• 5–9
● 10–19
● 20–29
● 30–39
● 40 +

▶ *Figure 19 Proportional circles map showing Scottish onshore wind farm capacities*

Isoline maps

An isoline map uses lines of equal value to show patterns ('iso' means equal). For example, isolines of equal precipitation plotted on weather and climate maps (**Figure 20**).

Desire line maps

A desire line map shows movements of people or goods between places. It shows direct movement from the place of origin to the destination, rather than the actual route (**Figure 21**).

▲ *Figure 21* *Desire line map of international flights from Heathrow, London*

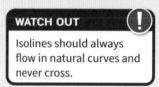

WATCH OUT ❗

Isolines should always flow in natural curves and never cross.

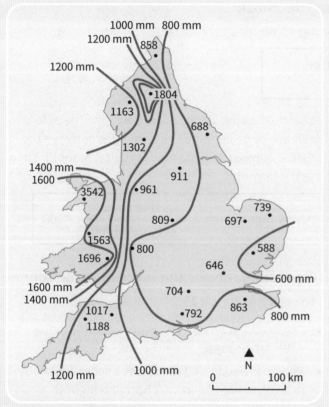

▲ *Figure 20* *Isoline map showing precipitation (mm) for England and Wales*

Flow line maps

A flow line map shows movements between places, often along a specific route. It uses arrows to show direction of movement, and different widths (drawn in proportion to the value being shown) to show volumes (**Figure 22**).

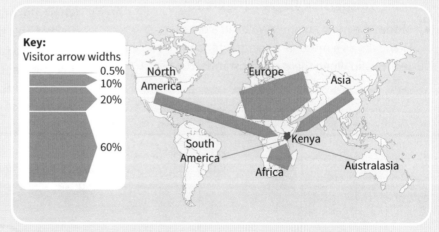

▲ *Figure 22* *Flow line map showing the origin of tourists to Kenya*

Knowledge

40 Geographical skills

Using numbers and statistics in geography

Geographers frequently use numbers and statistics, which help interpret patterns and trends.

Percentage calculations, including increase and decrease

The most common calculation is working out what percentage a number is of a total:

$$\text{Percentage} = \frac{\text{Number you want to find the percentage for}}{\text{Total number}} \times 100$$

To calculate a percentage increase, find the actual increase by calculating the difference between the original number and the new (bigger) number. Then use the formula:

$$\text{Percentage increase} = \frac{\text{Increase}}{\text{Original number}} \times 100$$

To calculate a percentage decrease, find the actual decrease by calculating the difference between the original number and the new (smaller) number. Then use the formula:

$$\text{Percentage decrease} = \frac{\text{Decrease}}{\text{Original number}} \times 100$$

Measures of central tendency – mean, median, and mode

- **Mean:** the 'average', calculated by adding up the individual values for a set of data and dividing by the number of values. But this gives no indication of how data within a set are spread around the average.
- **Median:** the central or mid-point value in a ranked data set. Half of the data set lies above the median and half below. Both ranking and spread are shown using a **dispersion diagram (Figure 23)**.
- **Mode:** the most common value in a data set. However, as a measure of central tendency it is only really valid when there is a substantial data set.

Dispersion, range, and inter-quartile range

Look again at **Figure 23**.

- *Dispersion:* refers to how data is distributed within the **range**.
- *Range:* the span of data across a set, calculated by subtracting the lowest from the highest value. The range therefore describes the spread of the data.
- *Inter-quartile range:* a statistical value to show where the middle 50% of the data lies within any set. It is based around the median and takes all data into account (discounting the effect of any anomalies). The inter-quartile range can be used to compare dispersions between two or more sets of data.

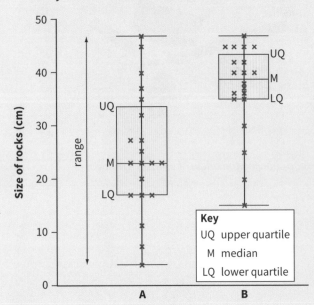

◄ **Figure 23** *A dispersion diagram showing the median and inter-quartile range*

Key
UQ upper quartile
M median
LQ lower quartile

Key terms — Make sure you can write a definition for these key terms

communications   correlation
dispersion diagram   function
latitude   longitude   mean
median   mode   range

Retrieval

40

Learn the answers to the questions below, then cover the answers column with a piece of paper and write down as many as you can. Check and repeat.

Questions	Answers
1 What is latitude?	how far north or south a location on the Earth's surface is from the equator, measured in degrees and minutes
2 What is longitude?	how far east or west a location on the Earth's surface is from the Prime (Greenwich) Meridian, measured in degrees and minutes
3 What are contours?	lines joining points of equal height, plotted at regular intervals on a (relief) map; they are coloured brown/orange on OS maps
4 What are spot heights?	indications of exact height above sea level on a map; on OS maps they are black dots with the height above sea level written alongside
5 What is meant by a linear settlement pattern?	the built-up area extends along a road or river
6 What is meant by a nucleated settlement pattern?	the built-up area is dense, and focused on a central point
7 What is meant by a dispersed settlement pattern?	the built-up area is spread out at low density
8 What is meant by settlement function?	the settlement's main identifying characteristics, such as 'market town' or 'heavy industrial centre'
9 What is meant by settlement situation?	the settlement's location relative to other places
10 What is meant by settlement site?	the actual land the settlement occupies
11 What is meant by communications on a map?	transport networks, such as roads and railways
12 What is a geographical information system (GIS)?	a database of located geographical information usually based on maps, satellite images and aerial photographs layered with digital information, statistical data, and written text
13 What is a correlation?	a relationship between two variables – shown on scattergraphs and/or tested statistically to see if the relationship is real or accidental
14 What is a residual?	a point lying a long way from the line of best-fit on a scattergraph (which must be explained separately); also called anomalies or outliers
15 What is meant by dispersion (of data)?	how data is distributed within a range
16 What is meant by the range (of data)?	the spread of the data calculated by subtracting the lowest from the highest value
17 What is the inter-quartile range?	a statistical value to show where the middle 50% of the data lies within any set – used to compare dispersions between two or more sets of data

Put paper here

Put paper here

Put paper here

Put paper here

Put paper

Put paper here

Put paper here

OS maps symbols

Symbols on Ordnance Survey maps (1:50 000 and 1:25 000)

ROADS AND PATHS

M 1 or A 6(M)	Motorway
A 35	Dual carriageway
A 31(T) or A 35	Trunk or main road
B 3074	Secondary road
	Narrow road with passing places
	Road under construction
	Road generally more than 4 m wide
	Road generally less than 4 m wide
	Other road, drive or track, fenced and unfenced
	Grafont: deeper than 1 in 5; 1 in 7 to 1 in 5
Ferry	Ferny: Ferny P – passenger only
	Path

PUBLIC FIGHTS OF WAY

Not applicable to Scotland

1:25 000	1:55 000	
		Footpath
		Road used as a public footpath
+++++++		Bridleway
		Byway open to all traffic

RAILWAYS

	Multiple track
	Single track
	Narrow gauge/Light rapid transit system
	Road over, road under; level crossing
	Cutting; tunnel, embankment
	Station, open to passengers; siding

BOUNDARIES

+ — + — +	National
+ · + · + · +	District
— · — · — · —	Country, Unitary Authority, Metropolitan District or London Borough
	National Park

HEIGHTS/ROCK FEATURES

50	Contour lines
· 144	Spot height to the nearest metre above sea level

outcrop   cliff   scree

ABBREVIATIONS

P	Post office	PC	Public convenience (rural areas)
PH	Public house	TH	Town Hall, Guildhall or equivalent
MS	Milestone	Sch	School
MP	Milepost	Coll	College
CH	Clubhouse	Mus	Museum
CG	Coastguard	Cemy	Cemetery
Fm	Farm		

ANTIOUITIES

VILLA	Roman	✕	Battlefield (with data)
Castle	Non-Roman	⁎	Tumulus/tumali (mound over burial place)

LAND FEATURES

	Buildings
	Public building
	Bus or coach station
⚑ Place ⎱	with tower
⚑ of ⎰	with spire, minaret or dome
+ Worship	without such additions
○	Chimney or tower
⌀	Glass structure
Ⓗ	Heliport
△	Triangulation pillar
	Mast
	Wind pump / wind generator
	Windmill
+	Graticule intersection
	Cutting, embankment
	Quarry
	Spoil heap, refuse tip or dump
	Coniferous wood
	Non-coniferous wood
	Mixed wood
	Orchard
	Park or ornamental ground
	Forestry Commission access land
	National Trust – always open
	National Trust, limited access, observe local signs
	National Trust for Scotland

TOURIST INFORMATION

P	Parking
P&R	Park & Ride
V	Visitor centre
i	Information centre
✆	Telephone
	Camp site/ Caravan site
⚑	Golf course or links
	Viewpoint
PC	Public convenience
✕	Picnic site
	Pub's
	Museum
	Castle/fort
	Building of historic interest
	Steam railway
	English Heritage
	Garden
	Nature reserve
	Water activities
	Fishing
☆	Other tourist feature
	Mornings (free)
	Electric boat changing point
	Recreation/leisure sports centre

WATER FEATURES

Marsh or salting   Towpath Lock   Slopes   Cliff   High water mark
Aqueduct   Canal   Ford   Flat rock   Low water mark   Lighthouse (in use)
Weir   Normal tidal limit   Sand   Lighthouse (disused)   Beacon
Lake   Bridge   Dunes   Mud   Shingle
Footbridge

========== Canal (dry)

OXFORD
UNIVERSITY PRESS

Great Clarendon Street, Oxford, OX2 6DP, United Kingdom

Oxford University Press is a department of the University of Oxford. It furthers the University's objective of excellence in research, scholarship, and education by publishing worldwide. Oxford is a registered trade mark of Oxford University Press in the UK and in certain other countries.

© Oxford University Press 2023

Written by Tim Bayliss and Andrew Crampton
Series Editor: Tim Bayliss

The moral rights of the authors have been asserted

First published in 2023

British Library Cataloguing in Publication Data
Data available

978-1-382-03981-9

10 9 8 7 6 5 4

The manufacturing process conforms to the environmental regulations of the country of origin.

Printed in the UK by Bell and Bain Ltd, Glasgow

Acknowledgements

The publisher and authors would like to thank the following for permission to use photographs and other copyright material:

Photos: p8: think4photop / Shutterstock; **p12(l):** Jonathan Saruk / Getty Images; **p12(r):** zahirul alwan / Shutterstock; **p13:** YOSHIKAZU TSUNO / AFP via Getty Images; **p16:** Richard Whitcombe / Shutterstock; **p17:** Jeff Gilbert / Alamy Stock Photo; **p20:** Neil Cooper / Alamy Stock Photo; **p24:** Ryan DeBerardinis / Shutterstock; **p25:** Neil Cooper / Alamy Stock Photo; **p30:** HadCET / Crown Copyright; **p36(l):** Gubin Yury / Shutterstock; **p36(r):** Ivan_Sabo / Shutterstock; **p37:** Heritage Image Partnership Ltd / Alamy Stock Photo; **p39:** RG Images / Stock4B / Jonas Krüger / Corbis; **p45(a):** Anna Veselova / Shutterstock; **p45(b):** Erni / Shutterstock; **p45(c):** Daimond Shutter / Shutterstock; **p45(d):** MIKO GARDEN / Shutterstock; **p49(l):** Erni / Shutterstock; **p49(r):** MIKO GARDEN / Shutterstock; **p55(l):** FRstudio / Shutterstock; **p55(r):** PARALAXIS / Shutterstock; **p56(l):** Chikena / Shutterstock; **p56(r):** Frontpage / Shutterstock; **p57:** iacomino FRiMAGES / Shutterstock; **p58:** Simon Ross; p59(t): Stephen Firmender / Shutterstock; **p59(b):** Wolfgang Zwanzger / Shutterstock; **p63(l):** Geoorgiy Boyko / Shutterstock; **p63(r):** Stephen Firmender / Shutterstock; **p65(tl):** Volosina / Shutterstock; **p65(tr):** PeJo / Shutterstock; **p65(m):** koonkhunstockphoto / 123rf; **p65(b):** Eye Ubiquitous / Alamy Stock Photo; **p67(l):** Memories Over Mocha / Shutterstock; **p67(r):** Sami Sarkis / Getty Images; **p68(l):** Eye Ubiquitous / Alamy Stock Photo; p68(r): Iryna Rasko / Shutterstock; **p71(t):** Iakov Filimonov / Shutterstock; **p71(b):** Andrei Stepanov / Shutterstock; **p75(l):** mikelane45 / 123rf; **p75(r):** Andrei Stepanov / Shutterstock; **p76:** Tyler Olson / Shutterstock; **p77:** robertharding / Alamy Stock Photo; **p79(l):** gillmar / Shutterstock; **p79(r):** Sandra Ophorst / Shutterstock; **p80:** Agencja Fotograficzna Caro / Alamy Stock Photo; **p82(t):** Gail Johnson / Shutterstock; **p82(b):** Andy333 / Shutterstock; **p88:** Peter Smith Photography; **p92(tl):** januszkurek. com / Shutterstock; **p92(tr):** dbphots / Alamy Stock Photo; **p92(b):** Charlesy / Shutterstock; **p94:** Ordnance Survey; **p95(t):** Jo Chambers / Shutterstock; **p95(b):** Liquid Light / Alamy Stock

Photo; **p100(t):** Rodger Tamblyn / Alamy Stock Photo; **p100(bl):** robertharding / Alamy Stock Photo; **p100(br):** Matthew J Thomas / Shutterstock; **p101(l):** Nigel Wiggins / Shutterstock; **p101(r):** DJTaylor / Shutterstock; **p103:** S B Stock / Shutterstock; **p104:** Washington Imaging / Alamy Stock Photo; **p106(l):** Ordinance Survey; **p106(r):** Webb Aviation; **p107:** Eag1eEyes / Shutterstock; **p112(l):** Simon Perkin / Alamy Stock Photo; **p112(r):** Kanuman / Shutterstock; **p114:** Tim Bayliss; **p115:** PA Images / Alamy Stock Photo; **p118(l):** ChrisV00 / Shutterstock; **p118(r):** Ordinance Survey; **p120(t):** Ben Latham / Shutterstock; **p120(b):** The Photolibrary Wales / Alamy Stock Photo; **p121(t):** John Schwieder / Alamy Stock Photo; **p121(bl):** Ordinance Survey; **p121(br):** Septemberlegs / Alamy Stock Photo; **p125(l):** Jeff Morgan 08 / Alamy Stock Photo; **p125(r):** Natural Retreats; **p126(t):** Racheal Grazias / Shutterstock; **p126(b):** JaneHYork / Shutterstock; **p133:** Elena Odareeva / Shutterstock; **p136:** Peter Tsai Photography / Alamy Stock Photo; **p147:** Tim Bayliss; **p148(tl):** Bristol City Council; **p148(tr):** Ordinance Survey; **p148(b):** PLEIADES © CNES 2016, Distribution Airbus DS; **p149:** Image Professionals GmbH / Alamy Stock Photo; **p151:** Ordinance Survey; **p152(l):** REACH PLC; **p152(r):** Gavin Roberts / Alamy Stock Photo; **p153:** Phil Wills / Alamy Stock Photo; **p169:** ricochet64 / Shutterstock; **p178:** George Osodi / AP / Shutterstock; **p181(l):** Construction Photography / Alamy Stock Photo; **p181(r):** AGGREGATE INDUSTRIES UK LIMITED; **p184:** Cambridge Aerial Photography / Alamy Stock Photo; **p188:** Jarek Kilian / Shutterstock; **pp193-227:** Tim Bayliss.

Artwork by QBS Media Services Inc., Aptara Inc., Mike Connor, Mike Parsons, Barking Dog Art, Simon Tegg, Lovell Johns, Kamae Design, Giorgio Bacchin, Ian West, Ian Foulis, Hardlines, Richard Morris, Angela Knowles, and Dave Russell.

Ordnance Survey (OS) is the national mapping agency for Great Britain, and a world-leading geospatial data and technology organisation. As a reliable partner to government, business and citizens across Britain and the world, OS helps its customers in virtually all sectors improve quality of life.

The publisher would also like to thank Adam Robbins, Claire Crampton, and staff and students at Heathfield Knoll School and King Charles 1 School in Kidderminster for sharing their expertise and feedback in the development of this resource.

Although we have made every effort to trace and contact all copyright holders before publication this has not been possible in all cases. If notified, the publisher will rectify any errors or omissions at the earliest opportunity.